The Missing Years

By Dick Clifton

With the best wishes of the author

Also by Dick Clifton

Love and Carnage

http://bit.ly/loveandcarnage

Very little if anything seems to have been written about the men who searched for and found prisoners of war that had been released when the armistice was signed (occasionally it would be a grounded pilot) and escorted them through the forward area in to Allied occupied territory. Without the cooperation of il Partito d'Azione and the willing assistance of the ribelli (rebels as the partisans were known), who often provided guides, they would not have been able to operate.

The story which is based on the author's personal experience takes place in Abruzzo. It is written as a sister book to The Missing Years, and gives an insight to the risks ordinary people were prepared to take in the midst of almost daily atrocities.

While the repeated betrayal of group activities points to the existence of a spy and forces the Leaf men (so called because of their method of contact) to suspend operations until new routes can be found keeps the reader guessing, the love element developing between some of the characters brings a little light relief from the activities of the ribelli and the atrocities committed by the governing forces

Neath blazing sun and pale moonlight
remote and far away.
When winds are high a mournful
song is heard by night and day.

The ghostly spirit wanders,
away from haunts of man.
Who knows what memories linger
in an empty petrol can.

Copyright © 2009 by Dick Clifton *All rights reserved.*
First published in Great Britain in 2008

CHAPTER 1

May 25th, 1942.

He stood, a lonely figure beneath the brazen sun, while the fine grey dust thrown up by the departing truck formed a swirling cloud and mingled with the sweat that trickled from his armpits and coursed freely down his back and chest. The deeply tanned face with its tell tale frown etched between the steady grey eyes, and the sun bleached hair, greying at the temples, belied his 22 years and gave him semblance of greater maturity. The two years spent in the desert had left their mark, bringing the self assurance and economy of movement so necessary for those who wore the Scorpion[1]. Basil Holden had joined the Unit in the early days of its formation and was on a special solo assignment.

It had been considered that, owing to the existence of two large Panzer Divisions in the area, the usual hit and run tactics carried out by a full patrol would be unlikely to succeed. One truck, however, stood a fair chance of getting within walking distance of the objective, a large petrol dump some 10 miles West of Segnali. Accordingly No.5 left A.B.2. patrol and dropped Basil about 6 miles west of the dump, the plan being to pick him up at a rendezvous the following day and rejoin the patrol which would hang around near Bir Hacheim.

Without waiting for the truck to fade in the distance, he turned towards his objective, his curiously short, high stepping walk, peculiar to those who roam the desert sands on foot, carrying him rapidly over the undulating ground with untiring ease. His shadow lengthening before him as the day neared its close.

It would be necessary for him to sight the dump while some daylight remained in order to obtain an accurate bearing before shallowing the sand to await the coming night. He prayed his estimate would prove correct, for the success of the venture and, with it, his own safety, would depend on timing. It was essential that the light be just sufficient to enable him to pick out the dump, but not bright enough for him to be easily spotted. Too well he knew the danger inherent in an approach from a sun just set, when the bright skyline could throw him into stark relief.

A light breeze fanned his cheeks and stirred the surface of the sand which had become a multicoloured carpet ranging from dark brown to delicate pink. Basil never tired of the glorious desert sunsets with their unbroken panorama of colour. The sun behind him, half hidden now behind the dunes, burned fiery red as if reluctant to go.

---

[1] The Scorpion: Emblem of the L.R.D.G.

Suddenly he saw the dump, looking rather closer than expected and covering about 1/4 acre of ground; this was larger than reports had indicated. He swiftly dropped to the ground and read off a bearing from the compass strapped to his wrist. The distance, he estimated, was about two miles.

Taking advantage of the last rays of light, he scanned the terrain through his glasses, noting with satisfaction the apparent absence of a nearby force. The fast fading light was still sufficient to study the movements of the sentries in order to get their approximate timing.

Nearby, a bivouac, invisible in the gathering dusk, was revealed when a small party of soldiers emerged and took up their positions at two strategically placed light machine guns. Between them, they commanded the areas to the East, North and South of the dump. Previous raids had taught the Germans to take no chances with petrol dumps even though they were behind their lines.

Calmly Basil transferred his gaze to the sentries patrolling the perimeter of the dump. Two sentries constantly encircled the barbed wire enclosure, each maintaining an even pace with his partner on the opposite boundary. At the same time, two more sentries patrolled in the opposite direction in a similar manner. The spacing allowed the two pairs to meet their counterparts at diagonally opposite corners. This unusual arrangement ensured that each boundary had a sentry constantly patrolling its length and no stretch could be out of view for more than half a minute. Furthermore, if a sentry was put out of action he would be missed immediately.

It was obvious that speed would be the all important factor in gaining access. A brief opportunity of cutting the wire and scrambling through would be afforded behind any one of the sentries as he converged on the corner. It was also obvious that the Western boundary would be the safest since this was out of sight of the two machine gun posts.

Even as he slid his glasses back into their case, his well trained brain was busy collating the information and formulating a plan of campaign. No useful purpose could be gained by further watching and, since he intended to delay his approach for at least an hour, he settled down as comfortably as possible in order to rest before continuing towards his objective.

When the time came, Basil traversed the distance between himself and the dump; finding shelter behind some scrub, he took up a position some 50 yards away, where the vague outline of the stacked petrol cans could just be seen silhouetted against the pale iridescence of the stars. Almost motionless, he listened to the many tiny sounds which travelled clearly through the still night air, patiently waiting for the increased activity which would occur before the camp settled for the night.

Although he had anticipated guttural shouts and odd snatches of song, the general cacophony of an Army encampment bedding down for the night smote his ears with an avalanche of sound which disturbed the tranquil desert night and startled him into renewed alertness even though this commotion was nothing more than expected. Quite unexpected, however, was the sound of approaching footsteps which set his pulses racing as, with every sense attuned to the dangers of the situation, and knife already in hand, he shrank closer to the sands.

His straining eyes scanned. the area methodically, picking out the almost invisible shadow of two figures approaching his exact position. The desultory murmur of their voices carried clearly to where he lay ready for immediate action. The figures halted a few yards from him and the familiar hiss as they urinated into the sand sounded unnaturally loud, as also did his own escaping breath as they departed.

Gradually, the sounds subsided and at last all he could hear was the steady tramping of the sentries' feet.

Prepared for the final dash, Basil held cutters in his right hand while in the left, his own speciality, a short length of flexible cable with a strong crocodile clip fixed securely to each end. With a bare 20' to go, he crouched awaiting his opportunity. The thick crepe soles of his 'desert creepers' made no sound as he glided swiftly to the wire. With practised ease he attached his cable close behind a barb on the lowest strand of the fencing, at the same time cutting the wire close to one of the supporting posts, and taking the strain of the loose strand to prevent it springing back. In one swift movement he raised the wire and slid inside then passed his short cable round the post and clipped it into position. To the casual observer there was now no apparent sign that the fence had ever been tampered with.

Silently he merged into the deeper black of the gangways between the stacks of cans and methodically made his way to the centre of the enclosure where he removed his pack in readiness to prepare the charges necessary for the completion of his mission.

Working by touch, his strong sensitive fingers speedily set the timing devices on the three small incendiaries, placing each in a hollow scooped out beneath the petrol cans. Then, replacing the disturbed sand, he carefully smoothed the area in which he had worked. Moving backwards he deftly removed all traces of his trail until he reached one of the other gangways which he walked quickly down, kneeling here and there and shifting his pack about in the sand to leave the impression, should anything go wrong, that this was where he had set his charges. Satisfied at last all that could be done was accomplished, he left as silently as he had come.

The luminous hands on the dial of his watch pointed to 1.35 when the explosion sent flames leaping high into the sky and lit the desert for miles around. The fierce glow even reached Basil who had covered nearly three miles in the hour allotted by the timing mechanisms. With scarce a glance at the conflagration he had caused, but with a strong feeling of satisfaction, Basil pressed forward, now intent only on reaching the rendezvous, a small outcrop of rock which lay some 20 miles S.E. of his operation.

CHAPTER 2

The first grey streaks of dawn found the four men from A.B.2. Patrol already astir; their bedding rolled and stacked in the truck. Brian Cruickshank coughed and spat disgustedly into the sand.

"Och dust", he complained "when this bluidy lot is o'er ye'd not catch me a ganging to the coast - the wee lads and lassies can ha' it a' to thimsilves".

Jimmy Bowles, the Sergeant in charge, 6'1" of bone and sinew with a Bulldog surmounted by crossed Union Jacks tattooed on his bronzed forearm, laughed.

"Why not Jock?

'To the seaside I shall go with a bucket and a spade to spend my life, my aim, my hate to mortifying sand.' "

The words of an anonymous desert poet brought a chuckle of merriment from the other two members of the party, Frank Page and Arthur Hart.

Every man in the L.R.D.G. was hand picked - when working together on a patrol they made an efficient fighting team, each individual member being not only expert at his own particular job, but also well versed in the mechanics of all operations. Thus any one was able to take over any given task should the occasion demand.

Grinning, Jimmy handed out the thin hard biscuits from the back of the truck.

"Possy anyone? - Airmail coming over"

he hoisted the small tin of jam into Jock's ready hand. The frugal meal was soon finished and washed down by a meagre ration of tea, brewed on a smokeless fire made from the special combustible tablets carried for the purpose. Not for these the usual Army method of a can of sand soaked in petrol; to them petrol constituted a life line which ranked second only to water - no wastage of either could be permitted.

"We move off in half an hour". Jimmy, a Regular Soldier and product of the Coldstream Guards, did not give orders and never shouted, he merely made requests of his man and obtained immediate obedience - despite this quiet manner, however, even these hardened veterans knew better than to risk his displeasure and the steely glint that could appear in his eyes. Each quickly checked his own personal equipment and saw that his water bottle was full. Then, while Frank tested the traverse of the Vickers machine gun mounted on the base of the truck and made sure that there was no tendency to jam, Jock checked over the engine, diving underneath for a last minute glance to ensure that all was as it should be. Meanwhile, Jimmy had checked the course, while Arthur attended to the radio. The daily routine took no more than ten minutes.

When all was set and ready to go, cigarettes were passed round for the brief wait before zero hour. Frank, resting back against a wheel of the truck, took a letter from his pocket, one of four he had picked up from Base H.Q. at Siwa two weeks earlier. He liked to save his letters, reading one a week, for in this way he felt closer to his wife, The almost effeminate face, so out of character, came alive with joy as he devoured the words written by the girl he had married two short days before he left England. "Jenny took two tiny steps" - he called out. He was inordinately proud of the little girl he had never seen and would never know, and passed on other titbits to his pals relating to the antics of his small daughter. The others were quick to share his pleasure and the inevitable teasing ensued. "Och mon, the wee bairn will gie ye no peace when ye get back hame", said Jock, "Ye're far better off in the grand solitude of this heathen paradise".

With this parting shot, he jumped into the driver's seat and started up the engine, while the others scrambled aboard, taking up action positions. The time to relax was gone.

Jock crouched over the controls of the truck sending it bounding across the blue, meanwhile, Jimmy busied himself checking the calculations necessary for accurate navigation in a world devoid of landmarks.

Strict radio silence was being kept, so Arthur didn't have much to do. At 23 he was the youngest member of the team, and had only recently joined the Group. He was not lacking in experience, however, having received his baptism of fire with the Northumberland Fusiliers during General Wavell's advance in 1940. This had been followed by a trip on the 'President Dumar' to the Sudan, and more fighting in Eritrea - where he received a mention at Keren - then back to Egypt and Libya in time for the relief of Tobruk. Wavell only had 30,000 troops to his Command at that time and, with the force split between the Western Desert, East Africa and Greece, our soldiers were kept very busy. Eventually, inspired by the tales of almost legendary deeds performed by the L.R.D.G. Arthur had applied to serve with the Unit and was now on his first patrol.

He kept a sharp lookout as also did the gunner Frank Page. Even in the most remote areas of the desert, it was possible to meet a stray force, particularly as the day following a night operation was often more dangerous than the actual raid itself, the enemy having recovered from his confusion, was almost certain to send out patrols to search the area. The danger of being spotted by an enemy plane could not be overlooked and was probably the greatest hazard these brave men had to face.

"That chap we dropped yesterday afternoon certainly made a bonfire last night" - he remarked to Frank, "I wonder if he got away".

"Oh, Basil you mean?" Frank replied, "I expect so, he might be mad but he's not stupid". Frank grinned boyishly, "A bit of a mystery really - how he gets back sometimes is a puzzle - but so far he always has. Used to play around with Penny's[2] lot and for all I know still does".

Suddenly Arthur stiffened,

"Alert", he shouted, pointing skyward. Jock immediately cut his engine and the truck rolled to a standstill.

"Report" - Jimmy snapped.

"Possible plane at five to one North up about 60°".

"O.K. don't lose it", he replied, "Take cover."

The camouflage net, especially adapted by Jock, was rolled in position on the tail of the truck, it unfurled in less than a minute on hinged supports much in the manner of the hood of a small sports car. The Sgt. swept the skies with his glasses, while Frank quickly brought the snout of the machine gun to bear on the rapidly growing speck. Presently the faint drone of an engine came to their ears.

"Sounds like a Mezzie", remarked Jock whose keen ears could detect the faintest deviation in the note of an engine and could recognise 'the song' as he called it, of most types of plane. Even if concealment had not been the object of the exercise, the machine gun could not possibly hope to reach the plane at the altitude it was flying. Nevertheless, survival would depend on their readiness, but all they could do at this stage was to sit tight and hope to avoid detection.

"Don't engage if it comes down, unless it's obvious we've been spotted", advised Jimmy. The swiftly approaching plane rapidly grew in size, passing to one side but, though low enough for the marking to be clearly seen, was well out of range. Suddenly it banked to the left, circling round the truck two or three times. Then, from out of the sun, it dived - the enormous shadow on the sand raced over the ground towards the small party - as the hideous roar of machine guns opened up, the sand erupted in little spurts of dust where bullets struck home. Frank, crouched behind his gun, cursed freely as he tried to train it on the target, the horrible staccato sound cut in over the roar of the plane to be joined in duet as Frank pressed his own triggers. Meanwhile, the other three had snatched up their own small-arms and taken cover behind the truck ready for any opportunity to score a hit. The plane overshot the truck, then climbed steeply, veering again into the sun and positioning for a new approach.

Jimmy scowled as he pressed home a fresh magazine in his rifle,

---

[2] Colonel Penniakoff - otherwise known as 'Popski'.

"I reckon he must have the eyes of a Shite Hawk to spot us from such a height," he said.

Once more the monstrous cacophony split the quiet of the desert as the plane again dived, coming in even lower this time - so low in fact that the goggled face of the pilot was clearly visible. Fascinated, the party saw the head disintegrate as Frank's bullet smashed home. The plane screamed overhead, lurched, then taking on a steeper angle, tore its way into the ground some half a mile away, where it instantly burst into flames sending a thick column of black smoke into the clear air.

After the noise of the preceding few minutes, the silence was acute. Jimmy scanned the sky and surrounding area to satisfy himself that all was clear.

"Alright, stand down", his voice unusually abrupt in the still tense atmosphere.

"Yon spalpeen's ruined ma bonnet", spluttered Jock, picking the tattered relic from the ground whence it had fallen after being plucked from his head by a close one.

"Bonnet?" queried Arthur, "Is that what you call it? I always took it for a dish rag".

"Awa wi ye, ye ignorant sassenach". Jock hurled the offending headgear, catching Arthur expertly behind the ear.

"Joke's over" - Jimmy's voice cut in on the horse play -"Let's get to hell out of here before that smoke attracts more visitors". Laughing they climbed back into the truck furling back the net as Jock pressed down on the starter. Getting no response, he jumped down and lifted the bonnet frowning intently into the engine. Two jagged holes, unnoticed before, had appeared in the metal body work, the petrol line had been severed and the starter motor wrecked.

"What's the trouble Jock?" Jim called.

"There's a bit of a mess here, but I think it can be fixed. Get the box of spares will you". Deftly he removed the starter motor and the parts that had jammed into the flywheel.

"From here on one of ye will wind her up" he cracked. The petrol pipe proved to be the lesser problem since a spare was carried and exchange was a simple matter.

While Jock was repairing the engine, Jimmy sent Arthur to the top of a nearby sand dune to keep watch, and took the opportunity to shoot the sun for an accurate fix. He frowned as he noticed the local time taken from a small sun dial which was used in conjunction with the chronometer showing Greenwich Mean Time to obtain the longitude. The plane had been sighted at 10.05; it was now nearly eleven o'clock; the party would be late at the rendezvous, but that was not important since Basil was not likely to wander off and contact was tolerably certain. The long delay in the region of the burning plane was the real problem since the Germans were bound to send out a party to investigate the cause of the smoke. Even if they knew it was one of their own planes, they were still likely to investigate in case the pilot had baled out. In either event, their discovery would be certain.

Jimmy's watch showed 11.15 when Jock shouted all was ready. Immediately he signalled Arthur to return and they lost no time in getting under way. They didn't get far, however, before the truck hit a soft patch of sand and, despite all Jock's experience, bogged down. Jimmy jumped down, grabbing the trenching tool, while Arthur unstrapped the iron channels from the side of the truck - Frank remaining on look out beside his gun. The sand flew as Jimmy busily dug out from under the wheels, while Arthur waited poised to slip the channel into position. They were in a bad spot for this to happen since they were in a gully between two sand dunes which restricted visibility to a mere 2/300 yards. The danger being that while they could remain hidden from sight of a patrol positioned 4/500 yards away - a patrol could equally well come upon them suddenly at an uncomfortably close range.

The truck moved slowly onto the channel, engine screaming as Jock fought the wildly spinning wheels, then continued slowly over the sand, only to bog down again as the two clambered aboard.

Desperately they started digging her out again, when suddenly Jimmy's fears materialised - Rat-ta-tat-tat, the menacing sound smashed through the air. Arthur stiffened seeming almost to leave the ground, then slammed into the side of the truck with the impact of the bullets, and hung grotesquely for a moment before crumpling to the ground - the huge fountain of blood smothered Jimmy and stained the clean sand. Quick as a cat, the Sgt. Rolled beneath the truck coming up beside Jock who held his sten ready for him. Two armoured cars had approached round the end of the dune and sped up on his right. Frank was hammering away with the Lewis returning the fire, his bullets clanging harmlessly against the armour of the approaching enemy. Jimmy emptied his magazine into the tyres and grabbed Arthur's weapon still standing in its clip on the truck. Still the cars approached, drawing apart as they came then yet another appeared from the other end of the gully. Abruptly the Lewis stopped, Jimmy glanced up as Frank, cut almost in two by the hail of bullets, rolled over the breech of the gun. Jimmy jumped up and, pushing Frank to one side, swung the muzzle back towards the enemy - meanwhile Jock grabbed a Molotov cocktail and lobbed it under the nearest car, following it with grenades. The fiercely burning liquid penetrated the damaged bottom of the car, and brought it to a standstill, the intense heat forced the Germans into the open in their effort to escape the raging inferno inside their car, only to fall like so many puppets with broken strings under the rapid fire of the Lewis.

Jock jerked up to lob another Molotov at the second car, now little more than 15 yards away, where it stuck and burnt fiercely, doing little damage. Suddenly he staggered out from the relative shelter of the truck, a grenade still in his hand, as he collapsed he raised his arm to throw it but his strength was gone, it rolled a few feet then exploded.

Jimmy, his right arm now hanging useless, continued to operate the gun. Dimly, through a red mist, he saw the armoured cars coming closer - waves of darkness and a feeling of nausea swept over him as he felt himself falling ... falling ... falling.

CHAPTER 3

Basil Holden pressed on through the night, savouring the cool light breeze and noting with satisfaction the way it stirred the fine surface of the sand, speedily filling the dimples left by his feet. By dawn he estimated he had covered about 12 miles from the scene of operation and if his navigation was correct would sight the rock formation by 8 O'clock.

The sun was high when Basil, tired now after the exertion of the night, reached the rendezvous. The cache of food and water still intact indicated that the spot had not been discovered. Nevertheless, he carefully scrutinised the area before taking a spade to scoop a hollow under the shaded side of the rocks to form an overhang.

Having completed his shelter, he lit a cigarette and settled down to wait. Secure in the knowledge that discovery was unlikely, he idly watched the smoke curl lazily in the now still air. His thoughts wandered back over the years. Was it really only three years, he asked himself, to that other world when, with all the gaiety of youth, he had dashed off to join the Army during the Munich crisis. The six months of peace time training had stood him in good stead, then the trip on the old "Nevassa" - "God! What a tub", he thought, and Egypt in April, 1939.

The declaration of war found him in the Citadel, before long he was posted to the 4th Indian Div., eventually becoming involved with the P.P.A[3] and by natural processes finally a part of the Organisation.

A movement in the sky caught his eye, just a speck in the distance but enough to break his reverie. Was it a bird or a plane, he raised his glasses and focussed them. At first he failed to pick it up again, then he caught the outline, it was a plane, but even when viewed through his glasses it was too small for him to decide whether it was friend or foe. Casually he watched the plane flying in a Southerly direction some miles North East of where he sat. Although it was getting imperceptibly closer, it was unlikely to pass even within hearing distance but it was something to watch in the dead world of land which surrounded him. Presently it curved gracefully round in a circular movement and he made a mental note for future reference to get the area checked for landing fields. Suddenly it dived out of sight behind the horizon to re-appear a moment later climbing fast and banking round into the sun, hovered for a fleeting instant then dived, and again disappeared from view. A moment later a column of smoke appeared gradually dispersing into a dark smudge against the sky. Basil noted the time - 10.05.

There was no point in staying awake as there was nothing he could possibly do about the drama just played out in the sky, he decided to catch up on

---

[3] No.1 Demolition Squad - (Popski's Private Army).

some sleep. Being a light sleeper he had no fears that he might miss the contact; as an old campaigner he knew the importance of seizing any brief opportunity for rest that presented itself.

It was 6.30 when he woke with parched throat and splitting head. A quick inspection of the ground around the refuge assured him that no living thing had been near while he slept. Evidently the truck had been delayed. He frowned thoughtfully, it was true the day was not yet finished, on the other hand, he would have expected relief long before this and experience had taught him that serious delay usually meant trouble. It was known that Rommel was massing his forces ready for a big attack in the very near future and though it was unlikely that his forces would come this far south even while employing their favourite pincer movement, there had been increased activity generally in the areas patrolled by the Group.

In the event of something having gone awry, the position was not too serious as the cache held sufficient food and water for a considerable period. The main problem would be how to get back to base since only a limited amount could be carried. The idea of staying until a chance patrol arrived did not enter into his speculations, all the evidence indicated that Rommel was preparing for a determined attack on the Gazala/Bir Hacheim Line and it could well be that many weeks could pass without rescue and the supply so necessary to life would be exhausted. He wondered whether the plane he had watched could have any bearing on the non-appearance of Jimmy and the others. Jimmy was usually such a punctual cove!

He considered the position carefully and decided to spend the night at the rendezvous in case the truck had been delayed, but he felt in his bones that this was not the reason for its non arrival. His intuition, sharpened by the risks involved with his present way of life, seldom let him down and it was working overtime at the moment. Even if he left immediately, it was unlikely that he could contact his patrol before it moved off.

The Free French Brigade was in the area of Bir Hacheim and it seemed to Basil that his best plan would be to try and make contact here. His return to Siwa would then be a simple matter.

CHAPTER 4

A Medical Officer, wearing the flash of the Indian Army Medical Corps, picked his way carefully between the rows of wounded; a few had the comfort of a stretcher, but the great majority lay on the desert sand without so much as a blanket to lend a pretence of comfort. All still wore their uniforms, or what was left of them, the khaki drill of the Allies mingling with the olive green of the Afrika Korps. Thoughtfully he surveyed the tragic scene and wondered, "would it never end?"

The three days since his Brigade had been over-run had been three days of nightmare activity. Meanwhile the battle raged without cessation, swinging with incredible speed and monstrous violence, from Acroma in the north to Bir Hacheim, 40 miles to the south, and from El Adem to the mine fields on the Gazala Line, sending a never ending stream of wounded back to the Field Dressing Station, which had become so hopelessly overcrowded that the German Medical Staff had been only too thankful for the assistance he and his two orderlies were able to give.

"Have we a catheter Sir?", the query cut across his thoughts.

Irritably he shook his head,

"Why?", he snapped the answer, then quickly, "I'll see what can be done". The risk to the bladder through retention of urine was a frequent complication with shock and had ever been a problem, particularly when proper attention was impossible. The harassed orderly bustled off to assist the unloading of a new batch of wounded just arriving.

Wearily the M.O. made his way to a large marquee, lifting the fly net to enter. The unmistakable stench of stale blood, sweat and grime intermingled with the heavy odour of medicants that assailed his nostrils as he entered, was overpowering in the confined space. He looked around, his eyes accustoming themselves to the comparative gloom after the glare outside. A table at one end held dressings and a few instruments, while all the paraphernalia used in first aid was dumped in one corner.

Some two dozen stretchers lay around the walls, each bearing its unhappy burden. Quickly he searched the table, but could find no catheters. Speculatively he examined a length of fine rubber tubing, apparently from a sphygmomanometer, and wondered whether it would do the trick.

"Oh well, can but try", he spoke aloud. Turning to leave the marquee his eye fell on one of the patients, blanket wrapped and properly bandaged, obviously attended to before everything got out of hand.

"Water", the request barely audible and coming in English surprised him, he had thought these were all Germans in here. Gently he raised the head, pressing his water bottle to the lips. The eyes, intensely blue and unnaturally bright, held more than a hint of fever. The patient drank greedily, choking in his eagerness. Firmly, the M.O. removed the bottle,

"Thank you Sir", then becoming agitated, "Get Basil-get Basil - clean swift click of ball on bat - whose Mary anyway" he lapsed into delirious mutterings.

Loud shouting and the noise of many lorries outside the tent brought the M.O. quickly to his feet. Hurrying outside he looked around him.

"Thank God", he muttered in relief, the promised convoy had arrived to start the Herculean task of shifting out the wounded. Already six vehicles were drawn up taking on their load. The remainder, some 60 lorries, a few ambulances and some open trucks, were deployed over a wide area. Despite his relief, the M.O.'s heart sank as he recognised many famous Division Signs for, in addition to the Palm Tree and Swastika, there was the Rhino, the Gazelle, the Desert Rat and others. Obviously the German net had been cast far and wide and returned a bumper haul. Small wonder the Hun seemed jubilant.

By the time he reached the sweating working party the first truck was ready to leave. Those able to sit being placed crocodile fashion on the floor, leaving a gangway down the centre for two lying cases.

The work of loading carried on for several hours, until at last only the walking remained. These were herded into two straggling lines ready to march off. The Germans and a few Italians in one party and the, British, now under armed escort, in another. At length they were gone, leaving only the dead and a miscellaneous accumulation of various bits of personal gear, mute evidence of the tragedy of war. The M.O. turned and strolled back to the marquee.......

Unbelieving, Jimmy felt the coarse clean sheets, that he was in a hospital was definite, but where? Vaguely, as in a dream, he remembered a British M.O. bending over him, then odd snatches of a painful journey in a truck along with several others. He tried to sit up, but the effort proved too much and he was thankful to relax back on the pillow. His left arm ached abominably, while his head felt like the Grandfather of all hangovers. Gradually his swimming head cleared and he began to take stock of his surroundings. As far as he could see from his prone position, he was in a hospital ward. A metal bracket at the foot of his bed held a glass bottle from which a rubber tube descended, which seemed to be attached to his foot. As his faculties returned he realised what it was, and-memory came with a rush. The armoured cars, Frank and Arthur had bought it. The kaleidoscope of jumbled meaningless events. An Officer bending over him. A jolting painful ride, which seemed to go on forever. The questing mind began to race, "Jock - what the hell happened to him, was he alright? Did anyone pick him up?

How long had he been here? Where the hell was he anyway and something important, what was it?" The doubt nagged at his brain.

"Nurse, nurse." His call brought an orderly hurrying down the ward.

Stopping by the bed, the orderly looked at him, noting with satisfaction the intelligent gleam now in Jimmy's eyes - all trace of fever seemed to have left.

"Hallo chum,"', he grinned, "Glad to see you're with us at last". Jimmy struggled to raise himself, but the restraining hand of the orderly stopped him.

"Name's Dick - what's yours?"

"Bowles, Jimmy Bowles".

"Alright Jimmy, what can we do for you?", as he spoke Dick deftly adjusted the flow on the blood set, mentally noting the level. Suddenly Jimmy remembered

"A bloke, Basil Holden, find out if he was picked up".

The orderly remained silent a moment - Jimmy began to get agitated, "I must know ..."

"Now then old son, don't you fret", Dick soothed, "I'll see what can be done, but you must be quiet and rest up. Perhaps the Oberstarztsargt will know something".

"Ober what?", Jimmy paled as realisation smote him -"Where the hell am I anyway?"

For a brief moment Dick contemplated lying, but the truth had to be told. Gruffly and almost brutally he said

"Derna Hospital - you're a P.O.W. now".

Having already suspected this, Jimmy's reaction was one of concern for the safety of his friend.

"For God's sake say nothing about Basil. Don't want Jerry patrols scouring the desert for him - what the devil you doing here anyway?" He scowled suspiciously "You're English aren't you?"

Dick laughed, "I got rounded up a month ago, being medics they kept me on here to help out." He glanced at his watch and straightened the bed, pumping the pillow to make Jimmy more comfortable,

"How's that?"

Jimmy smiled - "Grand".

"O.K. old chum, must buzz now, but I'll fill you in with all the gen later."

The conversation, brief though it was had made Jimmy incredibly tired, sapping his will to think; the heavy lids closed and nature took its inevitable toll.

When he awoke, some two hours later, a German Officer had entered the ward, accompanied by a British M.O. with the rank of Captain. Behind came two German Orderlies and Dick. The cavalcade advanced slowly down the ward, stopping now and then beside a bed to confer. Jimmy watched their approach, the sight of the German uniforms bringing home to him the full realisation that he had indeed been captured.

They stopped opposite Jimmy's bed; the Captain examined the chart, then looking at Jimmy, he smiled

"Well Bowles, you're looking fitter - are you comfortable?"

Jimmy nodded, "I'll survive".

"Good!" Then, sounding slightly embarrassed. "The Officer with me holds the rank of Major, and must be respected as such. He should be addressed as Herr Oberstabsarzt, but he will accept Sir". The German Officer stepped forward arrogantly but superbly correct, "Good morning Wachmeister, my name is Duncker, I am the Kommandant here, but I am also your Doktor. As Kommandant I must have obedience and I am strict. You will obey the orders given by the Sanitatsunteroffizier. As your Doktor, I will get you well - you understand? As Doktors your Captain Dark and I work together and we hope you will co-operate."

The haughty eyes bored into Jimmy for a moment then, softening - "It is understood, the fortunes of war."

His English held only the slightest trace of accent and Jimmy wondered where he had learned it, as he inclined his head by way of reply, the German acknowledging with a stiff little bow.

At the time Jimmy could not have spoken even had he wanted to, the idea of respecting an enemy officer's wishes was repugnant to him even though he realised that he had his well being at heart. Later he would have been the first to admit that Herr Oberstabsarzt Duncker treated him with the same care and attention that he gave the wounded of his own side, affording the British M.O. every facility possible within his resources and supervising the work as assiduously as he had when, as a civilian, he had been the Registrar of a large hospital in Germany. The superb care he received at Derna Hospital was very largely responsible for his eventual recovery.

During the next two or three days, Jimmy spent most of his time asleep. Eventually he rallied sufficiently to start taking an interest in his surroundings. That something very unpleasant had occurred was obvious from the high proportion of British wounded in the ward. The Germans were unlikely to put their own wounded into a ward reserved specifically for

P.O.W.'s; on the other hand, if, as he suspected, he was in the regular ward of a Military Hospital, then it was reasonable to suppose that there should be more of the enemy wounded than British. The implications depressed him. It is one thing to be a prisoner in the hands of the side that is losing the war, but quite another matter if the captors appear to be winning. The chances of release seemed remote and in his condition escape out of the question. It is probable that, had Jimmy's morale not been sapped by the debilitating effect of his terrible wounds, he would not have allowed himself to dwell on these morbid thoughts. As it was, he let matters prey on his mind and became more depressed day by day. One of the German orderlies, taking advantage of the black mood, deliberately taunted him with exaggerated accounts of how well the Afrika Korps was advancing. Dick, seeing what was going on, did his best to cheer Jimmy up, but having little or no accurate information of events in the field, was unable to refute the German's statements. Eventually, thoroughly disgusted with the action of his own countryman, one of the patients, Wachmeister Karl Braun, from one of the Panzer Divisions, put a stop to the taunting by complaining to the Oberstabsarzt.

Jimmy was virtually on his own as most of the Germans in the ward kept themselves strictly to themselves. By some unlucky chance he was the only Englishmen on his side of the ward, which made communication with the other British Soldiers almost impossible as they too were all seriously wounded. A few English lads did stay just overnight in transit to Benghazi, but apart from a word of 'hail and farewell' there was not much chance to speak to these. Dick was much too busy to spend any time chatting and, had it not been for Karl Braun, he would probably have continued to decline. As it was, the German Sgt., who had received his wound at Sidi Rezegh, befriended him and developed the habit of spending quite a portion of the day chatting, although his English left a great deal to be desired. The graphic gestures used to communicate succeeded in raising a laugh. Karl considerately kept away from the subject of the war, regaling Jimmy with many a comic anecdote of his exploits as a 'commi-waiter' in a London Hotel during the last year of peace. The lengthy discussions kept Jimmy's mind off his morbid thoughts and as his interest re-ignited, he began to ask more and more questions about his surroundings and the general progress of the war. In this way Jimmy learned of the German Bridgehead on the Gazala Line and the fierce fighting in the El Adam area leading to the isolation of Tobruk and the eventual surrender on June 21st. He was amazed to learn that this fortress had fallen with hardly a shot fired and wondered about the accuracy of his information. If he was crestfallen at this item of news he had so far advanced in his recovery that he didn't show it, but there was no mistaking the pride shining in his eyes when he heard of the magnificent stand put up by the Northumbrians at Got es Scarab when cut off by the establishment of the Bridgehead. The ensuing weeks passed swiftly in this manner so that, when the time came for Jimmy to leave, he really regretted parting from his German friend.

Although still confined to bed, he was much stronger when the ambulance carried him along the very road to Tobruk he had helped watch while on patrol more than 12 months before; he chuckled at the memory of the delayed action bombs thrown into enemy trucks as they passed.

By the time Jimmy had reached Caserta Hospital, near Naples, he was up and about.

Better food, supplemented by Red Cross parcels and a more clement climate, quickly built up his strength, while the comradeship shared with fellow P.O.W.'s soon restored him to his normal happy nature. The time at Caserta passed quickly and pleasantly enough, with nothing much to do except chat, play chess or draughts, or sit around the veranda and watch the young Italian girls visiting their boy friends in the wing of the hospital outside the wire. This last being a favourite occupation with nearly everyone.

With strength fast returning and a sane outlook on life, Jimmy's thoughts began to occupy themselves more and more with plans of escape. Realising a knowledge of the Italian language would be essential, he asked an Italian girl, one of the Red Cross helpers, to teach him. She readily agreed, visiting Jimmy daily, and conducting the lessons with such bouncing enthusiasm that she was quickly christened 'Flossie Bubbles' by the lads. With hospital routine to consider and other commitments on her time, she tended to bound in at approximately the same hour every day. This happened to coincide with the mid-day soup and afternoon coffee times, when the lads were in the habit of devouring some item of food from the Red Cross parcels. Food in the hospital was not very plentiful, in fact without the parcels it would have constituted a starvation diet. Thus it is not surprising that 'Flossie Bubbles' opening remark of "But you are always eating'", was not only awaited with hushed expectancy, but greeted with a howl of mirth the moment it had been uttered.

Twelve weeks after the action in the desert sand where Jimmy had received his wounds, he was considered fit for transfer to Prison Camp.

After so many weeks at Caserta Hospital, where life had been comparatively easy, Jimmy was understandably sorry to leave. He had made many friends there and the chances of linking up again were remote. On the other hand he welcomed the move. The sooner he was settled in a permanent camp, the sooner he could plan his escape.

The party of which Jimmy was a member was taken by truck to a transit camp at Capua, and thence by train to P.G. 59 near Gualdo di Macerata. The camp in which Jimmy eventually found himself was large, unsanitary and vermin ridden. The prisoners being housed in huge storage rooms originally built for the storing and processing of sugar beet.

Sleeping arrangements were by means of three tier double bunks, separated by a single plank of wood to give individual sleeping space and equipped with a straw filled bag as a mattress. Since the straw was never changed it was the ideal sanctuary of every type of infestation imaginable.

When Jimmy's party arrived, there was an immediate rush for the lower bunks. Jimmy, however, chose a top bunk in preference since he felt the mild exercise of clambering aboard would benefit him. In point of fact, he scored since the men on the lower bunks soon found to their disgust that they seemed to acquire twice as many vermin as those on the higher bunks.

The tiers of bunks were arranged in banks of 8 units, with a 3' gangway between each bank which constituted a platoon of 48 men one of whom was an N.C.O. in charge and responsible for discipline and the distribution of rations and Red Cross parcels. Jimmy found himself in a platoon under the care of a stocky and very tough Warrant Officer from the Tank Regiment whose real name was Cooper, but rejoiced under the not very imaginative appellage of 'Tanky'.

Tanky proved to be a likeable fellow who lost no time in introducing himself to the members of his platoon and instituted a rota system immediately he realised that the 50 gramme roll of bread constituting the daily ration for each man, varied in size. Under this rota system each man had his turn of first selection from the 48 rolls. The rota was also used in conjunction with first dip in the cauldron of skilly. This, soup was often so thin that frequently the last man served received vegetable broth with no body whatsoever.

The cutting of the daily cheese ration into 48 equal pieces, however, proved completely beyond Tanky's capabilities. The portions being so minute that he suggested each man should take it in turn to have all the cheese at once. Although this meant cheese only once in 48 days, the idea was unanimously adopted, proving so popular that other platoons were quick to follow suit.

With the adaptability stemming from his years of service, Jimmy lost no time settling in. By the morning after his arrival, he might have spent all his life in the camp. Always an early riser from years of habit, Jimmy was up with the lark - he dashed outside for his morning ablutions to find to his disgust a massive queue to the one and only tap shared between the 3,000 inhabitants of his section of the camp[4]. As soon as he realised the position he made a mental resolve that, by hook or by crook he'd be first at the brook on subsequent days. When at last he had finished his wash he returned his kit to the bunk and wandered into the compound to explore. The stone chipping

---

[4] Conditions at the camp were subsequently improved when a water tower was built and proper washing facilities installed.

surface outside his building gave clean walking and Jimmy welcomed the opportunity of exercise in fresh air after so many weeks of confinement to hospital wards and verandahs. The camp, roughly square, was split into three compounds, no communication being permitted between the prisoners of different compounds and the entire area surrounded by two barbed wire fences about 10' apart. The inner of these bore a warning notice that it was charged with a high voltage electric current. Jimmy decided there and then that he wasn't likely to test the accuracy of the warning. A small notice, found at frequent intervals along a trip wire placed about 3' inside the inner perimeter wire, bore the legend -

"Halt'. Stoppage and Demurrhage no allowed. You will be shotted."

Jimmy chuckled to himself on seeing this and wondered who the author was.

A tower equipped with searchlight and machine guns, stood at the corner of each compound. Sentries patrolled the outer perimeter and every gate, whether inside or outside the camp, had a double guard. Floodlighting completed the precautions against escape. To Jimmy, taking in his surroundings, escape seemed impossible, particularly if, as he suspected, the sentries were alert. Only a week earlier he had watched helplessly as a prisoner attempted to get through a similar arrangement at Capua. Somehow he got through the two wires in broad daylight and charged the sentry only to be shot dead before three yards had been covered. Furthermore, Capua had not boasted an electrified fence. Jimmy sauntered round the circuit of his compound, keeping a sharp look out for any possible loop-holes. Stopping to light a cigarette, he placed a foot on one of the posts bearing the trip wire, the better to shield the flame of his match. The immediate response of a sentry in one of the towers and his shouted warning, left no doubt in Jimmy's mind that the sentries were indeed alert.

After some half dozen tours round the compound, Jimmy began to realise he still had a long way to go before he could consider himself fit enough to attempt a break out. Feeling unreasonably tired from his brief period of exercise, and just a little depressed, he returned to his bunk for a rest. Throwing himself on the straw mattress, he was soon fast asleep.

CHAPTER 5

When Jimmy awoke about half-an-hour later, his gaze centred on bronze sardonic features creased in a smile, the cleft between the grey eyes seeming deeper than he had remembered. He sat up with a jerk exclaiming

"Well I'm damned - Basil Holden. Where the devil did you spring from?"

The two men clasped hands and, in the emotion of the moment, embraced each other.

"I might ask where the hell did you get to", Basil responded as they broke apart, his smile robbing the words of all offence. For a space of minutes they sat grinning at each other without a word. Eventually, Basil spoke.

"When I saw you going out to the compound this morning, I wasn't sure it was you. Somehow, without the sunburn, you looked. different, then again, you are a lot thinner. Anyway, I saw old Tanky who confirmed that it was indeed a Sgt. Jimmy Bowles, so I arranged for the chap on the bunk alongside you to swap places with me. From now on old bean we're together".

Jimmy grinned happily and said, "Brother, what a celebration we could have if only... "

Basil laughed outright before he could finish - "Why not? I've got some bits and pieces left, let's have a brew up". With all the agility of a cat, he jumped down from the bunk, grabbing a small tin stove, which he referred to as his blower[5], and a bag which had obviously been made up from the legs of a pair of desert shorts. The draw-string, originally designed to tie round the calf as a protection against mosquito and sand-fly, serving to close the opening.

"Come on Jimmy, see how the bloated rich live".

Leading the way outside, he soon had a fire going in the stove which he fed by scraps from the bag. Within five minutes the forced flames had boiled the Klim[6] pots and tea had been made. Basil quickly dowsed the stove, collecting the charred embers and placing them in a special tin he kept for the purpose.

"Can't afford to waste anything that burns round here", he grinned. Collecting the gear together, the two friends hurried back to their bunks where Basil produced biscuits, butter and jam and a revolting looking mess

---

[5] Blower: a brew stove constructed from old tin cans and equipped with a fan operated by winding a handle on the side.

[6] Klim: proprietary brand of dried tinned milk often enclosed in Red Cross parcels.

he referred to as 'Capua Tart'[7]. Even though eaten slowly, to spin out the enjoyment, the minute feast didn't last long. Jimmy fished out cigarettes,

"Have a Caporal". Basil shook his head -

"Today calls for Players" and with the air of a magician, he produced a packet of the English brand -"We can smoke those horrors later". Lighting his own cigarette, he quickly dowsed the match, placing the burnt remnant carefully in his brew bag and proffered a light from his cigarette to Jimmy.

"Well Jimmy my lad, what happened?"

Supping tea and drawing contentedly on the cigarette, Jimmy quickly recounted the events leading to his capture.

"I might add", he finished, "I've often wondered how you fared stranded like that."

Basil shifted himself into a more comfortable position - "Well now old chum, it's a longish story; there's still tea in the pot, so make yourself useful and I'll try and fill you in as closely as I can".

He sat silent for a moment, his forehead puckered in thought while Jimmy waited, watching every move of the lean face and noting the tiny creases around the mouth that had not been there before.

"First of all, the stunt was a rollicking success"

"Oh yes", Jimmy interrupted, "We saw the bonfire".

"Alright, so far so good", Basil continued, "When you failed to show up I guessed something had gone wrong, so decided to stay the night and push on to Bir Hacheim in the morning, hoping I might contact the Frenchies. As you know, they were on the southern end of the Gazala Line".

Jimmy nodded ,I thought you'd probably try that".

Basil grinned ,"It seemed the only sensible thing. Mind you, I did toy with the idea of making for the Jaghbub Track in the hope of seeing a patrol, but the distance involved was about 40 miles and the prospects of picking up a patrol remote."

Basil leaned forward, nipping out his cigarette, and carefully stowed the stub in a tin.

"Anyway, I kipped down for the night, but was woken up by the most infernal racket. I sat up in a hurry I can tell you. The moon had risen and the old blue was like daylight, you know how it can be".

---

[7] Capua Tart: Biscuits or bread, soaked in water, interleaved with raisins, and dried in the sun.

Jimmy nodded his agreement.

"About half-a-mile to the north east, literally hordes of tanks were moving in a south easterly direction, a line that would carry them south of Bir Hacheim. There wasn't a thing I could do but sit and watch. Some time later there were flashes in the sky and I guessed they had engaged our chaps.

All next day I hung around and watched the traffic, making a record of what I saw. It was like being on the Marble Arch road watch over again. That something big was going on was obvious, that patch of desert became as busy as a Sunday Coast Road back home. Supply trucks banging up and down almost nose to tail".

Basil paused and grinned ruefully, "It was a bit of a mess. To tell the truth I didn't realise at the time that I had been cut off. When the Lord Mayor's Show continued all through the night and next day I realised that this was more than just a skirmish and Rommel's push had started. To reach Bir Hacheim entailed filtering through the hordes of moving enemy vehicles so I abandoned the project. I could have sought shelter with the Arabs, but reasoned that, with a heavy action under way, they would probably have made themselves scarce and, in any case, I didn't want to hang around in the Gebel with our own chaps so near. If the distance involved had not been so great I would have made straight for Jalo but, of course, I was much too far east to use the chain of dumps running down from Marble Arch."

Jimmy looked astonished. "I'm surprised you decided against the Jaghbub Track, surely you would have stood a better chance there of being spotted by a patrol?"

Basil shrugged, "Normally yes, but don't forget, it was pretty certain that Jerry had a major offensive under way and what was more, from the amount of stuff passing, it seemed to me that he was pushing ahead pretty rapidly. I reckoned if I was in his place I'd be watching the tracks very closely and would certainly try to control such an important track. Then again, it would have taken me at least a week, probably much longer, to get to Jaghbub, during which time anything could happen".

He paused to light a cigarette, offering one to his friend.

"The Indian Infantry Brigade at Bir el Gubi were only about 50 miles away as the crow flies, and I reckoned I could probably detour south, well clear of the fighting, and be there in four days. I only had the four pints of water and rationed myself to half-a-pint a day. Even though I was travelling by day and sleeping at night, I didn't see a soul, not even a stray Arab selling eggs! The nightly firework display came closer and closer and I was forced to detour further south than I had intended. Anyway, the long and the short of it is I didn't reach Bir el Gubi until 11/12 June - only to find the birds had flown."

Jimmy laughed, "Sorry old chum, but you're a right Charlie and no mistake".

"Well yes! I did feel a bit of a fool and could have kicked myself. My food and water had got depressingly low. Anyway, as you know, there is a well at Bir el Gubi, and pretty foul stuff that water is too - but water is water and I was able to replenish my supply. Grub was the bigger problem, until I hit on the idea of finding where the camp had been. Scratching around in the sand wasn't my idea of fun, but it yielded a tin of bully, several scraps of biscuits, also believe it or not an Onion - trying to grow."

Jimmy chuckled. "Go on! True or false?"

"True enough", Basil affirmed, "I was a bit doubtful about keeping it but decided I couldn't afford to waste any grub and ate it on the spot. Boy was it a hot one! I had at last succeeded in getting east of the fighting, so planned to stay the night near the waterhole and march north in the morning. Sidi Rezegh was only about 25 miles away and I had high hopes of making contact long before I reached there. About midnight, I woke with a start. Armoured cars and trucks were buzzing around like flies and deploying over a wide area. From the shouting and general excitement, I gathered they were Italians. I suppose my first thought was to get out, but the possibility of grabbing a piece of transport was tempting so I hung around for a while, waiting for a suitable opportunity. However, every truck I looked at had a horde of bods bedding down around or under it, making it impossible to swipe one without raising a proper hullabaloo. Feeling thoroughly thwarted, I lit out just before daylight just about as fast as my legs would carry me, which, truth to tell, was not a very cracking pace. The padding around on meagre rations was slowing me down rather more than somewhat.

It never occurred to me that the enemy would get so far east and I had a nasty suspicion that if their advance continued to keep pace with me, I should end up by walking all the way to Alex.

The new conditions made a northward tack impossible, so I set course for Sidi Omar and hoped the little food and water I had left would last out. From this time onwards my memory's rather hazy and I believe I may have been a bit light headed at times. Somehow I lost my compass, when and where I don't know, and wandered around, missing Sidi Omar completely. The food I had found at Bir El Gubi was soon exhausted and I was at last forced to open the emergency ration."

Basil paused, his face suddenly grim. "The bloody thing held two pieces of wood and some earth".

"What!" - Jimmy's ejaculation was like a pistol shot. For a moment the pair were silent Jimmy's face reflecting his shocked horror, while Basil's normally good natured expression had given way to such a look of murderous hate that it even chilled his friend.

"Steady on Basil". Jimmy's quiet voice cut across his thoughts. Basil relaxed and smiled tightly.

"Sorry mate, but if I could get my hands on those thieving blighters back home..." He left the sentence unfinished.

"The main thing is I survived. When the water ran out the following day, I really began to suffer and started trying anything to keep me alive. I think the most disastrous effort was some cactus which I pulped down for the juice. It was as bitter as gall and left a burning sensation in my mouth and throat. Some snails I found gave a little relief, and a derelict truck provided a tiny drop of water from its radiator. The rest is a meaningless jumble with no sense of time or place.

Eventually, I stumbled on some Arabs who took me to their camp, and looked after me while I rested up. During the three days I was with them I learned that the Afrika Korps was at Solum, and that Tobruk had fallen. When one of the Arabs offered to guide me to a track which would take me to Gerawla I jumped at the opportunity. He was as good as his word and left me about five miles from the coast, having first made sure that my water bottle was full. Before I had walked a mile I fell in with some Indians, who took me to their H.Q."

"How on earth did you end up here then?" The puzzled look on Jimmy's face brought a chuckle from Basil.

"Sheer bad luck really. The H.Q. was deserted. While I was busy getting to Gerawla, Rommel's forces were equally busy getting round the place. The whole area was virtually cut off. Had I realised this when I actually arrived, I could probably have got out, but instead, I became involved in the most chaotic shambles it has ever been my misfortune to see. It was very definitely a case of every man for himself and the devil take the one without transport.

From what I saw of things, a little organisation would have got nearly everyone out of the trap, instead of which trucks half empty and sometimes completely empty, dashed down the road to the east, the drivers apparently only concerned with their own safety. It seems incredible I know, but one chap told me that he actually had his hand on the tail of a truck half full of his own mates. Rather than delay, the Lance Bombardier i/c booted him away and left him stranded.

Needless to say, when I realised the position, I had a dekko round for some transport myself, but was unlucky and started to walk. The following morning, June 28th, just thirty-three days after I had started my trek, a German Patrol picked me up. Having a pretty wholesome regard for my skin I didn't argue.

I must say the Germans treated us very well all things considered, but when we were handed over to the Italians at Tobruk things began to get a bit rough. We crossed the Med. in the hold of a coal boat, the Black hole of Calcutta had nothing on it, and finally reached Capua where I stayed some weeks while this camp was being prepared. One night about 50 chaps escaped, and though the full story never came out, it was rumoured that they had gone through the sewer. Did you come through that camp by the way?" Jimmy nodded.

"You will recall the latrines were sizeable holes communicating direct with the main sewer. It seems that some character had been an Inspector of the London Sewers and lowered himself down to investigate. He found it was possible to walk through the system and emerge well away from the camp. He must have been a bit of a lad because he returned and led a large party from his old Unit through. I expect he didn't like to risk imparting the news to anyone he didn't actually know for fear of betrayal - what a sight though, all those blokes literally going down the plug-hole!

I never did hear whether they got away with it or were re-captured, or for that matter how the story leaked out, but certainly the Ities were surprised at the large number missing next day on roll call and instituted a three times daily call for the next week, but despite interrogation, I don't think they ever discovered the truth."

As Basil came to the end of his story, Jimmy automatically went over it again, co-relating the salient facts with the knowledge he had gleaned of Rommel's advance from the Gazala Line to the outskirts of Alexandria. The ingenious series of thrusts aimed at the soft lines of communication with sufficient forces to effectively cut off selected areas, explained the reason for the sudden collapse of our front. His spirits soared as he realised that The Allies had not been defeated in face to face combat. Rommel's fantastically long line of communication would be an inevitable weakness and, for the first time since his capture, Jimmy began to believe that the tables would eventually be turned.

CHAPTER 6

Although the more energetic P.O.W.'s had organised a variety of activities which covered every conceivable form of entertainment from Chess to Concert Parties, many were too apathetic to take part. Resisting each and every endeavour made by the various organisers to energise themselves and refusing to take an interest in anything. They could be seen slouching around the camp or lying on a bunk, too lethargic to make any attempt to keep themselves neat or clean. If they spoke, which was seldom, it would be in a whine bemoaning their hardships, but usually their introspective self-pity made conversation impossible. All too many developed sores on elbows or back sides, caused mainly by the almost constant pressure of sitting or lying and because of a debilitated condition brought on by the combination of a psychological outlook and the totally inadequate diet, the sores, once started, would spread rapidly, in many instances becoming gangrenous. The almost invariable decline into death was alarming in its, rapidity.

Basil and Jimmy were determined that nothing like this should happen to them, taking part in everything that came along they kept their minds fully occupied throughout the long days. In order that they should retain their physical tone they mapped out a course of exercises which was strictly adhered to. The routine included two hours of brisk walking round the compound every day irrespective of weather conditions. The regular exercise kept them fit, but unfortunately increased their appetites, creating a perpetual hunger impossible to assuage on the scant nourishment available. The Red Cross parcels, well balanced though they were, had never been intended as more than a supplement to camp rations.

About six weeks after Jimmy arrived at the camp, the pair of chums were taking their duty walk when, suddenly, Jimmy stopped, drawing Basil's attention to a wooden shed.

"Isn't that the food magazine?" He resumed walking - "Have you noticed the construction of that shed?"

"No not particularly, why?"

"Well, I've had a bit to do with shed construction and I'll eat my hat if that's not just a wood frame-work with weather boards tacked on. Anyway it's given me the germ of an idea for supplementing our food stakes."

The shed, which was kept locked but unguarded, stood in the centre of an enclosure separated by a single fence of barbed wire from the compound. Although unprotected by the trip wire, entry to the enclosure would not assist an attempt to escape since it stood entirely within the bounds of the camp, the only guard was a Piantone at the gate which was in the Admin. compound.

"I believe it may be possible to remove three or four planks and rig them up so that they could be replaced without any obvious signs that they had been tampered with. I'll explain in more detail when I've worked it out properly."

As the two continued their walking, they fell silent. Basil liked the idea, and if Jimmy said there was a way of removing the planks then he was probably right. His mind began to tussle with the problem of how to get into the area. There was no telling whether the fence was electrified or not. It Probably wasn't since it bore no warning notices. Then again, if it was electrified it would surely be a source of danger to the Italians for, unlike the main fences which had an open area between the outer perimeter and the inner electrified fence, thus eliminating the risk of an accidental touch, this one had no such protective guard. However, he wouldn't care to test out his theory by coming into contact with the wire. That it was capable of being electrified was obvious since the wire was carried on insulators in a similar manner to that used on the inner boundary but, though Basil looked closely on each circuit of the compound, he couldn't see any obvious connection to the electric supply. A safe means of creating a direct short would have to be devised as a test before he could be satisfied that the fence was safe. He smiled as he pictured the ensuing scare if it proved to be alive, there would be a mighty flash and the Itie would go berserk. It wouldn't do to be seen close to the barrier then he mused. Occasionally a Piantone would sell a length of baling strip for an exorbitant number of camp money tokens; this strip was very popular for fashioning into eating knives. It was capable of being sharpened on a stone and when bound with string to form a handle, made a fairly satisfactory knife for buttering the bread rolls. Since it was quite useless as a weapon of attack, the authorities permitted its use. A length of this with one end stuck into the ground and the other lobbed over the wire should create a satisfactory contact and, if the fence did carry a current, it would become immediately obvious. The question was how to get a length sufficient for his purpose without rousing any suspicion. The obtainable material seldom measured more than 12" or so and he calculated that he would need a piece at least 9' length if every run of wire was to be tested.

Meanwhile, Jimmy's thoughts had been occupied with the shed, his searching glance taking in every salient detail each time they came abreast of the object of their interest. He was convinced that his impression was correct; he noted with satisfaction that a large number of short lengths of weatherboard had been used in the building, presumably he thought to use up existing timber and conserve supplies. At the rear end there were about half-a-dozen 4' lengths, adjacent to each other. If four of these could re removed it should leave an aperture measuring about 2' x 3'. Nothing had been done to cover the end join of the various planks. Jimmy reasoned that the nails holding the highest selected board would have to be removed in order that it could be slipped out of position. Once this had been achieved it would be a simple matter to pull away the remainder. He hoped the builders had not been too generous in their use of nails. Two nails for each board would then have to be replaced in the uprights to act as pegs and corresponding holes, one at each end of the weather boards, enlarged in order that they could be hung in position, leaving the structure apparently intact. Normally the task would be extremely simple, but the need for silence, coupled with the lack of suitable tools brought a pucker to his brow as he wrestled with the problem.

Scarcely a word was exchanged as, engrossed in their thoughts, they continued to walk briskly round and round the compound long after their minimum stint was finished was finished. At last as if by mutual agreement they returned to their bunks where, in low tones, every point of the proposed scheme was discussed until, after several hours, they had conceived a plan which promised a reasonable chance of success.

Before the plan could be put into operation, tools would have to be devised, first to cut the wire fence and secondly to withdraw the nails securing the weather boards of the shed. The first of these presented no real difficulty, since a small cold chisel, and cutting plate was easily fashioned from the steel tip taken from a pair of Army Boots. The original owner willingly accepted a tin of Peak Frean apple pie for the coveted article. If he thought the pair were mad he didn't say so.

An implement for withdrawing nails was a tougher problem many ideas were suggested and rejected as being unlikely to do the trick with sufficient speed and certainty. For three weeks they cudgelled their brains, experimenting with laminations of tin to form a jemmy but without success. Then, providence took a hand in the form of a gang of workmen who arrived to start the erection of a tower to provide the camp with an adequate water supply. Together they enviously watched a carpenter wielding his claw hammer as be built shuttering ready for the concrete mix, and determined between themselves that somehow they would secure this prize.

If the conspirators saw a solution to their problems in the tools brought by the workmen, their delight was as nothing compared to the glee engendered in the hearts of their comrades at the sight of so much valuable combustible material suddenly appearing in a camp where every expendable object had long since been fed into the brew stoves. That night the carpenters' entire days effort disappeared into a thousand brew bags. As was to be expected, the following morning became one of intense activity as the guards stamped between the serried rows of bunks vainly searching for the missing timber. Acting with typical herd stupidity they looked for planks of wood and found none. Puzzled, they searched all the likely places where big items could he concealed and ignored the insignificant little brew bags. Meanwhile the delighted prisoners grinned and winked at each other. When the disappointed guards left the compound the combined hoots of laughter that went up were so loud that the sentries at their posts alerted themselves fearful a mass break was about to commence.

A large proportion of Basil's time during the ensuing few days was spent watching the carpenter for an opportunity to steal his hammer. Eventually the opportunity came. The carpenter laid it on the edge of some shuttering surrounding a trough already half filled with concrete while he collected up some spilt nails. Swooping like a hawk, Basil scooped up the hammer, dropped a largish stone into the wet concrete and faded promptly from the scene. The carpenter missed his hammer immediately, but seeing the disturbed surface of the concrete, shrugged philosophically and went off to collect a new tool.

Meanwhile, feeling extremely elated Basil hurried to the barrack-like building where they lived and slept. On reaching his bunk he carefully hid the hammer in the straw mattress. Then, in high spirits, went off in search of Jimmy. He found him reading "Griff", a weekly news sheet, which was posted on a notice board and the labour of love of a group of men who spent a large portion of their time writing up the scant items of news that could he gathered within the confines of the camp. The combined talent was remarkable, providing regular cartoons, usually depicting the humorous side of camp life and a feature article centred on places of interest outside the wire. Printed carefully in pencil to resemble a sheet of newspaper, the product was a 'work of art and represented many hours of painstaking effort by the artists.

"Oh there you are". Basil greeted Jimmy.

"Hallo", Jimmy turned towards his friend, then indicating a small notice pinned up alongside the News Sheet-

"Have you seen this?"

Basil frowned as he read the notice –

Discipline

1. No prisoner will be allowed in the compound during the hours of darkness. A guard will be placed outside the door of each building and will shoot anyone disobeying this order.

Platoon Commanders will call the roll morning and evening and ensure that this order is complied with.

2. Brewing up in the compound will cease.

Basil swore with a peculiarly ferocious Arabic oath-

"I've managed to scrounge that damned hammer, now, this we shall have to plan new. What a blasted nuisance!"

"It is a bit of a bind" agreed. Jimmy mildly." I suppose they are penalising us for the nightly forays in the timber stakes". "Probably - I've half expected something like this." Then, as an idea struck him, he laughed -"A pencil, quick Jimmy. Have you one?" Jimmy foraged around his pockets until he found a small stub. Taking it, Basil wrote swiftly in a bold hand at the base of the offending notice -

THE BREW MUST GO ON!

Chuckling, the pair left the notice board making their way into the warm sunshine outside. Later when they returned for the evening issue of Fenuchi soup, they glanced at the notice board in passing and saw that someone had added -

WHATEVER HAPPENS

above Basil's contribution.

The full phrase became a slogan in the camp as the prisoners vied with each other in their endeavours to keep the practice going. Brewing began to take place between the gangways of the bunks, in the sanctuary of the latrines, and every imaginable place that could not be interpreted as 'Compound'. Eventually, fearful that a serious fire would be started, brewing was banned altogether but, by this time, the phrase had caught the imagination of nearly everyone in the camp.

Honour was at stake and the brew went on despite reprisals. Eventually the Authorities gave up all hope of ever implementing the order. In desperation, after John Hazelgrove, a New Zealander, attempted to make an electric brew stove from the lead of two pencils, and blew all the fuses in the camp, they lifted the ban.

Neither Basil nor Jimmy were idle during the weeks in which the brew stove feud raged, for despite the ban on entering the compound after dark they were determined to go ahead with the planned raids on the food magazine, and spent many hours together discussing the alternatives of carrying out the raids in daylight, or getting past the guard at night. Finally they decided on a plan which could be carried out at night but, as it required at least six men to operate with a reasonable chance of success they were reluctantly compelled to select four assistants. As each man would have to be extremely self reliant and possess more than the usual measure of moral courage the task of selection was not easy. The presence of spies within the camp could not be overlooked, so the fewer who knew of the scheme the better. Anyone who was approached would have to be relied upon to keep complete secrecy whether or not he accepted and only those whose history was known could be considered. Of the four extra men required, the selection of the first three presented no great difficulty for each had revealed by various actions in the camp that they possessed most of the qualities required. These were Tanky

Cooper, John Hazelgrove, the New Zealander, and his friend Brian Marsden, also from the Land of Milk and Honey. He had become famous for this description of his Homeland for, to him, no place was quite like New Zealand and the obvious ring of pride in his voice whenever he mentioned home, which was often, soon earned him the affectionate title of Immigration Officer. The sixth member took somewhat longer to select since there were a number who seemed to he equally worthy. Finally a bearded Gunner known as Porky was chosen. Whether he had another name or not no-one seemed to know. A case of, to them he was Porky, and Porky he remained till the end.

CHAPTER 7

In order to allay suspicion, Tanky approached the S.B.O. for permission to organise a Drama Group. Had he not done so, the frequent meetings of the Syndicate, as they termed themselves, would soon have drawn unwelcome attention from the more inquisitive prisoners in the camp and, ultimately, from the authorities in charge, who were forever on the watch for anything that might look like organised planning.

Neither Basil nor Jimmy had succeeded in obtaining a suitable conductor to test the wire round the enclosure, and this problem became the first item on the agenda; many ideas were put forward, most of which proved to be impracticable - somehow a method would have to be devised which would not lead to an enquiry should it fail. A scheme so simple that nobody could connect it with subsequent events. Despite several hours of discussion, the combined efforts failed to find a solution.

The following day was John Hazelgrove's wash day; as he bent over a trough in the ablution shed, his mind revolved round the problem discussed the previous day, but for the time being an answer evaded him.

"I'll think of something if it's the last thing I do" he vowed.

The day was warm and he took off his shirt and proceeded to wash it. The disgusting sight of the multitude of lice which came to the surface of the water distracted his thoughts from the question of the wire as he dealt death to the millions. Suddenly, as so often happens when concentration is relaxed, the solution came to him. He decided to try the idea straight away. Humming a gay little tune he continued his wash then, still humming, he carried it round to a spot near the fence, where he set up a Heath Robinson looking line and hung the garments up to dry. Apparently watching his smalls, he waited patiently for an opportunity, then, with such incredible speed that the action went unnoticed, he tossed his shirt onto the fence, where it hung caught most satisfactorily on the barbed wire. Simulating a look of dismay he waved his arms lustily in the air, pointing every now and then at the shirt. The pantomime of gestures designed to draw the attention of the Piantone at the, gate to his errant article of clothing brought gusts of laughter from bystanders, quickly attracting a crowd, glad of anything that would create a diversion in the monotony of their daily life.

Eventually the Piantone took note and came suspiciously forward. Then, in the mercurial way of the Italian, he joined good humouredly in the general laughter as he realised what John was trying to convey.

"Non fá niente, la puó prendere".

John fully understood what was said but, feigning ignorance, replied

"No understand - no capito"

whereupon the grinning Italian indicated by an amazing variety of gestures that he could cross the trip wire to retrieve his garment if he wished. This had not entered into John's scheme of events and, for a moment, he was nonplussed. He had presumed that the Italian would pick it off the wire and hand it to him if the fence was safe or, if not, switch off the current prior to retrieving it. Pointing to the notice on the outside wire, he danced up and down shouting

"Electric - electric" and, to the huge delight of his audience, acted out a mime of death.

The Italian, now thoroughly amused, shook his head and, between fits of laughter, spluttered

"Non ê pericoloso da toccare".

To demonstrate the meaning of his words he strode over and touched the wires. Smiling his thanks, John stepped quickly over the trip wire and rescued the shirt. Meanwhile the onlookers clapped and cheered hilariously. Grinning now, and immensely pleased with himself, John replaced his shirt on the makeshift line and sat down to await the drying of his laundry.

Some two hours later, he recounted the episode to Basil who immediately called a meeting to bring the Syndicate up to date and iron out the finer points of their programme. Now that they knew that the wire by the shed was safe, all were impatient to get started, unanimously agreeing that this night would be as good as any other night, so why wait? As the accepted leader of the Syndicate Basil briefed the small party carefully, re-iterating every man's part in the game that was about to be played. Distances and timing had been checked for the various movements and piecemeal rehearsals carried out during the preceding weeks, until every man was capable of performing any of the manoeuvres required. With characteristic thoroughness, he went into every detail of the Plan and finished by saying -

"Now remember, tonight's work will lay the foundation for all future forays. The method of getting out of the hut at night, if successful, will be the one that is always used. With care and average luck, the Italians will never know that anyone has ever stayed out. You must not underestimate the dangers involved. Remember, the entire venture has a high element of risk and the penalty of being caught will be harsh. If any of you have second thoughts and want to draw out, speak now and we'll not think the worse of you. Consider carefully that the slightest deviation from plan or minor error of judgement can jeopardise not only the entire enterprise, but also the life of each and every man of us."

He paused a moment to allow his words to take effect, looking carefully at each face for any sign of wavering. His own firm resolution was reflected in each one. Imperceptibly, his expression softened then, smiling -

"Thanks chaps, I knew I could rely on you."

Talking amongst themselves, and carefully avoiding any reference to the coming adventure, the party split up. Basil had insisted that he should make the opening in the wire and the shed, since this was the most hazardous part of the project. This had met with some protest from the others, John Hazelgrove being particularly vehement and declaring that the risky undertaking should be decided by drawing lots. Basil, however, by virtue of his greater experience in tasks of this nature, had finally got his way. Jimmy would be standing guard for him and the pair would be out from Lights Out until Roll Call the following morning, when it would be possible to slip in unremarked by taking advantage of the fact that, in order to facilitate washing, the prisoners were allowed to report to their Platoon Sgt. if they had missed Roll Call while attending to their morning toilet. Even though Tanky was the Platoon Sgt. it had been agreed that he wouldn't mark the two names as present until they had reported back. Should they be caught during the night Tanky would thus be protected from the risk of including two from his Platoon who obviously could not have been there. If that happened he would have a deal of explaining to do. The Italians were quick to jump on the slightest suspicion and would not rest until they arrived at the truth.

Stretched on his bunk, three hours later, Basil glanced at his watch. 8.30, Jimmy had just woken him and was now preparing for a couple of hours sleep before zero hour at 11 p.m. While he kept his vigil, Basil went over the plans again in his. mind. Every now and then the tick-tack of boots going down the gangways disturbed a sleeper, who would curse in his sleep.

"Lucky break. " he mused "The ban on going to the latrines at night being lifted. I suppose we should thank the filthy beasts who soiled the gangways until the stench was too much for even the Ities to bear! What fantastic depths of degradation man can sink to."

He scratched ruminatively. "Bad enough having these blasted lice without making matters worse. The five minutes allowed out of the hut gives plenty of leeway and in one minute the deception will be over". He looked again at his watch. "How slowly the time goes, only 10p.m." and lit a cigarette, there would be no opportunity for smoking later.

At the appointed time he woke Jimmy, then silently made his way to the others, finding them all awake and ready. The two New Zealanders opened the gambit by making for the door of the hut while the other four followed silently a few yards behind. On reaching the door Brian approached the Piantone for permission for the two of them to visit the latrine. Meanwhile, Basil led Jimmy to the pre-selected spot just out of sight behind the door. As soon as the New Zealanders had started across the compound, Porky also approached the Piantone and asked permission. The former nodded and Porky, by turning in the opposite direction, distracted his attention from the two crossing the compound. Believing he was about to relieve himself against the wall, the guard took a couple of steps towards him. At the same time Basil, with Jimmy keeping step beside him, slipped quietly behind the Piantone and together they broke into a run. The New Zealanders, who were halfway across, did likewise - not stopping until they had disappeared into the latrine, by which time the other two had dropped to a sedate walk as they reached the half-way mark. When the Piantone glanced back' all he saw was the two figures he expected entering the latrine. Well within their five minute limit, the two New Zealanders returned by the way they had come. Cheerfully bidding the Piantone goodnight, they made their way to their bunks.

While this had been taking place, Tanky had remained in the background ready to create a disturbance if Porky's ruse to occupy the attention of the Piantone for the brief moment required failed.

Jimmy checked that the coast was clear while Basil collected his tools which had been securely hidden during the afternoon in a cavity under the eaves of the latrine. Together, keeping well in the shadow of the building, they made their way silently to a point opposite the shed before parting company.

From where Jimmy stood, his back pressed against the building, he could see one of the guards keeping his vigil at the top of one of the machine gun towers and, presenting a greater danger because of his relative nearness, the Piantone at the gate to the Admin. Compound. Although the sky was overcast and the fence and shed could only be seen in the reflected light from the lamps, the boundary wires were clearly visible in the glare of the floodlights. Nevertheless, he felt secure in the knowledge that, while he could see from his position in the deep shadow thrown by the wall of the building, anyone approaching from out of the light would not be able to see either himself or Basil who was already stepping over the trip wire as he made for the fence.

Now that Basil was about to start cutting a way through, he was as cool as if he had been taking a stroll down a rustic lane in England. There had been a momentary chill as he stepped over the trip wire, when the appalling thought occurred to him that John's testing of the wire had only told him that the fence was safe during the day. Beads of perspiration started from his forehead as he realised this incredible slip in their reasoning. But too many had taken considerable risk that night for him to back out now. He swore softly under his breath, cursing himself for a weak kneed woman and steeled himself to carry on. On reaching the fence he touched each strand with a quick jabbing motion. He was well aware that this would not make any difference if the current was turned on, but, for once, his iron will failed to force the shrinking flesh to come into firm contact with the wire.

Gaining confidence with each touch of the wire, his tension relaxed as he became certain that the fence was really safe. Crouching close to the ground and pressing his body against the fence to kill any resonance, he took the bottom run firmly in his hand and placed one of two short lengths of wood which he carried, under the wire, making quite sure as he did so that the strands lay over the piece of steel heel tip that been fastened into the end. By placing the other end of the wood on the ground to form a vertical prop, he made a solid bench against which to cut the wire. Then, taking a home made chisel, he placed its sharpened edge across one strand of the twisted wire. Until this moment his movements had been completely silent. Even Jimmy who stood less that 15 yards away hadn't heard a sound. The sharp click as the hammer hit the chisel was inevitable, causing Jimmy to look quickly at the Guard who, to his relief, remained casually leaning over the rail of his platform. The procedure was repeated as Basil made a second cut on the remaining strand about 1" away from the first. By bringing into use the second length of wood he was able to raise the bench to the next run of wire and repeat the procedure. Having succeeded in making the gate, it was now imperative to fashion a means of closing it if regular use was to be made of the route he was preparing, and the fasteners would have to be inconspicuous. His strong nimble fingers worked swiftly, bending the longest strands back on themselves to form crude but efficient hooks. Having made his cuts on each side of a barb, it proved a simple matter to hide the join by threading the loose barbs into the joining hooks. Although Basil worked steadily, the need for silence made it a long job and it was almost midnight before he had the fence ready for use. Hoping the effect would be as good in daylight as it appeared to be in the dim light thrown by the lamps, he slipped through the wire and melted from Jimmy's view.

Thanks to the claw hammer he had filched from the carpenter, the removal of the weather boards from the shed proved easier than expected. Even though he had reduced noise to a minimum the hideous screech as the nails came out kept him on tenterhooks for it seemed inevitable that someone would hear and investigate. By 4.15 he had removed the heads from the nails with the chisel and pressed the shortened nails back into their holes to form pegs on which to hang the weather boards in their original positions, having first enlarged the original nail holes in the tops of the weather boards so that they would fit snugly. The noise as he drove each nail firmly home, amplified by the resonance of the wooden framework, sounded crudely loud even in the ears of the waiting Jimmy who stiffened in apprehension as he saw the Piantone come out of his box at the entrance to the compound and stare suspiciously in the direction of the shed. Scarcely daring to move a muscle, he watched the Piantone lean over the gate and crane his head forward in an attempt to penetrate the darkness. Every nerve stretched to capacity, Jimmy patiently waited for the Italian to make the next move. The risk inherent in driving the nails home had been carefully calculated and it would be his job to draw attention to himself by slipping round the end of the huts and running noisily to the latrine where he would inevitably be found. He could then swear that the Piantone on his hut door had been asleep and he was frightened of disturbing him. It was hoped that the noise created by his running would serve to warn Basil and, at the same time, subdue any suspicion the guards might have regarding the area of the shed. There should be plenty of time for Basil to cover his tracks and return to the compound before entering the latrine to give the same story thus backing Jimmy up. They felt the risk of a few days solitary would be a small price to pay, providing the secret remained undiscovered, and hoped that the maligned Piantone would not get into too much trouble.

While the Piantone continued to stare in the direction of the shed, Basil, now completely motionless stood, a vital figure, ready for immediate action. He glanced at his watch deciding to wait for five Minutes and, if no alarm came, enter.

Having satisfied himself that, as far as he could tell, all was safe and no alarm had been taken, he slipped softly through the aperture into the shed, grinning in satisfaction as he did so. The light showing through the windows facing onto the bright floodlights revealed a small counter which spanned the width of the shed near the door. Storage racks, which stretched to within a few inches of the roof, and were loaded with all manner of tinned foodstuffs, cheese and other edible fare, took up the entire centre of the floor space while, at the far end, stacked from floor to roof were the Red Cross parcels ready for the next issue, but Basil was not interested in these since to take some of them would be tantamount to robbing friends. Undoing his brew bag which he carried tied to his belt, he began to stuff it with loot. Grinning broadly he grabbed a mammoth string of hard thin sausages.

"Long time no see little doggy" he chuckled.

A dozen tins of meat and some packets of hard biscuits followed then, taking several handfuls of dried pasta, he stuffed it into every available space in the now bulging brew bag before tying the top securely. Barely twenty minutes had passed since he had entered the shed and again stood outside listening intently, before replacing the boards on the pegs, The shed now appeared complete once more.

Having checked that he had the right number of spare nails in his pocket in order that he should not leave any on the ground as evidence, he slipped quietly to the fence, fixed the wires into position and rejoined the waiting Jimmy.

"I thought it was all U.P for a while" whispered Jimmy, "the Piantone was deucedly interested in the shed, but I think he must have been very uncertain and scared of making a fool of himself as he eventually shrugged and returned to his shelter."

Basil chuckled softly -"Perhaps he was asleep in that box of his. In fact I think he must have been not to hear that racket!"

The first grey streaks of down showed in the sky as they once more entered the latrine, their night's work almost finished. Quickly, for time was now getting short, they transferred half the haul from Basil's brew bag into another taken from its hiding place in the eaves. Covering the tops with pieces of wood, scraps of paper and other brew rubbish as a precaution should they be told to open their bags. When the first early birds arrived for the morning splash, they were already washing and shaving and excited no interest.

Feeling refreshed after their wash, they made their way to the brew patch, a small area, well away from the huts where brewing was now permitted. Here they found Porky waiting as arranged with brew stove and materials for the fire. The temptation to prepare some of the loot was great, but they ruthlessly overcame it. It would be foolhardy to risk discovery before their gains had been distributed and would defeat the object of having Porky to hand.

While Basil got the fire going, Porky collected water in the Klim Pots, no mention of the night's work had been made, though Porky knew, by the bulging bags, that the sortie had been a success.

Returning, he put the pots on the stove while Jimmy, with a sigh of relief, sank to his haunches. He had been standing in the one position for nearly five hours and, apart from the abominable aching of his feet, he was extremely cold. Rubbing his hands together, he stretched them towards the fire.

"Hm! smells good". The fresh aroma of coffee tainting the air filled him with a sense of well-being as he anticipated the scalding beverage. Meanwhile, Porky slipped back to the wash-house for another two cans of water. When he returned Jimmy was already drinking from one of the cans, while basil continued to busy himself at the stove. "Alright, I'll look after that," he said, " you have some coffee, I reckon you need it".

Edging Basil to one side, he handed him the coffee from the stove and placed the two fresh cans over the flames. Hugging the pot between both hands, Basil sniffed the contents, relishing the humidity of the hot steam passing his face. Sipping slowly he stared moodily at Porky winding the small handle which operated the fan of the blower. The night's work had proved what could be done by organised planning and he wondered whether shouldn't have put their energies into an escape plot rather than the raiding of the magazine.

"The trouble is" he reflected, "Where the devil do we go if we do get out. The nearest British Forces would be at Malta and there isn't much chance of getting there. Rumour has it that the Line in Africa is somewhere near Alexandria and although, like India, I suppose it could conceivably be reached without having to cross the sea." He chuckled briefly as the absurd thought crossed his mind. "The war would probably be over and forgotten by the time we reached there," he continued, "Switzerland has attractions and many people have made it their goal, but I don't relish internment and eventual repatriation away from the fighting areas."

His mind wandered on thus for a while, until the train of thought was broken by Porky remarking,

"O.K., all set?"

Coming to with a start, he helped collect up the paraphernalia. Chatting amiably among themselves, the trio strolled casually through the compound towards their hut which lay just beyond the latrines. As they passed the front of the building they came face to face with the Camp Commandante, Colonello Arturo di Lorenzo, a heavy jowled obese man in his late fifties. Not unnaturally, he had long been dubbed Il Duce and was invariably referred to as Benito or Musso.

His brown eyes, almost hidden in rolls of fat, bored gimlet like into the three.

"Wait - why no saluta?"

"Because our hands are full you fat oaf" muttered Porky.

"What is that? What is that?" The harsh voice came angrily as he glared first at Porky then his two six footer friends, pulling himself up to his full 5'9" and sticking his chest out like a bantam cock.

"Our hands are full and hats off". Jimmy quickly supplied.

"So', you saluta next time without da hat, cosi".The Commandante threw up the Fascist salute.

"Si *Signóra*" - even now Porky could not resist a mild taunt by giving the feminine form of address in his reply. The Commandante glared momentarily at the speaker -

"Signóre: sentire Signóre".

Porky grinned happily - "Si Signóra".

For a moment the Commandante continued to glare, he would have liked to make an example, but the Red Cross Legation had made enough trouble last time. Muttering,

'Stupido - ignorante". He stomped off.

Together they resumed their walk towards the hut, Porky still chuckling over the incident.

"That was a damned silly thing to do!" Basil spoke sharply. "That man knows more English than you give him credit for. You can thank your lucky stars Jimmy supplied a quick answer."

A deep flush mounted to the roots of Porky's hair and, for a moment, his eyes flared in anger as he was tempted to make a retort. However, his sense of justice prevailed as he realised that if the Commandante had been so disposed, even a small happening like this could have landed all three in solitary. Inevitably the contents of the brew tags would have been discovered and there would have been the dickens to pay. He made a resolve to try and curb his irresponsible tongue in future, but he was destined to find that this trait in his character, which had so often landed him in trouble before was not so easy to hold at bay and would eventually land him in really serious trouble.

"Sorry old chum. I'll try to watch it in future".

"That's alright, but be more careful when we're on a stunt". Basil's smile robbed his words of any offence. "We don't want the apple-cart upset for the lack of a little common savvy do we?"

As they passed through the door of their hut, it was apparent that roll call was about to commence, so taking one of the two cans of coffee and his brew stove, Porky parted company to stand by his own bunk at the other end of the hut.

Soon after the roll had been called, Tanky clambered up beside Jimmy, who was reclining at ease while Basil shared out the coffee. On seeing they had a visitor, he emptied a portion from each can into a third before climbing up to join his friends. Smoking a cigarette apiece, over their coffee, Basil related the nights events and arranged with Tanky to contact the remainder of the Syndicate for a meeting at which the spoils could be distributed.

The daily exercise routine assiduously adhered to by the pair was so well known in the camp that Jimmy readily agreed when Basil suggested, a few moments after Tanky had left, that, tired as they were, they should carry on as normal rather then risk the inevitable ribbing which would ensue if they spent the morning catching up on lost sleep. The brisk walking in the mid-November air quickly cleared the soporific effect of the overcrowded hut from their heads and they were pleased to see, when passing their route through the fence, that even in daylight the join was not obvious and was unlikely to be spotted without close inspection. The shed too looked normal.

For the best part of the two hours spent walking round the compound they discoursed on any subject that came to their minds, eventually, still chatting amiably, they returned to the hut. As soon as they entered, it was obvious that something had happened to shake their co-prisoners out of their lethargy. The babble as everyone talked at once was deafening but above all a general air of excitement prevailed.

CHAPTER 8

"Oh, there you are," Brian Marsden's voice came from behind them - "I've been looking all over for you."

Basil frowned as the thought occurred to him that the raid had been discovered.

"What's the bother?"

"Bother?" Brian laughed, "Who said anything about bother. I've been looking for you to see what you thought of the rumour." Basil looked at Jimmy, who shook his head.

"I don't know what you're talking about Brian."

"Well, according to the rumour which is pretty strong, there was quite a battle at El Alamein on 24th of last month and our chaps are reckoned to be steadily advancing. The story goes that an attack was launched by General Montgomery, who is reported to have taken over at Alex, which developed into a battle for supremacy lasting about a fortnight and culminated in a victory for us. Incidentally, ever heard of Kidney Ridge?"

Without waiting for a reply, he went on -

"It seems Rommel counter-attacked with his armour there and a right royal fight ensued which lasted for two or three days..."

"Rommel?" Basil interrupted, then frowning, "I thought he was supposed to be ill or something."

"So he was and I suppose he still is; I must admit that part puzzled me until I learned that General Stumme was dead, and can only assume that Rommel was rushed back from Germany to take his place". Brian paused a moment to collate his thoughts. "Where was I?"

"Tank battle," Jimmy prompted.

"Oh yes. During the course of the action, he is reputed to have lost something like 200 tanks and is now galloping full speed back home, with our boys hot on his tail. Some of this has come from the Ities themselves who are feeling rather sore and reckon the Germans were so keen to get away from the fighting that they swiped all the transport and left half a dozen Italian Divisions stranded in the desert."

"No wonder they've been so glum all week," chortled Jimmy. "All the same, I can't believe the Jerry just ran off." "No" agreed Basil . "Far more likely they felt themselves more entitled to the transport and gave themselves priority, we all know how they despise the Italians - and you can hardly blame them," he finished.

"Anyway, to continue," said Brian "The net result was that several Italian Generals were taken prisoner and only one German, Von Thoma."

"What? not Rommel's lieutenant surely." Basil looked incredulous,"You're not extracting urine are you?"

Brian immediately became serious - "No old friend, I wouldn't do a thing like that - raise hopes for fun, not bloody likely! I've checked as far as is possible and wouldn't be telling you now if I wasn't pretty certain that the rumour is mainly fact. One of the Piantonies has already admitted to me that our troops are at Fuka which does suggest quite a rapid advance. Anyway, what about your Pommey saying. "There's no smoke without a fire" and Brother, what a fire!"

Laughing at this last remark, they fell into a general discussion of the news and how it might eventually affect themselves, until at length the call of 'come and get it' sent them scurrying for their rations.

Although Basil normally paid little heed to the various rumours that circulated the camp from time to time, the sequence of events recounted by 'the Immigration Officer' had the ring of truth and, as Jimmy had remarked, would certainly account for the serious expressions adopted by many of the Italian Officers who could be seen a passing too and fro in the Admin. block which lay just beyond the food magazine. Despite his determination to ignore the news until it could be verified, his spirits soared in the hope that it could be true.

The possibility of success in Africa making the invasion of Italy as a foothold to the Continent feasible could not be overlooked and he realised that it would be foolish to ignore it altogether. He felt confident in his ability to devise a means of getting out of the camp and it would be as well to be prepared against the eventuality of an escape route materialising.

He reasoned that there would he no point in leaving the escape until the Allied Forces were in Italy since the chances very strong that, in such a case, precautionary measures would inevitably be strengthened, and removal of everyone in the camp, to a safer area more than probable. The best policy he felt was to spend the winter behind the wires and plan an attempt in the spring, by which time the position would be clarified, and it would be possible to hide out in the hills. When the Allies succeeded in landing it shouldn't be too difficult to find them. If not they would at least be out of the camp and able to make suitable plans.

During the ensuing few weeks, as news of Anglo-American landings in Algeria and Morocco, with advances in Libya and Tunisia, filtered into the camp, Basil became steadily more thoughtful. Jimmy, who knew him extremely well by this time, noticed the occasional irritability when he tried to talk to him and guessed something was cooking in his mind, particularly as Basil seemed to spend a great deal of his time watching the arrival and departure of lorries in the Admin. compound.

He continued to lead the syndicate and organised a regular weekly raid, cunningly working a permutation between his available men and the various Piantonies so that it was very unlikely that any one of their number would have to work opposite a Piantone he had previously distracted. Only the minimum requirements from stock not easily missed were taken and the losses appeared to go undetected.

Christmas was approaching fast and, with only three weeks to go, it became imperative to do something to justify calling themselves a Drama Group. With a view to furthering the half formulated escape plans in his mind, Basil suggested a comic sketch, which he had persuaded a friend to write, depicting the Italian officer at work and play, and arranged to borrow appropriate equipment from the Italians to lend a semblance of authenticity to their appearance; the plan being to make scale drawings of the equipment during the few hours it was in his possession.

On the night of the concert, which was held a few days after Christmas, spirits were high in the camp, news had filtered in that Tobruk was again in the hands of the Allies whose forces were repute d to be somewhere in the Marble Arch area. The sketch put on by the Syndicate proved to be even funnier than intended, since not one of the cast had the slightest pretension to acting and Porky, who kept forgetting his lines but had a ready wit, ad-libbed unmercifully, saying the first thing that came into his head irrespective of whether it fitted or not. After a .few of his gems, the audience began to wait for him, greeting his sallies with howls of laughter, until even the performers were doubled up in mirth and the sketch spluttered to a finish.

A few days after the concert, Basil showed the drawings he had made of the equipment to Jimmy, who examined them carefully, noting the care which had been taken to record precise measurements. As he handed them back, his friend produced a bar of soap which he saw bore impressions of badges of rank and other insignia. A suspicion of a smile hovered round his lips as he thoughtfully watched Basil return his handiwork to its hiding place. Wondering what the old fox had up his sleeve, he continued to regard him with a quizzical look in his blue eyes. For a moment or two the pair sat each on his bunk, with knees drawn up under the chin, silently regarding the other. Then Jimmy laughed.

"Alright, tell me all about it, I suppose that Arts and Crafts Exhibition is not just for amusement."

Basil inclined his head, a trick he had when agreeing.

"Hardly" - he fussed around for a cigarette, proffering one to Jimmy as he lit it. Jimmy put out his hand to accept and was surprised to see that the tin was nearly empty since it was unlike Basil to run short midway between issue times.

"You've been bashing the smokes haven't you? - that all you've, got."

Basil grinned ruefully.

I've, been grinding the old noddle a bit just lately and it rather killed the ration."

Knowing that Basil would be offended, and not wishing to offend him, Jimmy accepted the cigarette knowing that he could. make sure Basil didn't want for a smoke later.

"I'll say you have." He chuckled. "You've been like a bear with a sore head."

"I know I'm sorry about that, but well you know how it is."

"Not to worry, now let's hear your ideas."

"As you have probably guessed, with the change in North Africa and a good possibility of driving the Germans clean out, it will leave a massive army doing virtually nothing but in a strategically good position to invade Italy. Now I don't know how the Powers that be will set about this job, but the logical thing would he to concentrate on Sicily, then cross the straits, of Messina and swarm up Italy. If this happens, you can bet your shirt on us being whisked off to Germany before we have a chance to get out and make our way South. As far, as we know, the war isn't finished in Africa yet, but I shouldn't think it will take very long now. In fact, I would never be surprised if a foothold in Italy wasn't established by June or July."

Jimmy showed his amazement. "You're being a bit optimistic aren't you? We don't really know if the rumours are true."

"Oh, they're true enough," Basil replied firmly. "You've only got to watch the Ities to realise that. In any case, we'd look a bit daft if we waited until the stories were confirmed and lost our opportunity through doing so."

"Alright, we'll assume the rumours are true. Firstly, when and how you plan to get on out and, secondly, where the hell do we go?"

"Briefly, there's not much sense in leaving before the winter's over, so we shall have plenty of time to prepare. I thought the beginning of April when the weather should be improving and with Summer before us, food will be more easily available. If my reasoning's right, we shall only have to remain hidden for a couple of months or so. As for getting out, I've been watching the Admin. Compound pretty closely lately and, believe that by dressing up to look like a working party with an officer in charge, we could bluff our way out in a truck. Incidentally, how's your Italian?"

Jimmy looked up - "Heh! steady on, it's not that good".

Basil chuckled, then treating Jimmy to a sly glance. "It had better be on the night or there are going to be some red faces around and no mistake".

His quiet voice became even quieter as he developed the theme so that, at times, Jimmy had to strain his ears to catch the words. Their discussion lasting far into the night as Basil weighed carefully each criticism Jimmy made before putting his own point of view, and vice versa, until they were both satisfied that the operation had a good chance of success and would stand up to the probing of the Syndicate.

During the following months of January and February, the cold wet weather instilled a general air of gloom into the camp, which was not alleviated by the conflicting rumours which circulated during this period. Few, if any of the prisoners had intimate knowledge of Tunisia or the areas where the fighting was taking place. There were no maps to refer to and the confusion added to their despondency. The capture of Tripoli they could understand and rejoiced in a victory where they could envisage the 8th army advancing through Libya, but Rommel's repulse in Tunisia during February, resulting in the capture of Kasserine Ferrane and Sbeitla could not he pictured. The advance to Djebel Abiod in the North sounded like a conquest in the Jebel. The Italians realising the general lack of knowledge, were quick to seize the opportunity for propaganda and represented the gains as great victories by Rommel. Few realised that this was merely a temporary set back and that the positions were retaken ten days later.

No heating was provided in the huts, which became damp with condensation mainly through a lack of adequate ventilation, nor was there any escape from the misery in the compound, which subjected as it was to the tramp of many feet, became a veritable quagmire.

Although the days passed slowly, they were not without some enlivening diversion as various individuals in the camp did their best to raise the rapidly declining morale, but their stoic efforts could not combat shortened rations coupled with a hold up in the issue of Red Cross parcels. Even the members of the Syndicate were forced to tighten their belt, during this time for any attempt to raid the store would have resulted in a trail of mysterious footprints apparently going straight through the wail of the shed. Since the Italians were unlikely to credit this to ghosts, it was decided that discretion should be the watchword for the time being. Although the Syndicate tried many experiments to get over the difficulty, they failed to find a solution.

Had the route to the shed not been an integral part of Basil's plan of escape it is probable that they might have risked a raid. The last bar of chocolate, carefully hoarded for use when they got away, had been eaten and they, like their comrades, were down to bare camp rations now reduced to 50 grammes of bread per day, about one pint of soup, which had become even more watery and seemed to contain no more than a dozen grains of barley. Sometimes a piece of meat was found at the bottom of the can, but this was a rarity and reckoned to be a valid reason for great rejoicing by the recipient: the minute cheese ration was halved and the proportion of burnt acorns in the coffee rose sharply.

A direct result of the lack of food parcels was the end of the Auction Mart, one of the highlights of the week which had helped to break the monotony, even those who didn't use its facilities to exchange items from their parcels for something which they preferred normally whiled away many an hour listening to the brisk bidding.

The camp spivs put away their decks of cards and crown and anchor boards; there was nothing left for even these to fiddle, and despair became the keynote of the day.

Fortunately, there is a trait in the British character which only comes to the surface when times are really bad. Imperceptibly the mood changed, smiles began to be seen - jokes to be cracked; some put their thoughts to paper and published them in 'Griff', when

> "There's a one eyed railway station to the north of Italy
>
> There's a. P.O.W. Camp below the town,
>
> Where the stouter hearted squadies walk around in twos and threes,
>
> And the mud around their ankles weighs them down.
>
> When the sun is at it's height and your shivering and white,
>
> And yer buckle's where yer belly orter be,
>
> Don't let it get you down, but wipe away that frown,
>
> And show the bloody Ities you'll be free!

appeared, it was followed by many others in similar strain, some printable others not, and sparked off a series where budding poets vied one against the other, in their efforts to beat the original.

The brighter weather, which arrived with March, played its part in lifting the depression. As more prisoners congregated outside to take the air, competition became keen for a position in the sun under the lee of the buildings, for the wind still blew in Arctic blasts cutting ,through their worn clothing and penetrating to the bone.

It was common knowledge that the work party formed up at a quarter-five every morning and departed in a convoy of trucks a quarter-of-an hour later. The trucks would then deliver small labour gangs at various outlying farms dispersed over a fairly wide area.

In order to obtain a knowledge of the work party routine, John Hazelgrove volunteered for farm work outside the camp, which took him away from his friends from early morning to 6p.m. The daily routine being the parading of the working party at a quarter-to-five, ready for the trucks which would leave a quarter-of-an hour later. The convoy would then deliver small labour gangs at various at various outlying farms dispersed over a fairly wide area. Thus he was unable to help with the making of the props required in their bid for freedom. A task which was occupying the major portion of the others' time. His contribution was nevertheless valuable for it was important, if Basil's plan was to succeed, that details of the area outside should be known.

John's main function was to find out if there were any irregularities which would provide the loop-hole Basil was looking for, he suspected that many a farm not on the official list received help from the camp, and in this his suspicion proved to be well founded. During his daily journeys John noticed that a truck would quite often leave the convoy before it had reached the dispersal point. Invariably when this happened an Officer sat beside the driver. The ribald comments passed between the guards when ever they saw a truck depart in this manner left him in no doubt that it was not unusual for a labour force to be supplied in return for favours from a Lady at a farm.

Back at the camp, Tanky proved to be adept with a needle a skill acquired, so he said, by years of darning his own socks, so the majority of the necessary needle-work fell to him. A collar and tie for the Officer was contrived from the tail of Jimmy's shirt; he protested vehemently at this sacrilege but was politely informed by all and sundry that if he must have these luxuries he must pay for them. Buttons and badges were carved from wood, using the patterns taken from the soap impressions, and suitably coloured with grease crayons. Belts, and bandoliers etc. were made from cardboard and lethal sandbags from the despised toe-rags. Finally, a remarkably realistic gun was produced by dipping a rough carving into melted grease crayons and carving the details into the grease coating.

By the end of March all was ready then, as if to add encouragement, news of Montgomery's victory over the Mareth line and the rapid disintegration of resistance south of a line from El Hamma to Gabes, reached the camp. It seemed to the jubilant Syndicate that the war in Africa would soon be over.

The intervening days until the small party met in the shadow of a gangway soon passed. Although Basil had carefully gone over the plan and meticulously discussed each man's tasks with him, he still continued to check over the details while patiently waiting with his companions for the last relief of the night to come on duty. He frowned as the thought crossed his mind that the forays on the food magazine had, by comparison, been simple, providing a time was elected between the regular two hourly relief of the Piantonies, the risk of being caught was reasonably slight. The very factor of the constantly changing face had been of assistance in avoiding recognition, it was a definite hazard and prohibited any move in the plan being put into operation before 4 a.m. A shadow fell across the door and Basil glanced at the luminous dial of his watch –

"Only a few minutes late - it seems as many hours!"

The tense crew held their breaths and cursed silently to themselves as the relief exchanged a few words with the Piantone going off duty, then wasted more of their precious time hanging around outside the hut. Eventually, he entered and the syndicate went into action. As Tanky approached the Piantone, Basil slipped silently behind him, his arm rose, silhouetted for a brief moment in the rectangle of light framed by the door, and the sandbag he held landed with silent precision behind the unsuspecting Piantone's ear. As Tanky caught the unconscious man, John came forward to assist Basil with the removal of overcoat end equipment, and the other three quickly made their way to the latrines.

Five minutes later, the unfortunate Piantone lay securely bound and gagged behind the door of the building and John, now wearing overcoat end cap, with rifle slung negligently over his shoulder, took up his position at the entrance.

"Good luck - see you anon." Basil's whisper just carried to John's as they clasped hands before, accompanied by Tanky, he sped away to join the remainder of the party.

The routine through the wire and into the food magazine had been performed so often that it was accomplished without incident. Within 15 minutes of the commencement of the operation Jimmy was fitting himself out with the prepared accoutrements of a Major in the Italian Army, while Basil, assisted by the others selected a few easily carried provisions.

By the time Jimmy was ready, it was half past four and the sound of arriving transport could he heard outside the shed. Followed by the others, he stepped outside then, leaving them in a tight bunch in the shadow of the shed, he walked quickly towards the Admin. Block turning as he neared it to approach a truck close to the shed, as if he had just left the buildings. On coming abreast of the truck, he addressed the two guards in the back in Italian.

"You two, come with me." By virtue of much practice, he had succeeded, in eradicating practically all trace of accent. Without questioning his authority to give the order, the guards jumped to the ground, and saluted. Returning the salute, Jimmy turned on his heels and marched briskly in the direction of the shed. Unsuspecting, the two guards followed him into the trap, where the waiting crew pounced simultaneously, attacking silently in commando style but, taking heed of Basil's instructions not to kill unless absolutely necessary, contenting themselves with merely stunning their unfortunate victims before dragging them into the shed, where they stripped them of their overcoats and equipment. The time spent by Basil teaching his men how to truss a man efficiently was amply rewarded by the expert way in which Porky, assisted by Tanky, secured the unconscious Italians before Basil and the Immigration Officer had finished kitting themselves out with their effects.

Jimmy, who had remained on watch outside to shear off anyone who approached too closely, scowled as Brian's voice came clearly through the thin walls, of the shed.

"It might have been tailor made."

The speaker who was donning an overcoat turned to look at Basil then his eyes bulged as he choked back a loud guffaw.

"Heck man! You can't wear that."

Although the coats were normally worn long, the one Basil had, ended a good inch above the Knee - his bony wrists protruded from the sleeves with inches to spare, making the gangling 6' frame look ridiculous. He grinned ruefully, taking off the coat as he did so. Porky was the nearest fit, but Basil dare not risk having him exposed to close scrutiny since his cutting remarks and general antagonism had made his face too well known. Tanky, 5'10" was perhaps an inch taller; Basil beckoned him over.

"We'll have to change roles," then holding the coat out, "try this for size."

Though a little short, the coat was a passable fit, as he did the buttons up Tanky grinned appreciatively.

"It's nice and warm," then passing his hand over the fabric. "Nearly new I think. I wonder what they call their 252."

Porky laughed a trifle too loudly. "Trust a bloody Sgt. Major to think of that - bung it in his pay-book".

Fortunately a sudden clamour from the vehicles outside drowned Porky's laugh. Nevertheless, Basil admonished him quietly as he urged the party to remember where they were and that time was getting short. Then, seeing that Tanky had finished dressing.

"Come on, get a move on," he stepped outside waiting for the others to follow, then replaced the boards in the shed and watched for Jimmy's signal that their intended driver was looking in the opposite direction. As soon as the signal was given basil and Porky sped for the truck and waited quietly behind the tail for the pseudo guards to join them before climbing in so that, if the depression of the springs caused the driver to glance round, he would attribute the movement to his escort returning to their positions.

Meanwhile John, who had been left 'on duty' at the hut, waited for the formation of the work party at quarter-to-five and hoped that their escort would not try to have a word with him. Precisely on time the Italians arrived accompanied by Cpl. Baggaley, a British N.C.O. enjoying special privileges and rumoured to have Fascist leanings. Keeping well in the shadow John watched the men hurry out of the building and form into a ragged line between the two guards each calling out his name to the Cpl. who, obviously enjoying himself, stood to one side ticking off their names from a list. A sly smile marred the over handsome features of the Cpl. as he realised one had not arrived. The penalty for being late could he severe and it was high time he reported this lazy Kiwi to the Commandante. The malicious thought twisted his features as he wondered what form the punishment would take.

"Hazelgrove - Hazelgrove." Simulating a note of anger to impress the guards, he started to shout the name. Dropping the rifle behind the door, John slipped off the overcoat end ran out, taking up his position at the end of the column.

"You blasted Kiwis are all the same" snarled the Cpl. "Get a move on you idle bastard" then, turning to the squad "Quirk march, left, right, left, right", he marched them through the compound, swaggering beside them as if on a show parade ground and screaming with thwarted rage as the lads continued to talk amongst themselves despite his repeated order of "No talking in the ranks".

As soon as the squad reached the Admin. compound, the N.C.O. stalked into the office to report the gang was ready, taking the opportunity while he did so to lay a complaint against Hazelgrove. Mimicking the despised N.C.O. the men sorted themselves into small groups containing, their personal friends in readiness for going aboard the vehicles.

Seizing his opportunity, Jimmy strode across to John and rapped him smartly across the shoulder with a riding crop curtly telling him to get in the truck by the shed - indicating the one he meant with his crop. As he did so, one of the men standing alongside looked him straight in the face.

Jimmy recognised him as Bob Chester, a likeable, happy go luck type and one of the few who had been considered when forming the Syndicate six months previously. Bob allowed a slow wink to close his eye, then in the strange way prisoners learn to communicate without appearing to do so.

"Give my love to the missus."

Jimmy was used to quick decisions.

"Jump in that truck if you want to come," he whispered.

Almost imperceptibly Bob shook his head,

"Got my show next month, but thanks and good luck!"

Then, sprinting across the compound he rejoined his friends who were already climbing into one of the vehicles.

By this time the front of the convoy was beginning to move out of the gate, so Jimmy clambered up beside the driver of his truck, who, busy with the controls, took no notice. As they got underway Cpl. Baggaley came out of the office, and made off towards the prison compound. Seeing him slinking off, one of the escort guards grabbed him and, despite his protestation of special privileges, bundled him unceremoniously into the back of Jimmy's truck. Turning to explain the mistake to the guards on the truck he recognised one as 'the Immigration Officer'. Startled dumb he looked at the other and seeing who it was, stood for a moment dazed,

"Grab him."

Basil's terse command rapped out as Tanky sent the N.C.O. sprawling on the floor of the truck. Quickly Porky pinned his arms while John forced his jacket into his face to smother any outcry as they passed the gate. Within a few moments the truck was sailing down the road at the tail end of the convoy. Thinking it safe to do so, Porky released his prisoner, whose face was white with a mixture of fear and rage.

"You're mad - bloody mad:" he shrieked. "What do you think you're up to?"

To a man the Syndicate grinned at him happily.

"This is your lucky day mate." Porky slapped him on the back rather harder than necessary.

"Not if I know it" he snarled, "I'll stop your little game."

With unexpected suddenness he made a dive for the tail of the truck, eluding the grasping hands, and landed on all fours in the road. Getting to his feet he started to run back towards the camp shouting

"Escapees, Escapees".

Tanky, raising the rifle to his shoulder as drawing a bead he began to squeeze the trigger, felt no regret over what had to be done. Nor did he hesitate, it was one life against five of his comrades and anyway he had no time for traitors. At that moment, one of the machine guns at the camp opened fire. Cpl. Baggaley staggered, fell and lay still.

Subdued by the suddenness of the tragedy, the five sat looking glumly at each other and not saying a word. Meanwhile, Jimmy was keeping his eyes open for a turning on the right that John had described to him as being a cart track about six miles from Sforza-costa on the Tolentino Road, recognisable by a large farm house backed by Poplars which stood on a knoll nearby. John had been down the track on a work gang and had noted that it forked about half a mile from the road, one branch leading to the farm that had employed them, the other apparently continuing for some distance in the general direction of some higher wooded ground which could be seen in the distance.

Jimmy, who had been wondering what the shooting was about and concerned whether he should stop the driver or not, nearly allowed the truck to overshoot the turning before ordering the driver to leave the convoy. In taking his eyes away from the road to acknowledge the order, the driver realised for the first time that the Officer sitting next to him was a stranger, the suspicious look on his face suddenly tinged with fear as his eye fell on the gun nestling in Jimmy's right hand.

"Keep quiet and do exactly as I say and you wont get hurt," Jimmy rapped, bringing the gun an inch higher.

The driver gulped and hastily obeyed Jimmy's instructions as he slowed for the corner and turned down the track. On reaching the fork, they took the left branch following the rapidly deteriorating surface as it meandered through a heavily wooded valley for about one hour, by which time, the speedometer indicated they had travelled some fourteen kilometres. Seeing a small opening on the left, Jimmy made the driver turn down it. If the previous track had been bad, this was atrocious being little more than a goat path which petered out within a hundred yards. Jimmy told the driver to stop and get out of the truck, calling to the others in the back,

"Alright lads, I think this will do nicely."

Keeping his gun still levelled on the driver, who had gone grey in the face, he jumped down joining the rest of the party as they poured out of the truck.

Motioning to the Immigration Officer to relieve Jimmy with his rifle, Basil began to collect lengths of ginestra, a form of bass which grew in profusion in the immediate area, and fashioned the lengths skilfully into a rough broom which he threw to Porky,

"Get cracking on those wheel marks."

Catching the broom expertly and with a cheery "Aye, Aye, Sir", Porky nipped down the path while Basil busied himself making two more brooms before joining him in the task of sweeping out the tell-tale signs left when they turned off the track. For the next half hour the little party worked hard. The truck was driven into some thick undergrowth and covered with small branches, already bearing their new spring leaves, and all evidence of its presence removed. When all that could be done to conceal the vehicle had been accomplished, the party climbed into the back and sat down to a meal of raw sausages and bread, generously inviting their prisoner to take part. Realising by now that he was not going to be killed unless he made a false move, he began to brighten up considerably. Accepting a piece of bread but refusing the sausages, he munched it as he covertly watched his captors apparently thoroughly enjoying their meal.

During the course of the day nobody passed down the path where the Syndicate lay hidden, the only sound disturbing the peace of the forest being a solitary motorcycle about midday and the clamour of bells as a shepherd with his flock passed down the track on his way home during the evening. The day was passed in desultory conversation in which they took care not to raise their voices or mention their plans.

The Italian's name, they learned was Ercolene - he was Uno di Reggio and anti-Fascist. He seemed to have a good grasp of current affairs in Italy and considered Mussolini's days of power to be almost over. The Italian people, he declared, were fed up with a war that was taking all their young men to be used as buffers for the Germans and blamed Mussolini for joining Hitler in an enterprise which was not to their liking. He thought that if Mussolini did fall the King would assert his rights and try to arrange an armistice with the Allies. Strikes and rioting had been going on in Milan, Turin and other cities in the north and the feeling that the slaughter of Italian soldiers in Russia and Tunisia could only lead to invasion and the ultimate defeat of Italy had become widespread. Peasants and Townsfolk alike bitterly regretted the loss of their Empire and placed the blame for this squarely on the head of Mussolini for dragging them into a war on the losing side.

The possible existence of dissenting groups, ganging up in opposition to Il Duce and his followers had not entered into Basil's calculations. No whisper of the political unrest having been allowed to reach the ears of the P.O.W.'s. Certainly it had not occurred to him that numbers of outlaw gangs composed in the main from Army deserters, brigands and political refugees were already formed, their members living apparently normal lives in the scattered houses and small villages to be found around the foothills of the Appenines. Since he had no means of knowing whether they would accept his small party into their organisation, or simply turn them over to the nearest local authority, and didn't care to place too much reliance on what Ercolene might say, he decided to give them a wide berth until more was known.

CHAPTER 9

The light breeze which sprung up, rippling the branches of the trees, passed unnoticed by the party now busy preparing to leave and the half light of the forest rapidly faded to complete darkness. Having first made sure that the truck was demobilised and distributed the small supply of food equally amongst themselves, they returned to the track which, according to Ercolene, connected with another road about 7 kilometres away. Basil estimated that it would be about 9.30 by the time they reached it and sent the two New Zealanders ahead to scout and make sure that the Italian was not deliberately misleading them. As they advanced Porky covered the rear approaches to the party while the Italian, with Basil on one side and Jimmy on the other, stood scant chance of escaping under the eagle eye of Tanky who, with rifle ready, walked a few paces behind. Although all could speak and understand Italian, they hadn't the same facility as that acquired by Jimmy. Nevertheless, it had been agreed that, unless explicate and clear instructions were required, this language should be the one used until safely home.

In order to learn more about the political situation, so that he could judge the position for himself and its likely developments, yet, at the same time, practice his Italian and keep Ercolene's mind occupied, Basil asked him to explain the position as he knew it. Ercolene, glad of the opportunity to talk, and now more confident that he would eventually be released, pulled a wry face.

"It's a long story and to give it justice I would have to go back to the beginning of the war" he began. "You see, even before last July, when Mussolini returned from Libya looking like an old man and desperately ill, there had been growing unrest in Italy. Despite this, however, until quite recently, we still held him in high regard and I believe if he had shown himself more often during the past few months instead of retiring from the public view, he may well have kept the affection of the public, even though the old magnificence was gone."

"Surely he must have known about the unrest?" interjected Basil."I would have thought he would have done all in his power to put it down. I know I would in his place."

Making a typical Latin gesture with his hands, Ercolene continued,

"Well, yes, I suppose he did. He railed against the people, comparing us unfavourably with the 'brave German soldiers', though it is said that he stuck up for us when the Germans made the same accusation of cowardice and reluctance to fight that he did." Pausing for a moment he went on - "You know, I think his scolding helped turn public opinion against him as much as anything. Of course what he said was largely true. We were reluctant to fight in a war that we didn't want alongside an arrogant and overbearing ally who appeared to be more lord and master than friend. Returning soldiers from Russia brought tales of how the Germans commandeered all the transport and left them to tramp through the snow."

"I hear they acted similarly at Alamein" Basil commented, then smiling, "Though, of course, there was no snow there."

Ercolene nodded. "We seem to be regarded by the Germans as an expendable item of war. Even so, we accepted the sacrifice for Il Duce, but when the Germans began to enter Italy, ostensibly for training, and used the excuse to set up Nazi Cells in the larger towns, everyone began to get alarmed, particularly when word went about that we were to suffer military occupation with a puppet government under Roberto Farinacci, who is renowned for his allegiance to the Germans."

"But surely Mussolini had something to say about this" protested Basil. "I was always under the impression that he could be quite ruthless if his authority was threatened."

Ercolene shrugged. "Normally yes, and in the old days he would have been, but by this time he had become so apathetic that he just ignored the situation and didn't even bother to appear in public in an attempt to allay our doubts or bolster our morale. It wasn't long before people began to say he didn't care or he would surely put a stop to the bad treatment of Italian workers in German labour camps and were asking each other why did he allow the export of so many of our beautiful works of art to the Reich."

Basil smiled to himself at this, thinking how typical it was of the Italians to count the loss of their beloved masterpieces as a major calamity and could well imagine them overthrowing Il Duce for this alone.

"By the Autumn," Ercolene continued, "the uneasy feeling had blossomed into widespread opposition to the German and Fascist Regimes, with arrests taking place almost daily."

Basil looked surprised. "Then this didn't really start with the reversals in Africa? which surely didn't commence till October."

Ercolene shook his head. "Oh no, the loss of our Empire out there only precipitated matters, everyone was already fed up and had been for some time. You must realise that the peasants in the south were nearly starving and came to refer to the last hole in their belt as 'foro Mussolini', they even coined a slogan 'lavora, lavora, Fascisti mangia'. In the towns the Fascist slogans were being removed and posters demanding liberty and peace appeared in their place. Secretly printed news sheets were distributed and from these we began to learn the true facts; on top of all this many were desperately praying for a defeat to end the war. By the time the British had occupied Tripoli at the end of January, our only hope seemed to be a disengagement from the German Alliance, but as long as Mussolini remained in power this seemed to be an unlikely solution. Inevitably the people turned against him, the more militant types forming secret bands, often under Communist leadership, and organised assistance for the Army deserters who were already hiding in the hills, some of whom had joined Yugoslav Guerilla elements operating inside Italy."

By the time the Italian had finished talking, the party had caught up with the two New Zealanders who had been waiting for them. Crisply John made his report.

"The road is about 100 yards ahead and beyond that there is a river which I think must be the Potenza." Then, turning to the Italian. "Is that so?"

Ercolene nodded.

"Can it be forded?" Basil asked.

Ercolene shrugged. "In the normal way, yes it could be easily crossed on foot but the heavy rain combined with the snow thawing out higher up makes it doubtful. There is the bridge at Treia but you will have to be careful, as I should think you will have been missed by now and, if so, sentries might be posted." The logic of this was sound. Looking at Jimmy, Basil said, "Do you know, I believe the Italian is really trying to help". Jimmy pulled at a loose button on his jacket, and toyed with it for a moment before replying -

"I don't know, he may be reasoning that this is what we would think but, in reality, be trying to prevent us from crossing."

"Maybe you're right; I think we'll have a look at the river first then decide what to do in the light of what we find."

First having sent the two New Zealanders ahead once again to check that the road was clear and received their signal that it was so, they quickly crossed over, grouped in a tight bunch, and were soon stumbling down a steep bank between the road and the river which was now visible as a silver ribbon a short way before them. Suddenly, the sound of a dog barking caused them to look alertly about them. An oblong rectangle of light appeared as a door opened in a nearby farmhouse and an irate voice shouted

"Piscifuoro!" [8]

The sudden silence which followed made the bang of the door as it was abruptly slammed sounded louder than normal. For a moment all was quiet, with only their heavy breathing breaking the stillness of the night. Then the dog began to whine and they relaxed. Each man had stood perfectly still during this interval, their minds distracted momentarily from the river. Bringing his attention back to the men, Basil started counting heads, then swore his Arabic oath under his breath as he noticed the Italian was missing.

---

[8] Dialect used expressly to dogs.

"Anyone seen the Italian?" he asked.

Staring in dismay at each other they started to look about them. "If he's gone, he's gone", Basil remarked, "and there's not much point trying to find him."

Just then a faint crackle of twigs in the immediate vicinity caused him to swing round, while Tanky gripped his rifle more securely bringing it to the ready. Each and every one strained their eyes as they tried to pierce the almost impenetrable darkness.

"Don't be alarmed." Ercolene's voice came to them in a whisper. "I've been to the edge of the river and it's practically a torrent, we could never cross here".

Basil smiled grimly to himself as he noticed the 'we' indicating that Ercolene was apparently identifying himself with the party. "If he comes over to us", he thought, "he might be quite a valuable asset."

Telling the others to keep an eye on the Italian and stay where they were, Basil slipped quietly out of sight, making his way down the steep slope towards the river. The smoothly worn soles of his desert creepers slipping from under him on the wet muddy surface making it difficult to retain his balance. The rush of water which filled the air and drowned out all other sounds seemed to indicate that Ercolene had told the truth. Unexpectedly the ground became steeper and Basil's feet shot from under him defying his frantic efforts to keep upright. As he landed in the mud, one foot dipped into the water where it swirled round the roots overhanging the bank, its icy clutch seeping through his boot. Previous rains and melting snow had swollen the river as Ercolene had predicted for although not wide, it was obviously much deeper than normal. Basil could just make out some of the trees which would normally grow out of the banks submerged for about 3' in the water. Even had the temperature been reasonable Basil thought he wouldn't care to try and wade through it. Already the foot that had been submerged had begun to feel numb. Disappointed, since he didn't like the idea of spending several days travelling upstream until a point to cross was found, he returned to his friends. "You mentioned a bridge just now," he said to Ercolene "How far would it be?"

"Well, the river is so close to the road here that it can't be more than two or three kilometres. Come, I will show you the way."

Followed by Basil and the others who were keeping a wary eye open for any tricks he led the way back to the same point on the road that they had left some half-an-hour previously and stepped out briskly towards Treia remarking as he did so, "This road isn't used much at night and we should be safe walking along since the sound of vehicles at night travels a long way and we would have plenty of time to hide".

Some forty minutes later, on rounding a bend, they saw the bridge. Nothing had passed them whilst walking along the winding road and their luck seemed to be holding since the bridge appeared to have nobody on it.

Motioning to the others to stay where they were, Basil crept forward to investigate at close quarters in case someone was actually on the bridge but out of view. On finding the way clear he stood at the approach waving to signify that all was well. As he did so, his keen ears picked up the hum of approaching vehicles. By the time the others had caught up with him the distant sound had drawn closer and reached a crescendo, the easily recognised roar of motorcycles mingling with the heavier sound of lorries.

"Come on, put a move on," he urged, as together they raced across the bridge. They had almost reached the other side when a light appeared in the road ahead, followed quickly by two more.

"Scapa!" The Italian's voice sounded shrill above the ear splitting roar of the motor cycles which, by now, were converging on the bridge at both ends. The desperate Syndicate had not waited for Ercolene's shout but raced flat out tumbling over one another as they reached the sanctuary of the bank on the other side. Ercolene, who had kept up with them, panting heavily as he crouched down in the underbrush, his face white with exertion. They were not a moment too soon, from their hiding place they saw two motorcycles pull up at the bridge, seconds later these were joined by a third machine and a small truck which scudded to a standstill and disgorged a party of Carabanieri. The shouted orders of the officers and the scuffle of feet on the gravel road as the Carabanieri took up positions on the bridge and its approaches at either end effectively drowned any other noise but, despite the clamour, they took care to leave the area as silently yet as quickly as possible then, on finding a small path, followed it for about half a mile where it opened out to fairly level cultivated ground. Looking at his watch Basil saw that it was approaching midnight.

"Phew! I think we deserve a rest."

Suiting the action to the words, he squatted down on a log as the others found perches around him.

"Well chums, that was a near thing and I think you'll agree we should be grateful to Ercolene for refraining from giving the alarm when he could so easily have done so."

The Italian, who had remained standing, grinned in sheer pleasure at these words.

"It's nothing. Since the desertions started we soldiers are watched very carefully by our Officers and I'll never have another chance to get away like this."

While he was speaking he fumbled around his pockets then, finding a packet of Tre Stelle, he offered the cigarettes round.

"These are much better than Caporal but not as good as your Virginias." Taking one each they lit up, making sure as they did so that the flare from their matches would not be seen from across the valley.

After about fifteen minutes rest, during which time they talked animatedly about the recent scare, they set off once more across the open ground towards some dimly seen mountains ahead. In view of what had occurred there didn't seem much point in continuing to guard the Italian, who walked happily alongside apparently quite content to stay with them. By morning, having crossed one more road without incident, they found themselves again in heavily wooded country which seemed to be ascending steadily. Selecting a spot near a small stream, Basil called a halt. By making use of the abundant material at hand, a hiding place was easily prepared. Then, after the remainder of their food had been shared out and eaten, the seven tired men lay down exactly as they were and, worn out after the exertions of the night, were soon fast asleep.

Dusk was already beginning to descend when Jimmy, who was the first of the Syndicate to awake, sat up rubbing his eyes as he looked around the sleeping party, a worried frown creasing his brow as he noticed that the Italian was missing. Urgently he shook Basil who seemed to come awake on the instant but, before anything had been said, Ercolene re-appeared, followed by a young girl of about seventeen who carried a round wicker basket covered by a white cloth on her head. To Basil, who had not seen a girl for nearly three years, she looked exquisite. The rounded golden tanned face blended harmoniously with her deep brown hair which was wound in a ring on the top of her head. With all the natural grace of a young peasant girl, she lifted the basket easily and placed it on the ground. Smiling shyly, she revealed small even white teeth.

"Buongiorno siete svolate?"

Basil, who was wondering whether Ercolene had been foolhardy, nodded then, as the girl quickly spread the cloth on the ground and prepared to empty the contents of her basket, Ercolene explained that he had told La Donna at the farmhouse that they were all deserters from the Army in Russia and were making their way to their homes and families in the south. Although very poor, the kind hearted people had helped them because they said there were other mothers' sons trying to get home.

By the time the rest of the party had woken up, freshly made pasta, mixed with beans and maize was being ladled into small earthenware dishes which the girl placed beside each man, murmuring as she did so the conventional

"Buon pranzo. Mangia!"

Bread, in chunks from a huge home baked loaf, was cut with a knife which Basil said later would have done credit to a Ghurka, cheese and a rather sour vino completed the meal.

The girl, who quickly overcame her initial shyness, told them her name was Franceschina. In the course of conversation over the meal, they learned that, as the youngest daughter of a peasant farmer she looked after the sheep and turkeys but there were so few of these left that she had also to help her mother in the household chores. Since her Father had been taken to a German Labour Camp after some trouble involving the Fascists in nearby Colcerasa, she had been on her own with her mother and sister. The other two members of her family, Mario and Gianni, were both in the Army, but no news had come from Libya for some months. Her pathetic look as she said, "We don't know whether they are alive or dead," brought home to Basil a facet of the cruelty of war that hadn't previously occurred to him. It made him rage inwardly over the impartiality which affects everyone involved, whether in the fighting line, at home in a city subjected to bombing or the quiet peace of the countryside apparently away from it all. No word basil or any of the others could say could eradicate her deep laid fear and grief so, changing the subject as quickly as he could, he got her chatting gaily enough on events around the farm and in the nearby village. Many of the older people in the area, she said, had already come forward to offer their help in tilling the ground. When the meal was finished, Franceschina collected up the remains, expressing as she did so her concern that they had eaten so little. Deeming it politic not to mention that after many months of meagre rations in a prison camp they were not yet capable of eating the huge repast offered, Basil, backed up by Jimmy and the rest, assured her that they had eaten more than sufficient. However, she insisted that they take the remains of the loaf and some small round cheeses made from sheep's milk with them. Then, having invoked St. Christopher and bid them 'arrivederci' she suggested they should try and contact a man known as Quintale, who was said to be in touch with the Rebelli, and might be able to help them. She added that if enquiries were made at the Dopolavoro on the Strada Nuova entering Cingoli, someone would be sure to know him.

Although it was not yet eight o'clock, it was quite dark when Basil looked at the patches of sky showing through the leaves overhead and anxiously noted the scudding clouds. Since leaving the camp, luck had been with them. The clear sky on the previous night had made walking pleasant and allowed him to take occasional bearings from the stars, but this, their second night, he thought, showed all the signs of being nasty. Basil's fears were realised when the rain started some two hours later, but fortunately the terrain they traversed had easy gradients and they made good progress. Gradually, the rain increased in intensity, quickly soaking through their clothes and reducing Jimmy's cardboard trappings to a pulp. No longer talking and with heads bowed, they trudged over muddy fields, along rain soaked woodland paths and splashed uncaring through small rivulets and streams. Their sodden clothes inducing a chill which even their exertions failed to disperse. The rain still beat heavily on them when, at three o'clock, they crossed the little used Cingoli road and started climbing into the hills beyond so that it was with some relief that within a short half-an-hour, they found a crude shelter in the form of a charcoal burner's hut and decided to go no further.

Although damp inside the shelter, it served as a refuge from the worst of the elements, but, lacking any facilities to dry their clothes, they were forced to huddle miserably together to await the dawn hoping that a fine day with a warm April sun would dry them out.

Despite their weariness, they found it impossible to sleep in their miserable condition and whiled away the remainder of the night discussing the possibility of contacting Quintale. Ercolene pointed out that, while Cingoli was by no means large, it was a sizeable place and would be sure to have a strong Fascist organisation, and as he was the only one with identity documents, it would be safer if he made the enquiries, while the others remained hidden in the woods. If questioned by one of the Fascist Police, he could always say that he was visiting a relative and, following his usual custom, had gone to the Dopolavoro for a drink in congenial company.

At first the Syndicate was reluctant to accept Ercolene's suggestion, but had to admit that his argument about the identity documents was very sound and eventually agreed that he should go ahead on those lines. Although, by this time, Basil felt reasonably certain that Ercolene could be trusted, he had no intention of taking too much at face value and secretly arranged with the others that a watch should be kept on the approaches to the shelter during the Italian's absence, and for a further half-an-hour after he had returned, so that, if Ercolene betrayed them, they would have a sporting chance of getting away.

When the rain eased off shortly before mid-day, Basil, helped by the two New Zealanders, collected all the dry kindling they could lay their hands on from the shelter and a nearby hollow tree, and after some effort succeeded in getting a good fire, which when fed from the charcoal burner's stock of charcoal gave out a good heat with practically no smoke.

Later, sitting round the fire, the blues of the night faded as their clothes dried out and, once more, prospects were viewed with equanimity. The welcome heat, combined with a meal of toast and cheese and a sleepless night had a soporific effect so that it was not surprising that Basil was eventually left viewing his dozing companions alone with his thoughts... If Ercolene succeeded in contacting the man Quintale and, through him, they could join an organised band, the major problems of survival until British Forces should land in Italy would be solved. That they would land eventually he had no doubt. The successes in Africa all pointed to an early invasion, while the decline of Mussolini's popularity clearly indicated that, given half a chance, the Italians would seek an Armistice. If, by joining an anti-Fascist organisation, they could expedite Mussolini's fall or strike a blow at the enemy, their time would be well spent.

Inevitably his thoughts became muddled as the heat of the fire overcame his desire to stay awake - the heavy eyelids closed - and his head nodded forward onto his chest.

CHAPTER 10

Shortly after 10 o'clock that night Ercolene returned from Cingoli and reported his mission a failure. He told them that when he had first entered the Dopolavoro and ordered a glass of Vino, his reception had been friendly and sociable, as was to be expected at such an establishment, and that he had experienced no difficulty in striking up a conversation with a few of the regulars; he had even joined in a game of dominoes with them. Later, when he introduced the name of Quintale into the discourse, they had seemed a little less friendly and tried to evade the issue. When pressed for an answer, they made an excuse to leave.

Subsequent enquiries had led to blank stares, or emphatic denials, some had merely shaken their head and hurried away. Finally, realising that he was not likely to find out much there, he had returned. As Ercolene finished his narrative, a light footfall caused Basil to swing round in time to see a stockily built figure block the entrance to the shelter, while the shadows of two more men proclaimed that the visitor was not alone.

The sight of an automatic rifle gleaming dully in the faint light outside brought Basil to his feet, while Jimmy, with a lithe movement arraigned himself alongside him. Their visitor stepped quickly inside the shelter and, at the same time, switched on a powerful torch, motioning to his assistant to keep the party covered. Sick at heart, Basil could only gape in dismay, as the strong light dazzled him. Reluctantly he raised his hands wondering as he did so what could have happened to John and Porky who should have been guarding the approach.

The stockily built intruder, who appeared to be the leader of the trio, advanced further into the shelter while his assistant remained a menacing figure, blocking the entrance. The third member of the party stayed outside. As the leader advanced, he directed the beam of his torch on each face separately, pausing a moment at each one as if to memorise the details, coming to rest finally on Ercolene.

"You who would know Quintale. Who are you? and who told you of him?" the harsh voice vibrated with menace. Before Ercolene could reply, Basil interrupted.

"Don't answer, let him find out for himself."

The beam of the torch was immediately switched to him and the rasping voice continued.

"Are you the leader?"

The light passed from head to foot and back again, as Basil's apparel was noted.

"P.O.W. by the look of you." He added.

As Basil nodded a sudden commotion outside caused the speaker to spin round. Simultaneously Basil attacked, using a flying tackle, which carried his opponent and himself through the entrance, so suddenly that the assistant was bowled over with the force of their passage before he had a chance to realise what was happening and open fire. The next moment Basil was fighting for his life, his opponent proved to be extremely powerful and though, at one time, Basil may have been the stronger of the two, months of low rations had sapped his splendid physique. Despite his maximum effort, the grip he had on the other was remorselessly broken. Bringing all his weight into play, he lashed out with a vicious jab, the painful jolt in his wrist as he landed on the other's jaw giving him a glow of satisfaction. Then he felt an agonising pain as a boot crashed into his groin. Temporarily winded and doubled with pain, his arms groped as he tried to come to grips with his opponent, who brought his knee up, but Basil saw it coming and rocked back, riding the blow, only to trip on a tree root which brought him crashing to the ground on his back. Instantly the other pounced and fastened a vice like grip on his throat. Frantically he tried to break free, while the blood throbbed in his temples and a red mist swam before his eyes. Suddenly, when all seemed lost, the grip relaxed and the enormous weight pinning him down rolled away.

Dazed, he staggered to his feet and stood swaying a moment as he tried to gather his senses. A friendly hand on his elbow and John's voice saying,"You alright Basil?" steadied him. He looked about the moonlit scene. The man he had been fighting lay stunned at his feet and a slow trickle of blood oozed from a small wound on the back of his head. Porky, with a twinkle of pure joy in his eyes, held the automatic rifle pointed unwavering at the two strangers. Brian, Tanky and Ercolene formed a trio by the entrance of the hut, apparently waiting to see if Jimmy and the Immigration Officer, who were already advancing on his fallen adversary, would need assistance. Picking the unconscious man up they carried him inside and, having fixed up a light with the torch, started attending to the cut on his head.

Telling Porky to stay outside with his new acquisition, Tanky carried out a quick recce of the area then, satisfied that nobody else was about, returned to find the remainder grouped inside the shelter. Basil, still feeling a little groggy, had sat down while he recovered his wind and John was explaining that when Ercolene had returned along his approach, he had seen someone follow him almost to the camp then return. After two or three minutes, the follower had reappeared, this time with two companions, one of whom carried a spandau. The light at that time had not been good enough to risk a shot, so he had collected Porky and stalked them to the shelter. As long as one of them was inside he had felt sure the weapon could not be used without the risk of wounding their comrade. Together they had crept up behind the man left outside and Porky had knocked him out with the butt of his rifle. Here John paused in his narrative and chuckled.

"When Basil came hurtling through that door driving the other two before him, it nearly upset our plans, however, Porky made a grab for the gun and after that it was virtually all over. I could see Basil was in a bad way and, forgetting chivalry and all that, tapped his man over the head."

By this time, the leader of the trio was beginning to come round. Basil, who had recovered, but was still in a cold rage, jerked him unceremoniously to his feet. Jimmy's quiet voice, however, caused him to pause.

"Let him be Basil, you're not yourself old man!"

Realising the truth of this, Basil let his victim go and, with shaking hands lit a cigarette as he fought to control himself. Then, to the amazement of all, the other chuckled.

"You're a ruthless man and I like you my friend."

Getting to his feet and thrusting his hand out he grabbed Basil's.

"Meet Quintale,"

Nodding to his companions, he introduced them as Ernesto and Gabrielle. "Had you not been so quick I would have told you who I was," he continued, "but these are troubled times my friend, so when a stranger comes asking for Quintale. Quintale must be careful."

His cold eyes gleamed but the grim line of his mouth relaxed, transforming his features as he laughed outright and slapped Basil on the back.

"Dio! but you're quick, like a tiger." Then squatting on the ground, "Come we should talk."

When all had settled themselves comfortably and introductions had been completed, Quintale took a foul appearing earthenware pipe from his pocket which he packed with an even more repulsive looking tobacco. When this was drawing to his satisfaction, be began to speak in a voice no longer rasping, but carefully modulated, though Basil thought he detected a certain timbre of hardness.

'In order that you should obtain a clear understanding of the Rebelli," he began, "you should realise that Italy is no longer united. Everywhere there are plots. Anti-Fascist plots. Anti-Royalist plots. Anti-German plots. Nearly everyone of importance seems to be involved so that it becomes difficult to tell who is siding with whom and for what purpose. The sole common factor being the overthrow of Mussolini and the return of justice and liberty."

Quintale paused and chuckled.

"The general situation could not suit the Commissars better and The Committee has only to wait for the right moment. Opposition to Mussolini has spread until even the King himself has become involved in the various schemes."

"But surely Mussolini must have seen the red light" protested Basil.

Quintale smiled. "There has, of course, been a complete reshuffling of the Guards due to a tip off which is reputed to have come from Guido Buffarini. If he is the culprit, you can bet the crafty fox has his own reasons. As you probably know, all the important officials were changed last February and General Ambrosio succeeded Cavallero as Chief of the General Staff. From Mussolini's point of view the choice could hardly have been worse, since, according to certain well informed circles, he is said to be in contact with Marshal Badoglio who is not only anti-Fascist but also anti-King and would favour an abdication as a prelude to negotiating a separate armistice. These two are also said to be in concert with Castellano and Carboni, both renowned for their anti-Fascist views. As a personal adviser to the King, Ambrosio, together with Due Pietro D'Acquarone has the confidence of the Princess Maria Jose; she too is reputed to be in touch with various Generals who would like to see the end of Il Duce.

Count Dino Grandi and Guiseppe Bottai have both been replaced, though they retain their seat on the Grand Fascist Council. Both of these are said to be involved in yet another plot to overthrow the Dictator, as also is Count Ciano, who has been made Ambassador to the Holy See and seems to have a finger in every pie. Mussolini has taken over his post as Minister of Foreign Affairs.

Taking advantage of this, the Communists have seized on the growing unrest to ferment strikes and demonstrations against the Fascist Regime, their doctrines appeal to the hungry population so that large numbers have been converted to their way of thinking. Nearly every district in Italy now has its band of Rebelli, mainly centred round a small nucleus of political exiles but as yet these have not been united, though many are armed and in contact with other leaders and when the time comes the Committee of National Liberation will know how to use them."

He then went on to explain that Quintale was not his real name and that he had been a Professor of Economics in Milan often lecturing on politics, his radical views had led to exile from the City and for some years he had lived at Cingoli where he now held a minor Municipal post. Working under his nom-de-guerre, he had built up a secret organisation, on communistic lines, aimed at the overthrow of the present regime. Because of the conviction, now prevalent, that the war was lost and Mussolini's days numbered, he had been able to come into the open and was recruiting a band of armed and desperate men who would be prepared to fight the Germans, should they attempt to take over Italy when the Fascist Regime ended. Already he had a score of these hidden out in lonely farms around the area. Working as an agent provocateur, he had organised the printing and distribution of subversive propaganda but, later, he hoped to become more active. However, much as he would like to have Basil and his party to assist, the introduction of half-a-dozen escaped British P.O.W.'s into the area would attract too much unwelcome comment but, if Ercolene cared to join forces, he would be pleased to have him. He then finished the long discourse by saying that he would tell Ernesto to guide the others to a cave in the mountains where they would be safe pending the arrangement of identity documents and civilian clothing.

Although disappointed by the decision that they would not be able to join in the activities of Quintale's organisation, Basil could see the soundness of his reasoning. Nevertheless, he was delighted at the prospect of civilian clothes and identity papers which was more than he had dared to hope for when they planned their escape. The cave, if suitable, would probably make an excellent H.Q. where they could remain hidden while they decided what to do.

Thus it was that a week later Basil stood on a ledge high in the hills near the village of Ugliano. A short way below him the crag like rock formation gave way to grass dotted with a large variety of wild flowers, many of which, he thought, would have held pride of place in a garden back home. Beneath a bright sun in an incredibly blue sky, he filled his lungs with the keen mountain air as he allowed his gaze to take in the scene. Looking out over the forest below he caught a flash of light as the sun glinted on a river in the distance. Then a moving puff of smoke brought his attention to a railway which followed the course of the river. Idly he watched the miniature train pass through the outskirts of a town he believed to be Matelica, following its progress until a more condensed billow of smoke indicated it had entered a tunnel. Since arriving at the cave five days previously, the Syndicate had occupied themselves learning the geography of the area, enjoying as they did so a freedom which still seemed strange. In the nearby forest a small stream, actually one of the small tributaries of the river Musone, provided adequate water and, as Quintale had generously furnished them with a large copper urn, they were able to keep a supply for immediate use in the cave. Glancing down at the well worn but serviceable home-spun trousers he sported, and feeling the warmth of the thick pullover and hill-type jacket, he reflected that they had indeed been fortunate to gain the confidence of such a man who, true to his word, had produced fake identity papers for the whole party in addition to the clothing. Basil felt that, short of very ill luck, they should be able to get by quite easily. However, neither Basil nor any of his friends were of a type who could just sit around and do nothing. The brief surveys of the area, while occupying their time, failed to satisfy the driving urge that was in them, so Basil had not been surprised when only that morning the two New Zealanders had voiced his own thoughts when they approached him with the suggestion that they should form a fighting unit and hit the enemy as often as they could. Saying he would think about it, he had wandered out to where he now stood in order to concentrate without interruption.

The mountains with their heavily wooded slopes provided the ideal setting for the hit and run tactics that would have to be used and though their sole armament was only two rifles and a very scant supply of ammunition, one successful raid would look after this discrepancy. Apropos to this, he wondered whether Quintale would be prepared to lend him the automatic rifle that Porky had been so reluctant to hand back and resolved to ask him when he called for Ercolene on the morrow.

A faint smile hovered round his lips as he thought of Porky who, already indignant at handing back the cherished weapon, would have to shave off his beard if they followed the suggestion of the New Zealand pair. Ruminatively he passed his hand over his own ten day growth. To operate successfully would entail a certain amount of intelligence work in the scattered villages and could even necessitate entering one of the towns in the area, particularly Castelraimondo which he knew to have a railway junction; it followed, as a logical sequence, that a reasonably well groomed appearance would be less conspicuous. Moustaches were so prevalent that these could be permitted but the little gunner's glorious growth would be noticed wherever he went.

Later, when he returned to the cave, he discussed the project with Jimmy before seeking out Tanky and Porky only to find, as he suspected, that all were as keen as he to make up for the lost ten months. Ercolene, however, when invited to join in, said that he preferred to help Quintale with the propaganda work as already agreed but, in any case, did not wish to get involved too deeply with the political issues so would probably try to get home as soon as it seemed safe to do so.

Towards the evening of the following day, Quintale, dressed as a peasant and driving a pack donkey laden with provisions, arrived at the camp. Accompanying him, similarly garbed, were Ernesto and Gabrielle. After a meal prepared by Porky, who had proved to be quite a fair cook, Basil raised the question of the automatic rifle. Apart from a barely discernible narrowing of the eyes, Quintale gave no sign that he had heard the request but sat quietly drawing on his pipe until Basil had finished outlining their plan. Picking up a stick he traced an intricate pattern in the ashes of the fire round which they sat, then, with a small quick movement he erased his work and bringing his gaze up as he did so, met Basil squarely in the eye. For a long moment the two wills clashed as Basil's unflinching grey eyes met the tawny ones of the Rebelli leader but it was Quintale who finally dropped his gaze.

Shrugging his shoulders he said,

"I might have guessed that you couldn't stay passive."

Then, beckoning Ernesto over, he spoke rapidly to him in a dialect which the others couldn't understand. After a short conversation Ernesto nodded his head as if agreeing to something, then settled back on his seat but Basil noticed with dismay that he had taken up a position closer to the cave entrance. The three men had not brought their arms with them so he was not unduly worried about these actions, nevertheless, he did wonder what it was all leading up to. Deciding it was best to keep a wary eye open, he passed a signal to the Immigration Officer to do likewise.

Quintale, whose keen eyes seemed not to miss a trick, frowned, then evidently guessing that Basil had not understood the dialogue, explained that he had asked Ernesto whether he would be prepared to loan out the rifle. The latter had replied that he would be glad of an opportunity to use it himself but, before deciding, would like to be satisfied as to the true aim of Basil's project. "You see", said Quintale, "Ernesto has every reason to hate the Fascists who only recently shot his wife and took off his children. Neither has he any love for the Germans. I have already mentioned the formation of armed insurgents, who are prepared to enter into Civil War if necessary to rid this country of the Fascist yoke. There are also many bands in Italy today using the political situation as a cover for brigandry, while professing to raid Fascists; these thugs come into the villages and towns armed to the teeth with modern weapons shooting and pillaging. Their definition of a Fascist appears to be any person with sufficient wealth to make their raid worth while. In Partisan activities, as in all forms of war, it is inevitable that some innocent people must perish, but this fact does not excuse deliberate robbery, nor the killing of Fascist minded villagers who are peaceful folk. Understandably, these thugs are viewed as outlaws by all decent thinking people and only those who are not aware of the true facts applaud their actions. If you can assure Ernesto that you intend to operate only against strictly military objectives and genuine Fascist Cells then, and only after he has given it some consideration, will he agree to come along, but you can't have the rifle without him."

At first Basil was reluctant to accept the gun on these terms since, as far as he was concerned, Ernesto was an unknown factor. He thought it quite possible the man was sufficiently ruthless for his purpose but, at the same time, was reluctant to introduce a hate complex into their midst doubting whether the stability required would be present. A too early burst of firing from an impatient member of a raiding party could easily spell failure or even disaster. On consideration, however, he decided that the danger was one that would have to be accepted since the efficiency of such a weapon in the right hands would increase the chance of success, so, in this instance, he felt justified in taking a calculated risk. While pondering over these points, he asked Quintale what Ernesto's reactions had been when he discovered his loss and learned that he had come home on leave from the Army some twenty-four hours after the tragedy. For the whole of that day he had remained at the farm too numb to do anything, then spent the next few days making enquiries. During this time it was revealed that his wife had been suspected of being involved in subversive activities. Knowing this to be completely untrue, he had vowed that he would no longer support a regime that would permit such heinous treatment of a woman on suspicion alone. Deadly, but calm, he had sought out Quintale and offered his services, proving himself to be extremely reliable and unfailing in his dedication to the cause. His one ambition seemed to be the end of tyranny.

The brief summary did much to reassure Basil, who considered that as Ernesto had not run amok as soon as he heard the news, he was probably stable and could be relied upon not to open fire prematurely. Much relieved, he thrust out his hand to clasp Ernesto's who embraced him in the Continental style declaring that actual participation would be more to his liking than the distribution of leaflets then, turning to Quintale, he thanked him for providing the opportunity.

By the time they had finished deliberating it was nearly 10 o'clock and, as Quintale wanted an early start in the morning, he announced his intention of retiring for the night. The remainder sat around the fire for a while talking about the war and its near end in North Africa, then they too sought their beds.

CHAPTER 11

During the next fifteen days every path and track in the immediate area was conscientiously explored and a road watch set up some three miles west of their H.Q. between Matelica and Castelraimondo.

Most of the vehicles which passed down the road proved to be supply lorries, usually in groups of two or three, travelling to small outposts between the two towns. There was only one isolated incident of a large convoy which was followed by troops on the march but, in the main, traffic was sparse, probably owing to the proximity of a railway which Basil marked down for early attention. The problem of the moment was to obtain weapons as a prelude to more belligerent work. When the watch had been operating a few days, a definite pattern began to emerge, the regular users of the road becoming easily recognisable. Among these was a patrol car which passed their position at fixed intervals four times per day. The crew of six, dressed in the grey-green uniform of the Fascist Militia, sat three a side in the open back of the car, each staring woodenly at his counterpart on the opposite seat. Basil guessed they were so bored with the monotony of travelling back a forth over a stretch of road they had grown to know well that they were no longer interested in the surrounding countryside. Their apathy made them an ideal subject for an ambush and Basil was sorely tempted to make an immediate attempt, instead of waiting for Ernesto with his Spandau. However, he realised that even with the element of surprise to his favour, the chance of a successful engagement with only two rifles and a very limited supply of ammunition was remote.

When Ernesto returned on the sixteenth day driving the pack donkey heavily laden once again with provisions, the warm May sun was beginning to take effect, making even the air in the hills balmy with its rays. Porky, who had removed his 'glory' seized on the excuse to sunbathe saying that he must match his skin with the rest of his face, nonchalantly ignoring the fact that high winds and an open-air life had done this naturally within two days.

On the third day of the month, almost twelve months after he had blown up the petrol dump at Segnali, Basil briefed his small party. The spot selected for the ambush was narrow and winding as the precipitous road followed the contour of the hill, leaving the railway to pass through a tunnel cut into the solid rock. The boulder strewn area above the road provided the dual advantages of height and protection should they meet resistance. In order to disperse his fire as much as possible Basil stationed Tanky and the Immigration Officer, both of whom were exceptionally good shots, about fifty yards apart, with Ernesto a little lower down the hillside approximately mid-way between the two. Porky who had drawn "donkey" in the ballot at the H.Q. on the previous evening, stayed under cover in the heavily wooded slopes below the road, while the remainder positioned themselves ready to take over if any of the firing party were hit.

From his position above a bend, Basil thrilled anew as he felt that strange explosive effect in the blood vessels of his nose once more, followed, as usual, by a sensation of almost unreal clarity and energy. He glanced at his watch thinking,

"The patrol will be along any moment."

A careful check at the road watch had indicated that the time seldom varied by more than a minute or so. Punctually the car came into his view and slowed as it approached the acute hairpin bend. Basil's arm rose above his head and the three guns, responding to his signal, were steadied in readiness for their target. The Fascists never knew what happened, for both the rifles found their mark in the driver and as the truck swerved Ernesto opened up with his automatic rifle, spraying its lethal hail from stem to stern of the car and contemptuously walking forward into the open as he did so; he continued firing until the magazine was empty. The watching Basil cursed under his breath for, apart from the completely unnecessary risk to his life, he wastefully pumped bullets into dead men. The driverless car with its unhappy burden veered to the side of the road, bounced off the rocks and careered back again, finally coming to rest precariously wedged on the concrete dragons teeth which protected the outer edge.

From his position above the hair-pin bend, Basil commanded a view of the road from both directions so that, by remaining at the post, he was able to maintain a look-out while the others streamed-across the road and commandeered the equipment.

As he caught sight of Porky leading the donkey onto the road the corners of his eyes creased while his lips momentarily lost their grim line.

"If only 'Muvver' could see him now looking more like a peasant than the Ities themselves," he thought and grinned broadly as he pictured the scandalised face of a fond parent.

Wearing an old slouch hat and a violent check shirt, his trousers tied with string below the knees and jacket worn like a cape across the shoulders with the arms hanging loose, Porky ambled up to the group in the road, swishing the stick he carried from side to side as he did so. The work of loading the loot into the panniers was quickly accomplished then, turning the donkey round, he went back the way he had come, while the car was set on fire and tilted over the edge, where it plunged, a flaming torch, down the steep bank until it finally came to rest up-side-down and blazing furiously.

Basil glanced at his watch once more. The whole operation had taken just six minutes. Feeling very pleased with the success of the ambush, he rejoined the others in the road and accompanied them to a pre-arranged rendezvous with Porky in the forest below.

By the time they reached the meeting place in a small glade, Porky had already sorted out the load and packed the panniers more evenly. The two rifles and the Spandau were dumped on top of the new equipment and logs and brushwood arranged to conceal everything. As soon as all was ready, Porky set off on his own, to all appearances a simple farmer returning to his home with a load of firewood at the end of a day in the forest. The remainder, who had split into three parties of two, following at short intervals.

By the time they had re-assembled at the H.Q. the excitement, coupled with the activities of the day, had tired them rather more than they had expected. However, this did not prevent them from examining their prize straight away. They were mildly disappointed over the quantity of ammunition for not one of the six rifles captured from the patrol carried more than five rounds in the magazine, while the clumsy looking Glisenti type revolvers had only two rounds apiece in the chamber. Seizing on a pair of these, Porky twirled one in each hand in true Wild West style and leaped astride the donkey shouting.

"There be rustlers in them there hills,"

he goaded the startled beast into a reluctant trot.

"Giddy up - giddy up" he chortled and, sticking the guns into his belt removed the battered relic of a hat to fan his mount. Whereupon, the indignant donkey promptly stopped causing Porky to lose his balance and, to the immense glee of his audience, he toppled to the ground.

"O.K. Cowboy! Get back to the ranch and hand in them shoot'n irons afore you go." chuckled Basil.

If the quantity of ammunition had been disappointing, they were nevertheless delighted with the haul and were agreeably surprised to find that the Villar Perosa, which had been mounted beside the driver of the car, was fully loaded. Picking up one of two pairs of field glasses, Basil stepped up onto a large boulder and tried them out on a distant hill, noting with pleasure as he did so that they were not only powerful but also sharp.

He was not unduly worried at the lack of ammunition since the raid had supplied arms for all and future raids would rectify the deficiency, but the fact that the patrol carried no spare ammunition and their guns were inadequately loaded, caused him to wonder whether the Italians were running short on supplies.

Ernesto, who had enjoyed the opportunity to work off some of his hate, stayed with the Syndicate for the ensuing weeks, taking part in several hit and run raids. Sometimes it would be an isolated Carabinieri post and sometimes a patrol car or supply column. Whatever the target, they took care to operate well away from their H,Q, and even roamed as far south as

Campolarzo and Urbisaglia to draw attention away from their hideout. The inevitable search parties combing the wrong areas were a tribute to their caution and a source of entertainment as they watched the frantic Italians through their glasses.

One evening during the second week of June, some six weeks after the initial raid on the patrol, Basil was sitting on an ammunition box outside the cave entrance, cleaning his latest acquisition, a 9mm Beretta sub-machine gun, while he joined in, an animated discussion of the recent landings in Pantellaria and their resultant effects on the chances of invasion.

"Undoubtedly," Tanky remarked, "the island will form a wonderful base for bombing operations. There seems to be no reason as far as I can see why it shouldn't be used as a flying base to cover an invasion towards the North of Italy which, I should think, would be far more effective than a landing in the toe with its inevitable risk of a short heavily defended line."

"What you say is all very true" agreed Jimmy, "but, as Basil has just pointed out, this would entail long lines of communication over a sea route, with the added difficulties of landing supplies as well as men at several points up the coast. Short of landing simultaneously on east and west coasts, they could well find themselves up against an enemy firmly entrenched in these hills. No old chum, I'm inclined to go along with Basil, the logical sequence would surely be via Sicily and across the Straits."

"Well don't !.."

The sharp click of a rifle bolt cut Tanky short and as Basil hastily loaded his Beretta, the other two snicked back the safety catches of their own weapons before springing to their feet. With one accord, they peered warily down the narrow path which led to their H.Q.

John Hazelgrove, who was on watch at the lower post, was not the type to get panicky and bring a round into the barrel of his rifle unnecessarily. The search parties had been increasingly more active throughout the preceding week and although they seldom operated at night, a guard had been set as an obvious precaution.

In one lithe flowing movement Basil slipped behind the cover of some boulders and cast his eyes towards the cliff like rock face opposite his position. There was just sufficient light left to see the vague shape of Porky already ensconced behind the Villar Perosa which had been set up in a niche a short way up the face. Although fitted with a strap to hang round the neck of the gunner and obviously intended to be used in this manner as a sub-machine gun, due to its extremely rapid fire it had proved impossible to use effectively. Even when a loop to take the Bipod had been contrived they still found the gun unmanageable. However, when supported on its Bipod and equipped with a shield, it promised to be a deadly piece of mechanism, and was capable of commanding the only two paths leading to the cave.

Methodically Basil checked each position within the range of his vision. Jimmy a little to the right and just below Porky, Tanky a few yards to the left of the cave entrance, with Ernesto on a narrow ledge some 50' above them. He felt a glow of pride in the slick way his team-mates had reached their stations, every one of which had been carefully chosen for its cover, range, accessibility and, most important of all, means of escape in the event of a really determined effort being made to flush them out. The Immigration Officer, who was on duty at the top entrance to the gorge, was not in Basil's range of vision, but nevertheless, he was confident that the New Zealander was also alert.

John's challenging shout sounded crisply in the pregnant silence that had descended over the camp, causing each to take a firmer grip on their weapons as they strained their ears to catch the response.

"Ercolene" - the voice sounded weak and out of breath.

"You stupid idiot! You could have been shot creeping up like that". John sounded exasperated. Why didn't you whistle or something?" The New Zealand twang, always more noticeable when John was excited, sounded absurd when the words spoken were Italian, and was indicative of the strain Ercolene's stealthy approach had caused.

"Where's La Volpe?" Ercolene asked ignoring John's rebuke.

"Who?" John frowned in puzzled bewilderment as he asked the question.

"La Volpe. That's what they're calling Basil in the villages."

As Ercolene stopped to regain his breath John noticed a dark stain seeping through the cloth of the Italian's jacket. The angry note died out of his voice as, feeling more than a little guilty, he took Ercolene solicitously by the elbow and asked what had happened.

"Everything .., everything. I must see Basil, they've taken Quintale." The distracted note in Ercolene's voice brought a worried frown to Basil's forehead as, coming level, he spoke.

"Alright, don't fret. First we'll get you fixed up and then you can tell us all about it."

Ercolene's relief on seeing Basil was so great he burst into hysterical tears and clung to his arm.

"That's enough!"

Basil spoke sharply and shook him off but, at the same time, slipped an arm under Ercolene's shoulder.

"Come on mate, you look about done in," he added in a softer tone.

Pulling himself together Ercolene thrust his jaw out and shrugged himself free of Basil's support.

"I'm alright now," he said as he followed Basil to the cave where all except the two New Zealanders had congregated. While Porky, who had somehow got landed with all the cooking chores, prepared coffee, Basil, helped by Jimmy, stripped off Ercolene's jacket and shirt revealing a gash along the ribs under his arm, a little higher than the elbow. Bringing the oil lamp closer, Basil examined the wound critically.

"You're lucky," he grunted. "Half an inch closer and your ribs would have gone, as it is you've got away with a nasty burn."

With remarkable tenderness for so big a man he dexterously dressed the wound and only when satisfied that Ercolene was comfortable and had recovered from his shock did he ask him what had happened. In a voice at first trembling, but gradually strengthening as he told his story, the Italian described how, during the early hours of the morning, a squad of Militia, accompanied by Carabinieri had raided a meeting, killing six of the members and arresting Quintale, together with two others. Their printing press had been smashed up and the office wrecked. Seizing an opportunity he had jumped out of the window and run for the sanctuary of the nearby forests, but had been hit before he was clear away. After reaching the forest he had lain hidden for some hours trying to decide what to do, then he had thought of Basil.

For perhaps ten minutes after Ercolene had finished talking no-one spoke. The arrest of Quintale was serious and meant the loss of valuable information which he had been able to furnish. Also there was no telling whether, under duress, he might not divulge the secret of the hiding place. The Fascists were not fussy when it came to their means of obtaining information. However, this was not the point that occupied the minds of each and every one of them as they sat around a crude table, some smoking, others not, but each alone with his thoughts. It was natural that, being the type of men they were, their thoughts should be centring on whether a rescue could be effected for it seemed the very least they could do in honour and loyalty for a friend to whom they owed so much. Eventually, Basil gave voice to their thoughts.

"I think a council of war is indicated," he said. Then added. "We must devise a means to snatch him back."

Looking round the tense faces and receiving the nods of assent, he was not surprised, it was no more than he had expected. Then, addressing Ercolene, he said,

"Do you know where they have taken him?"

Ercolene nodded..."O.V.R.A.[9] has an office with the Police and I recognised one of their agents in the party that raided us, but you will never get him away:"

Basil raised his eyebrows but otherwise his face remained impassive.

"You don't understand, they handed the prisoners over to the Germans who have set up an interrogation centre at the Casa Bianca".

For once Basil was jerked out of his calm.

"Germans. What Germans?" he rapped.

"There are no Germans in Cingoli that I know of," supplied Ernesto.

"A few came in from Matelica last week," explained Ercolene. "When you shot up that convoy between Falcioni and Gli Angeli, one of their Colonels was killed and they have used the excuse to place S.S. men in several of the towns and villages in the area."

"I don't see why the presence of a few Germans should make any difference," interjected Jimmy. "The problem is essentially the same and it makes no odds whether they wear the uniform of the S.S. or the Militia. Either way, success will depend on surprise, coupled with a really speedy operation."

Then, taking both Italians into his glance. "Do either of you know this house?"

Ercolene shook his head. "I have only heard it referred to," he admitted but they do say it is used by O.V.R.A. and that the cellars are confini."

Ernesto, who had been silent throughout the discussion got to his feet and started pacing rapidly. "I know that house." He said bitterly. "The cellars have been turned into prison cells. The interrogation room, which is sound proof, is at the end of a passage. Inside the room is a door which leads to a yard surrounded by a brick wall. It is ideal for secret executions so we must hurry even though already we may be too late."

"Now, let's not go into this bull headed," cautioned Basil. "Quintale has been in their hands for some hours, if they haven't shot him yet they aren't likely to until the dawn". He glanced at his watch. "We have about eight hours until then. I suggest you draw a plan of the building and we discuss the exercise. Don't forget that Cingoli is a stiff three hours walk away and we've all had a busy day. It's only common sense to get some sleep. We can plan our attack to take place half an hour before first light and in this way will probably catch them unawares. Being refreshed will make us more capable of success."

---

[9] Opera Vigilanza Repressione Antifascismo.

After some discussion, with frequent reference to Ernesto's sketch, a plan was evolved. Ercolene was to stay near the hideout but hidden at a point where he could watch so that he could warn the others if the cave and its contents was discovered during their absence. Basil thought this unlikely but the Italian was in no condition to help and it was a kind way of getting rid of him. Porky, accompanied by Tanky, would leave immediately with Guiseppe the donkey and tether him at the charcoal burner's hut where they would sleep then, leaving him tethered, join the main party at a point in the forest just outside Cingoli.

The first phase of the plan went smoothly with Tanky and Porky already waiting at the rendezvous when the others arrived. Then, Ernesto leading the way, they followed a series of paths through the forest until they reached a bullock track by which they entered the town through a narrow cutting between the buildings. At the main road running through the centre of the town they halted. The bright moon which lit the sleeping houses accentuated the shadow in which they stood, throwing the Casa Bianca into sharp relief. Two sentries dressed in the uniform of the Militia, lounged against the door. Jimmy grinned, his teeth gleaming even and white in the reflection from the moonlit buildings opposite.

"Just like the Germans to foist guard duties onto the Italians" he whispered. "Not very soldier like are they."

Basil chuckled softly as he flicked out the hinged bayonet fitted to the Beretta and checked that it had locked into position.

"They certainly aren't Guardsmen, but don't rely on it" he quipped.

During the tense moment which followed, the two friends gazed into each others face in that mutual understanding which comes to those who have shared the same experiences and realize that they might not meet again.

CHAPTER 12

The mood changed as Basil's smile revealed for a brief instant some of the boy that still remained beneath the hard exterior.

"All set?" he asked.

Jimmy nodded, then motioning to Tanky and the two New Zealanders to keep close, he followed Ernesto who led them by a devious route to a rear door of the S.S. Headquarters. Only one guard was on duty here and, like those at the front, appeared to be half asleep. After a whispered resumee of the layout of the interior, Ernesto returned to Basil then, leaving Porky to cover them should anything go awry, they dashed across the road piercing the surprised guards with their bayonets before they had time to realise that they were being attacked. The fearful scream that rent the air as Ernesto failed to make an instant 'kill' ruined Basil's hope of a silent attack. Wrenching his bayonet free, he placed a single shot into the dying man as Porky crossed the road to join them. Bunched together, they burst through the door of the building and were surprised to find the corridor deserted. Then, while Porky guarded the entrance, Basil and Ernesto raced to the end of the passageway passing several doors on the way, reaching the end just as Jimmy and his party came bursting in.

Calling to John to protect the rear entrance, Basil spun round and, closely followed by Ernesto, dashed down a flight of three steps near the end of the corridor, which connected with another passage ending at a heavily reinforced door. Cautiously Basil tried the handle and allowed himself a grim smile when he realised the door was not locked. Cautioning Ernesto to be absolutely silent, he eased it open about a quarter of an inch. A low murmur of voices in the guttural accents of the German reached his ears then, stepping away from the door, the index finger of his right hand gently caressing the rear trigger of the Beretta and with Ernesto standing beside him, he kicked the door open. A dark film of rage momentarily blurred his vision at the sight that met his eyes. Two Germans in the uniform of the S.S. sat at one end of a large table, while an Italian, wearing the hated black shirt, sat opposite writing something on a large sheet of paper. In one corner Quintale hung by his wrists, suspended from a hook in the ceiling with his toes just touching the floor. His head was slumped forward and the hair so matted with blood that he was rendered almost unrecognisable. As Basil gaped at the scene shocked into immobility, one of the Germans made a grab for a Mauser automatic which lay in front of him on the table. The cold rage which had seized Basil made his reaction quicker even than usual. The transition from his trance was immediate and the short burst of fire from his Beretta filled the room with noise and deadly effect. The German crashed heavily to the floor and the sharper more staccato note of the Spandau added to the din as Ernesto swept a murderous hail over the other two.

Somewhere outside an alarm sounded. Scooping up the Mauser from the table, Basil's glance fell on the sheet of paper now spotted with blood protruding from under the body of the Italian who had fallen across the table, and noticing that it seemed to be a list of names, he rolled the dead man aside and stuffed the sheet of paper into his pocket. Meanwhile, Ernesto, who had released Quintale and lifted him over his shoulder, muttered a short prayer of relief as he realised that his friend was unconscious and not dead as he had feared. Before he even reached the door, a sudden clamour of running feet and shouted orders from outside the building brought him to a halt. Then everything seemed to happen at once. Jimmy appeared in the doorway.

"The street is full of Carabinieri, he shouted. "We'll try to stop them from entering while you get out the back way." Then he dashed off.

As Ernesto staggered up the steps under the weight of his burden and made his way to the back door, the sharp cough of rifles mingled with the short staccato bursts of fire from sub-machine guns as one or other of the Syndicate found a target. The acrid tang of cordite already tainted the air. As he stepped outside a rifle spat and the bullet fanned his cheek as it buried itself into the wooden frame of the door an inch from his head. Someone in the excitement of the moment shouted

"Get that bloody light out!"

Crouching almost double he ran awkwardly for the sanctuary of an alley between the buildings where he was joined a moment later by the Immigration Officer.

Pulling a whistle from his pocket, Basil blew three short blasts, the signal that Quintale was safely away then, as if in answer to his summons, a group of five S.S. men appeared around the end of the building. Hastily stepping inside he reloaded the Beretta calling to John as he did so to check the interrogation room for another exit through the door to the courtyard. As John sped away to do his bidding a renewed burst of firing announced the arrival of reinforcements in the front. The light in the interrogation room still shed its strong glare over the debacle when, having tried the door in the wall behind the table and found it locked, John cast his eye quickly round the room. On the corner of the table lay a bunch of keys. The second key he tried fitted so, switching off the light, he opened the door, and stepped through into the small courtyard described by Ernesto.

Huddled against the wall were the bodies of two men, one of whom he recognised as Gabrielle. Striding over to a wooden gate secured by a simple catch, he opened it and peered out at a conglomeration of back yards which appeared to be deserted. Having closed the gate he returned to Basil to report his findings then dashed off again calling to Porky and Tanky to follow him through the interrogation room.

The first grey streaks of dawn where showing in the sky when Basil felt that sufficient time had passed for all to get clear. Slamming the back door, he bolted it and shouted to Jimmy to do likewise at the front entrance, who then joined him in a desperate bid for safety. As they sped towards the interrogation room, the brooding silence was rudely shattered by a resounding crash which reverberated through the house.

"They're assaulting the front door" groaned Basil "run like hell!"

They raced through the courtyard, separating as they reached the sanctuary of the narrow thoroughfares and. slipped quietly through the fields into the forest below the town.

Although the last to leave the building, Basil and Jimmy were the first pair to arrive at the shelter where the tethered Guiseppe still waited patiently. A few minutes later John arrived, then Porky. Half an hour passed and there was still no sign of Tanky. Basil was beginning to feel concerned for though he had expected Ernesto to be delayed there had been ample time for Tanky to reach the rendezvous.

"I wonder what's keeping him" he muttered aloud, then, addressing the others, "Did any of you see him leave?"

They looked blankly at each other for a moment and tried to recall those hectic moments as they made their dash through the courtyard and into the open country.

"He was alright when I warned him to leave," put in John, "but I can't remember seeing him since." he finished lamely.

Porky said he thought he remembered seeing Tanky in the courtyard but couldn't be sure. Reluctantly Basil gave the order to leave thinking that there seemed to be no point in waiting for a comrade who may have fallen when by so doing he risked the safety of half his band. Inevitably a hornets nest would have been stirred up and an intensive search of the forest was a logical sequence. Having first attended to Guiseppe's needs, they left him tethered as transport for Quintale and despondently started on the long walk back to the hideout.

Not one of the four spoke as they trudged wearily through the forest using little known paths as was their custom. Even the irrepressible Porky was silent, a fact which served as a constant reminder that one member was unaccountably delayed. Basil had not expected the two with Quintale to arrive before the allotted time elapsed so he was not perturbed by their absence. The donkey was available for their use and he reasoned that it would only be a matter of time before they returned. He had complete confidence in Ernesto's knowledge of the area and his ability to carry out the mission entrusted to him, particularly as he was assisted by Brian who, like the other New Zealander, was exceptionally self reliant even when judged by the high standards of them all.

He reflected that there had been plenty of time for them to get clear before any search party could be instituted. Tanky was a different matter, however, no-one could remember actually seeing him leave the courtyard and the possibility of his capture or even death could not be overlooked.

The cleft between Basil's grey eyes deepened as he puzzled over the mystery and tried to make up his mind whether he was doing the right thing by sticking steadfastly to the schedule. There had been so sign of either Italians or Germans either in the backyards or the narrow streets which separated the houses, all their efforts seemed to have been concentrated on the front and back doors of the Casa Bianca. The fact that Porky thought he remembered seeing Tanky in the yard was reassuring, for it would have been out of character if he had not left when told to do so. What could have happened in the interim? The persistent question returned to his thoughts again and again throughout the long trek and he cursed the fate that had played this scurvy trick, for it seemed they had rescued one but lost another and though risk was expected and willingly accepted by all, the loss of a member was difficult to bear.

Ercolene, looking drawn and nervous, greeted them hysterically on the path leading to the cave, irritating Basil who gave vent to his feelings in no uncertain manner as he roughly told him to pull himself together. The dejected Italian slunk into the cave where he sat watching Basil's every movement and regarding him with a dog-like devotion which irritated Basil even more, until, unable to stand it any longer, yet feeling ashamed of his outburst, he stormed out of the cave working off his anger as he furiously climbed the rocky path to the ledge overlooking Matelica.

The distant splendour of the Sibilline mountains with their peaks etched against the sky or shrouded in mist, fitted perfectly with the harmonious lines of the colourful hills which, blending with the amazing geometry of cultivated ground and arabesques of Oak, seldom failed to soothe him. The pine scented air filled him with a sense of well-being creating a condition in which he could relax.

Standing motionless the stern clean-cut features seemed a part of the rocks. Gradually his tension eased as he felt himself unwind. Remembering the sheet of paper he had stuffed into his pocket he took it out and smoothing the crumples from it against the flat surface of a rock, examined it. Roughly foolscap in size, with a number of names written in blue pencil down the left margin, it was clearly a list of wanted persons. Most of the names had been crossed through and against one the pseudonym Quintale had been inserted in red ink and three new names appeared to have been added to the list in the same handwriting. Thoughtfully folding the sheet of paper, he returned it to his pocket frowning as a conviction dawned that Quintale had talked. If this was so, it was possible that he may have divulged the secret of their hideout. As there was no way of knowing whether Quintale's interrogators had had time to pass on any information gleaned, Basil decided to move camp to Pioraco where, among the rock filled gorges, he and his party could remain hidden almost indefinitely.

As always when a course of action was decided, he moved quickly descending the rocky path with a speed and agility that would not have shamed a mountain goat and arrived at the cave in time to see the Immigration Officer approaching with Guiseppe. Noticing that the donkey had no passenger, Basil glanced down the track.

"Where's Quintale?" he asked, "Surely you did not leave him to walk up with Ernesto!"

Brian shook his head.

"No, he isn't here, but don't worry he's quite safe." Then, going into the cave, he dumped a Schmeisser on the ground.

"Even this ersatz sten gun gets heavy after a few miles" he remarked as he helped himself to a drink of water from the copper urn. Then, sitting down on one of the boxes that served as furniture, he rolled a cigarette. The tobacco, a coarse home cured variety, proved a little trying and took two or three attempts before the cigarette was made to his liking. Lighting it, he smoked contentedly for a few minutes while Basil seated himself and patiently waited till he was ready. "Anyway," to explain, Brian began, "We hadn't gone far after leaving you when it became obvious that Quintale would not survive unless professional help was obtained. He had been badly beaten up by the swine and I didn't like his colour. I got the impression too that some ribs were broken. It seemed to be out of the question to bring him up here as planned, so we hid in a thicket just outside of town until we could organise some help. Ernesto was getting increasingly worried lest he should die with his sins still on him, so I agreed to stay and look after Quintale while Ernesto called the local Priest to administer the last rites. He said that, as the Priest was an old friend of Quintale's, he would certainly not give them away to the Fascists." Brian chuckled, "I don't mind admitting," he went on, "I didn't feel too happy sitting like a clay pigeon waiting for Ernesto to return, but I could hardly leave a joker in the bush to die. I sweated there for about an hour and all the time it was getting lighter. With the road only about a hundred yards away I could see the activity our raid had stirred up and I got more and more edgy as I watched groups of Militia and S.S, men searching some of the houses just outside the town. Meanwhile, Quintale lay like a corpse beside me. Fortunately, it didn't seem to occur to anyone to search the woods. I had just about given up and was considering my next move, when Ernesto returned accompanied by an ancient Priest who walked with a stick. After examining Quintale and saying some prayers, he said he thought he would recover with proper treatment and asked us to wait while he arranged to have him carried to a place of safety. Then, leaning heavily on his stick, he hobbled off towards that church just outside the town. After what seemed an age, a much younger man, wearing the black habit of the Domenicani, arrived leading a bullock cart. He said that the Priest has asked him to take the sick man to the Suore Ospedagliere where he would get proper treatment and safe sanctuary. We placed Quintale into the cart and the friar drove off while we watched him head for the town."

Pausing a moment, Brian's eyes twinkled.

"You know, that joker took that cart right through a group of Militia pushing them out of his way as cool as you like. Incidentally, Ernesto said he wanted to warn a few friends that things have 'blown up' and we could expect him back here in about two days."

Having made up his mind that the area should be abandoned for the time being, Basil was reluctant to delay the departure, all his instincts warned him that delay would incur unnecessary risk. However, he felt duty bound to await the return of Ernesto.

As Basil had feared, the delay was fraught with peril for not only was a systematic search made of all the houses in and around Cingoli, but Aplini Troops were brought in to comb the hills, and Basil and his party were forced to keep on the move throughout the, daylight hours to avoid capture. Although the cave was searched Basil's foresight had enabled them to remove all traces of its use and they were able to return for the night. When the Italian failed to make his appearance on the third evening, Basil decided they could delay their departure no longer and, under cover of night, moved his small force across the valley to the comparative safety of the area he had chosen.

Meanwhile, Ernesto, who hesitated to risk betraying his friends by inadvertently leading a spy to the camp, moved about Cingoli freely and unsuspected, joining in the general conversation about the raid. It seemed that scarcely a man in the town was not an eye witness, or the friend of one, and the versions varied considerably. While one would solemnly talk of the parachutists he had seen descending in hordes over the valley during the early hours of the morning, another would profess to having seen Volpe with about 50 followers, marching through the town. Ernesto added his share to the many rumours, elaborating his tales with a careful disregard to the truth.

It was two weeks before Ernesto was able to visit the cave in safety and realised that he had lost touch. Deeming that, after all the trouble Basil had taken he would almost certainly seek news of Quintale, he visited the Priest who received him affably with the news that his old friend was progressing favourably at Gubbio, where the Suore Ospedagliere had him in their care. Inviting him in for a chat over a glass of wine, the Priest tottered into the cellar to fetch the refreshment, while Ernesto seated himself at a plain deal table wondering how best to approach him about news of the gang without revealing that he was actually one of them. "Have you seen anything of my friend who was with Quintale?" he asked as the Priest carefully opened a bottle of Chianti. Pouring the wine out before answering, the old man regarded him quizzically, the deeply Crenelated skin around his eyes giving them such an appearance of penetration that Ernesto squirmed uncomfortably under the gaze.

"You are playing a dangerous game my son" he said severely, "these are violent men and it has been written that those that live by the sword shall die by it"

"Someone must fight the evil of torture," retorted Ernesto, "you saw what they did to Quintale."

The Priest nodded. "Even so, it is apt that he should have gone to Gubbio, for it was there that St. Francis rebuked the Wolf that had been creating havoc in the area. If you know the story, the wolf was so ashamed at having earned the anger of the Saint that he wept and vowed he would raid no more."

Ernesto smiled, he knew the tale and had heard it often. "These tales are very fine to point the error of our ways" he pointed out "and I know we should turn the other cheek, but we have never been taught what to do if that cheek is also slapped."

The Priest chuckled. "Agreed! and I must admit that philosophy will not so easily prevent atrocities, but I haven't answered your question. Your friend was here last night and wants you to meet him at the Dopolavoro on Wednesday evening. Since it seems I cannot prevent you from joining them, I offer you the sanctuary of this roof should you ever require it."

By the fitful glow of an oil lamp, they discoursed on this and that together until the wine bottle was empty then, thanking the Priest for his hospitality and in return receiving his blessing, Ernesto bid him arrivederci returned to his lodgings in a mixed frame of mind.

CHAPTER 13

Domenico wearily followed the Maremma[10] team along the earth track which led to his home at the top of a small oak clustered knoll. The weight of years fell heavily on his shoulders, and the plough he followed seemed heavier than it had in the days of his youth. Even the hills seemed steeper. As was his wont, he kept up a running commentary to his beasts.

"It's the food shortage" he almost shouted. "Quando finira la guerra? What do all these politics matter anyway? It's the Contadini who take the brunt every time. It was the same all those years ago when I was a boy and my father used to say it to me, and it's the same now" he added bitterly. "It was like it when Mussolini came and it will always be so."

The beasts plodded on unheeding, their graceful horns swaying from side to side with the rhythm of their gait, for they were used to the old man's tirades and the sound of his voice soothed them.

As Domenico's thoughts roamed back over the years in the way an old man's will, he recalled the early days when be brought the young Filomena home as a bride. Then came the war in which, as a Corporal in the Bersaglia Regiment, he had helped fight the traditional enemy when the English had been allies. The early twenties when the Communist, Mussolini, was becoming known and his sudden rise to power. The war in Abbysinia during the thirties which had taken his only son Bruno. Pausing at the memory, he brushed a tear from his ageing eyes. Now this war which could only end in defeat and which had brought the hated Germans to Cingoli.

Suddenly the team stopped, bringing Domenico out of his reverie as he realised they had reached the well at the bottom of a slope which led to his home. Taking an ancient bucket, he dipped it in the clear water fed from a spring and as he drank his fill, thanked the Good Provider for a supply that never failed during the summer months. He felt very proud of the well..Not all could boast such a possession. One of the 'oxen' aroused him from his dreams as it pushed him gently in the back bringing his wandering thoughts to their needs.

Muttering "Wait for it can't you?" he placed the bucket before the beasts and fondly watched them drink. "Who else has such wonderful beasts?" he mused, "they work well and, God willing, in a few weeks the Vacca will provide a calf. Then there will be milk for cheese and later a young one to sell." Cheered by the happier thoughts, he resumed his homeward trend.

---

[10] Breed of Ox-like Bovines noted for their hardiness; though lacking the strength of some other draught cattle need not have supplementary feeding and are popular, for this reason, among 'lie poorer peasants.

Squat and ugly, built of stone, the house loomed into view. Before entering, he led the animals into the stable which was built onto the side of the house. The warm familiar smell of ammonia and hay assailed his nostrils and he sniffed appreciatively for he always associated that smell with home. Then taking a wooden pitchfork, he tossed a truss of hay into the manger, forking it over as he spread it along the trough. It doesn't look much, he thought, perhaps a little more. As he sorted out another truss, the fork fouled, meeting with unexpected resistance, and he looked suspiciously at the cow wondering whether she had lost her calf. Muttering to himself he stooped to clear the hay with his hands, then frowned in puzzled bewilderment as his hands came in contact with the warm body of a man. Stepping back he spoke sharply.

"What are you doing here?"

On receiving no response, he took a lamp from a niche in the wall and having lit it, peered more closely. There was no doubt that it was a man but 'Dio' he thought, he lay so still he might be dead. Crossing himself he stooped to investigate more closely holding the flickering light and gazing into the stubbled face to see if it were anyone he knew. Not very old he mused, about 30 I suppose. Then taking the stranger by the shoulders, he shook him roughly shouting "Wake up! Wake up!" Then noticing that the cloth felt sticky to his touch, he removed his hand and found it was covered with blood. Feeling a little frightened, he ran out of the stable and into the house where his wife was busy preparing the evening pasta in a large iron cauldron set over the fire.

"Who is that in the stable?" he demanded.

Filomena straightened from her task. " Who is who in the stable," she countered."You dream too much old man."

"If you think that, come and see who's dreaming," he answered roughly as he propelled his wife through the door. The stranger still lay in the same position as when Domenico had left him, filling Filomena's heart with compassion as she realised that he was hurt.

"Povera Gente, povera gente, we must help" she said. "Come on now, don't stand around, help me carry him in."

Although the stranger was not a large man, he was heavily built and it took the combined efforts of the two old people to get him into the house and upstairs onto a wooden chest which stood alongside the bed. Then shooing her husband out of the room, Filomena set about undressing the stranger. The shirt was stuck to the shoulder so, with the wisdom of her kind, she cut away the cloth, leaving the clot until she could devise a pad. Then bustled down the rickety steps to place a pot of water on the embers. Goading her husband to fetch more fuel for the fire, she returned to her task.

While washing the mud and stable filth from the unconscious man she paused to wonder over the soft texture of the hands thinking they would have done credit to a young girl from the city and compared them with her own hardened and calloused members. The fair skin where the sun never reached the body reminded her of her son when he was a boy. Even after the wound had been dressed and her charge tucked snugly in the huge communal bed, she lingered in the room gazing sympathetically at the pallid face. Pulling herself together, she picked up the soiled bundle of clothes and carried them downstairs ready for washing in the morning, rejoining her husband who, despite the warm June night, sat beside the now blazing fire smoking a pipe.

Heaving a tired sigh she lowered herself onto a rough cane bottom chair, her hands automatically busying themselves as she spun wool into yarn, manipulating the small hand spinner and smoothing the yarn with a dexterity born of long practice. Without raising her eyes from her work she said,

"Who can he be?"

Glancing toward the blackened rafters of the ceiling, Domenico shrugged his shoulders.

"'Who knows. Deserter or refugee from the bombed cities, but what are we to do with him.

"Then becoming uneasy again his eyes bulging slightly as his fear increased. "We daren't give him up lest we should be accused of sheltering him, yet it will be fatal to let him be found here.

"Filomena bridled speaking sharply."Whose to know he's here?" she demanded. "Of course if you go around yapping like a chiacchierone[11] ,then all will know."

For a short while Domenico stared moodily into the fire then, without saying a word, stood up and made his way to the bedroom. Removing only his jacket, trousers and boots, he climbed into the bed, barely looking at the stranger lying beside him and was already snoring stertorously in the grip of sleep when his wife came into the room a few minutes later.

A cock crowed from the roof of the pig house as Domenico splashed his face with water before descending to the lower room where his wife, who had risen before him, was already preparing a basket for the meal he would make in the fields. All that morning as Domenico worked, his thoughts frequently dwelling on the stranger under his roof, Filomena was kept busy with the

---

[11] Great babbler.

routine tasks which are the lot of peasant women. The pigs had to be fed and water carried from the well up the winding path to the house. The bread had to be baked and the sheep grazing on the fertile grass of the slope below the dwelling tended. Even so, somehow she contrived to keep an eye on the stranger who lay as if dead with only the slight rise and fall of the broad chest indicating that he lived. Shortly after midday while on one of her frequent visits to the bedroom, she chanced to glance across the valley while adjusting the heavy wooden shutters at the window. A squad of Carabinieri crossing the valley caught her attention, and she idly watched their progress for a moment thinking how much more useful they would be tilling the soil. Suddenly she tensed and her hand flew to her mouth as, with feminine intuition, she guessed their purpose. For a moment, with heart fluttering, she stood stock still incapable of any thought then, panic stricken, looked about the room forgetting in her dismay that, even had there been a hiding place, without Domenico's help it would be impossible for her to lift the stranger on her own.

. . . .

Captain Carvello of the Carabinieri, led his section of the search party over the uneven cultivated ground as he made for a heavily wooded knoll nearly a mile away. He felt warm and irritable and wished he was back at Perugia. The task of searching for the raiders seemed a futile waste of time. obviously, he thought, they would be miles away in the mountains by now and he privately hoped that they were never found for the Nazis deserved their fate, but he was a soldier and orders had to be obeyed. As he approached the farm house the evidence of neglect was immediately apparent. A shutter hung loosely on its supports and the stable door needed a latch. The old Donna who stopped her work to regard his party, looked careworn. The war is bad enough for us, he thought, but it's worse still for old peasants such as these deprived of their young men to help farm the land. Then, noticing a wreath on the door, even that looks as if it has been used before.

'While he had been taking all this in, his men spread themselves around the house. With arms akimbo Filomena glared at the intruder.

"What do you want soldier?" she demanded "Can you not see the wreath on the door?"

The Captain looked at her coldly, "Dio, how distasteful this is." he thought. Then, without showing his feelings demanded if she had seen any strangers. As she mutely shook her head her knees seemed to go weak. Ignoring the silent reply, the Captain strode brusquely to the entrance and attempted to enter, but Filomena dodged into the doorway to bar his passage. Irritably he pushed her to one side and clumped into the low ceilinged room. On finding it empty of people and devoid of any possible cover, he pointed to the trap in the ceiling.."I shall go upstairs" he said and, suiting his actions to the words, commenced to climb the rickety steps. Filomena stood dumbly by, she had done all that she could. Now, the thing must take its natural course.

Pushing up the trap, the Captain stared into the room which the shaded shutters had rendered pleasantly cool. Four candles burned at a small shrine in one corner and a figurine of The Madonna stood on a wooden chest beside the bed. The flickering glow of a single candle illuminated both the Madonna and the shrouded figure, throwing into relief the pebbles which weighted the eyes. A small rosary had been placed beneath the right hand which was folded over the other on his chest. Uttering a small prayer, he crossed himself, then searched the room only to find, as he had expected, that the only entrance was via the trap door. Satisfied by his inspection that no fugitive could possibly be hidden, he descended and with muttered apologies, hurried outside to supervise the search of the stable and surrounding area.

. . . .

The dull thud as the trap door closed penetrated the subconscious of the inert figure lying on the bed, who groaned and shifted his position slightly. Someone seemed to be pummelling his shoulder which throbbed painfully from the repeated blows, while looking on, Cpl. Baggaley, dressed in a weird mixture of German and Italian uniforms, leered down at him. Somehow he broke loose and ran into a small room where the scent of incense hung heavily in the air and the shriek of machine guns was appalling. He looked wildly about him but could see no-one. Above the din, Basil Holden's voice was shouting,

"One and sixpennies queue here."

Then he saw him standing on the mantelpiece and tried to reach his side but instead found himself walking backwards. On gaining the open country he started to run, but still the noise of the machine guns followed deafening him with their din and he ran faster, his heart thumping furiously until he felt it must burst. Suddenly there was a loud thud, followed by absolute silence. With his ears straining Tanky lay still, aware only of his wildly beating heart and an oppressive weight over the eyes. The nebulous fear he felt subsided as his mind cleared from the spectres of his dream and he began to sort fact from fancy. He now remembered the raid and the hurried exit which followed. He also remembered being wounded, and thinking it could not be much more than a scratch he had pressed on intending to attend to the wound later. Then again, he recalled following the undulating curve of a small valley where he had hidden his gun in a thicket when it became too heavy to carry. After stumbling around for a while, he had come to a well which refreshed him and he had followed a winding track up a hill. The stable door adjoining a stone cottage had been open and he had gone inside, then he supposed he must have passed out for the rest was a blank.

He began to wonder where he was for not a glimmer of light broke the total darkness and be became alarmed lest he should have been thrown into the cellars of the Casa Bianca. Then, realising that his eyes were still closed, he tried to open them, but the oppressive weight prevented him from doing so. He thought perhaps he was still dreaming and shook his head to verify that he was awake. The weak movement was sufficient to shift the pebbles from his eyes and a glimmer of light showed through the half opened lids. It was with a feeling of relief, mixed with increasing bewilderment, that he realised he was lying on a bed in a small stone walled room. Bright sunlight filtering through the cracks of a shuttered window indicated it was daylight outside. A strong smell of incense pervaded the room and from his position he could see the wreath of smoke rising steadily from a joss stick, forming fantasies of intricate patterns in the illumination of four candles at a shrine in the corner. He tried to raise his head but finding he was too weak to do so, lay still.

A scraping noise in one corner of the room distracted his wandering thoughts and he turned his head in the direction of the noise. A trap door in the floor was opening and the head and shoulders of a woman appeared, followed by the rest of her as she came into the room. On seeing his eyes open she smiled and the careworn wrinkles were transformed to an appearance of jollity. Placing a gnarled finger on her lips she crossed over to him, picking up a jug of water as she did so.

When Filomena had attended to Tanky's immediate needs, she told him to stay where he was and on no account to open the shutters at the window then, assuring him that she would be back shortly, left closing the trap door after her as she descended the steps.

Feeling more comfortable now that his burning thirst had been eased, Tanky grinned quietly to himself at the very idea of tottering weakly about the room just to open windows when it was an effort to even raise his head from the pillows.

Meanwhile, Filomena gazed speculatively at the few chickens scratching away around the stable door. Suddenly, as if divining her intention, they scattered with flapping wings and loud squawks as they tripped over one another in their haste to reach safety. With a speed of movement that would have astonished her husband, Filomena grabbed a straggler and, with a deft twist, wrung its neck.

The hot chicken and herb broth which Filomena concocted and patiently fed to Tanky quickly restored some of his strength. When he had finished eating, she sat on the edge of the bed and regarded him solemnly until, unable to restrain her curiosity any longer.

"Who are you? Where do you come from? How did you get hurt?" she asked. The questions came rapidly. Without pausing for answer she continued,

"We found you in the stable, how did you get there?"

As Tanky, smiling weakly, was about to answer, she interrupted with

"Why did you come here? Don't you know that it's dangerous for us?"

Then inconsequentially, as if regretting the impulsive words.

"Would you like some more broth?"

Tanky shook his head. He felt muzzy again and very very tired. Ignoring her questions he thanked her for the broth and said he would like to sleep. Full of contrition now, she helped him to lie down then, smoothing the dank hair from his forehead, she whispered,

"At least tell me your name that I may know you." Somehow he conjured up a smile and, giving the name on his false identity papers said,

"Bruno - Tocco Bruno from Milan."

Filomena, who nostalgically identified Tanky with her son, was not surprised to learn that he bore the same name because she had almost succeeded in deluding herself that he was indeed her lost boy. The years of frustrated motherhood culminated in a torrent of tears.

During the days that Tanky lay helpless, Filomena tended him with the devoted care of a mother, foreseeing his every need and, with selfless disregard to herself, spent many wakeful hours comforting him when the pain from his wound prevented sleep. She even dipped into the few lire representing her carefully hoarded savings and persuaded her husband to go to the town to purchase thread from the black market so that she could repair the rent in Tanky's jacket.

Torn between the desire to please his wife and his instinctive fear of strangers, Domenico visited Cingoli and wandered furtively about the town dreading that at any moment he would be arrested either for dealing on the black market or for harbouring a fugitive. When at last he obtained some thread and carried it triumphantly home, Filomena berated him for wasting her money on such poor quality. Angry in her disappointment, she tugged the cotton viciously several times and punctuated each tug with a shout of

"Fiacca!" as it broke. Then screaming,

"Fiacca! fiacca fiacca! - good for nothing, I ask you to do one little thing." she hurled the offending reel at her husband who diplomatically slipped outside to escape her rage.

The enforced rest, aided by Tanky's excellent constitution, combined for rapid recovery, consequently, by the time the Allies long awaited offensive began with its heavy bombing of Sicily during the first week of July, followed up by the parachute landings on the 10th, Tanky was up and about. The need to keep within the immediate vicinity of the house was burdensome but he wisely refrained from venturing very far during daylight hours as he impatiently waited for the day that he would be strong enough to rejoin the Syndicate. During the evenings, when the old couple had nothing much to do, he whiled away the hours telling them of the places he had seen and describing the streets of Milan with their buses and trams. With gay abandon he ignored the fact that he had never been to that city and hoped that a description of London with a slightly Continental flavour would suffice. Having been an avid reader, with Catholic tastes, he had a ready fund of stories with which to entertain his host and as the Italian peasant loves a story, he built himself quite a reputation as a raccontatore.

Not to be outdone, Domenico, in return, would embroider the titbits of gossip he had heard from friends but he was happiest when discoursing lengthily on the merits of different types of vacche, or the mysterious ailments of sheep. In keeping with farmers the world over he would vow with regular monotony that last year's crop was the worst ever and this year's promised to be even more disappointing.

On Sunday, Filomena would rise earlier than usual and bustle through her work in time to put on her best clothes to attend Mass. Then, carrying her shoes in her hand, for to wear them before she arrived at the church would be extravagant, and these, her only pair of real shoes must last, she would set off with the wooden soles of her Zoccoli clacking on the baked earth of the path. Domenico would usually hint,

"One at church is enough."

and invariably find an excuse not to attend. As far as he was concerned, Tanky's presence provided the perfect alibi and, with a roguish look in his eye, he had volunteered to miss church and keep him company throughout his stay.

One Sunday, while Filomena was at Mass, Tanky noticed that Domenico seemed nervous and preoccupied so asked him what was worrying him. At first Domenico hedged a little then, seeming to screw up his courage, he took a loosened brick from the wall and produced an automatic pistol from a cavity which lay behind it. Then, speaking rapidly, as if eager now to get the business over, he said,

"Is this yours?"

Recognising it for a 9 mm Beretta similar to the one he normally carried in his pocket, Tanky replied guardedly.

"Where did you get that?"

"It was in the straw of the stable. Filomena knows nothing of this but I think you should leave soon. I believe you to be no deserter, but English. If you are it would go ill with us if you were found here."

Tanky could only gape in dismay at this revelation and sat down temporarily unable to think of a reply. The old man looking suspiciously at him, and imbuing a note of authority into his voice as he gained confidence, said,

"Who are you? and how did you get that wound? I saw too many in France not to know a bullet wound when I see it. You have told us much about the city of Milan and places you have seen but nothing about yourself or why the Carabinieri were searching for you that day. It was different when you were sick and we cared for you as we would our own son, but now you must tell us the truth."

"I have told you, my name is Bruno and that I left Milan because of the bombing" protested Tanky.

The old man grunted disbelievingly and scowled at his pipe as he started to fill it.

"And I say I don't believe you. I was in Cingoli the other day and heard many strange things. I heard. that on the very morning we found you English parachutists killed many men then jumped into their planes and flew away. I believe you may be one of these."

As Domenico unfolded his theory, Tanky listened incredulously and rapidly considered whether to brazen it out or not. He had no wish to risk hurting the old man if he threatened him with a gun which now lay in his lap, on the other hand, he had no intention of being handed over to the authorities. Eventually he decided to mix propaganda with sufficient truth to satisfy Domenico and gain his confidence. With this in mind, he asked him to sit down while he explained. When Domenico had obeyed his request and he was sure he had his attention, he outlined the political events leading up to the war and the repercussions accruing from the German Alliance, he then went on to say,

"As you know, the war, for Italy, is now nearly over. Already the English are in Sicily, the Ferry is out of operation and the rail routes are chaotic. We and many others, believe that while the Fascists are in power the Germans will stay in this country and the war will be fought on Italian soil. If this happens no-one will be safe and Italy will become a part of Germany with Jackbooted Nazis tramping through our fields and into our homes. Like all true Italian patriots we hate the Germans who have always been our enemy. Our aim is to fight and kill them wherever they may be and so help to drive them from our land. You believe the raid in Cingoli was carried out by the English but you are wrong just as you are wrong about so many other things for the newspapers only print what they are allowed to print. They speak of great victories which in reality are terrible defeats. Knowing this Mussolini has lost heart so remains hidden from our eyes too ashamed to meet us as once he did.

One night, the night you speak of, Fascists, acting under German orders, raided a printing shop and arrested the men who would have told you the truth. These men were handed over to the Nazis who shot all except one who they tortured. Volpe, of whom you may have heard, received news of this and rescued the man from his tormentors."

Developing his theme Tanky watched Domenico for every reaction to his words. He skilfully changed the trend as a salesman might and took care to present only the opinions which seemed to meet with approval. One of Tanky's great attractions was his ability to instil his own enthusiasm into others, so it was hardly surprising that, as his arguments became more persuasive, Domenico found himself agreeing with every word and convinced that Volpe and people like him would bring the war to a rapid close. When he judged the time to be ripe for his disclosure, Tanky at last admitted. that he was one of Volpe's men and concluded by asking Domenico to bear with him for a further week when he thought he should be strong enough to re-join his friends.

Fired with enthusiasm, Domenico jumped up and embraced Tanky as soon as he had finished speaking then, with a roguish twinkle in his eyes, gaily crossed the room and returned a moment later with two small glasses and a bottle of Strega. Saying,

"We must drink to our brave friends in the hills," he poured the drinks, then with a firm "Alla saluta" drained his glass.

Tanky enjoyed his more slowly, savouring the new flavour which pleased his palate. After the glasses had been refilled, Domenico winked slyly as he topped the bottle up with water and said,

"Not a word to Filomena about this, she keeps it for the special occasions that never come".

Watching Domenico wash out the glasses Tanky grinned conspiratorially, then chuckled in amusement when Domenico carefully replaced them in the exact position that they had been before and blew gently along the dust laden shelf to raise a fine cloud which soon began to settle on the glasses. Highly pleased with himself, Domenico roared with laughter and, with eyes dancing with merriment, smirked,

"I too am cunning like the Volpe."

CHAPTER 14

As the Mass drew to a close Filomena looked around the little church and breathed out a sigh of contentment. It was good to be back and hear Don Pasquale preach again. Why it must be two years, she mused, since I started using S. Esuperanzio because it is nearer and my legs are not what they were.

Casting her eyes up to the old priest who was just giving the Blessing, she sighed again thinking, he doesn't seem to change with the years and looks no different to when he called last year, which was before he started using that stick to walk.

As soon as the service was over, Don Pasquale Diovetti walked slowly to the door of his church so that he could exchange a few words with each of his flock. Passing Filomena he thought how nice it was to see la Donna Tornelli in her usual place and smiled tolerantly as it occurred to him that that rascal Domenico was still conspicuous by his absence. Although he was feeling tired by the time all except Filomena, who had remained behind in the church, had gone their separate ways, he waited patiently for her to emerge welcoming the opportunity for service. It seemed incredible to him that six decades had passed since he had baptised her and he remembered the wedding to Domenico as if it were only the previous day. What a graceful creature she was then, he thought. The intimate knowledge of her lifetime had taught him her every mood and he could sense when she needed advice so, when at last Filomena dipped her fingers and made the sign of the cross, he didn't greet her with the usual conventional words, but suggested that she should accompany him to his house and talk awhile before returning home. Remarking how nice it would be to hear how Domenico and she had fared during the past twelve months, he accepted her arm gladly as she lent her support for the scant half-a-mile to his house.

Later, in the seclusion of his home, Filomena spoke of the man she knew as Bruno and told how he had been found in the stable and of her fears for his safety.

"I know that he is not really my own Bruno" she said, "and that I should not regard him so, but I can't feel in my heart that it is wrong. My husband says he may be a bad mad but no man could be bad and have such kind eyes for are they not the window to the soul?"

While she haltingly spoke of her sentiments towards the young man, Don Pasquale watched the emotion on her face and wisely refrained from interrupting as he waited patiently until she had finished, and allowed a few minutes of silence to elapse before giving his advice. Then, when he had complimented her on her compassion and berated her for the risks she incurred on her house, he suggested that Bruno would be safer in his home and warned her not to mention their conversation to anyone, including Domenico her husband. He asked her to give him the small St. Christopher which he knew she always wore around her neck and said that she could tell Bruno to accompany the man that brought it.

The following day, Monday, 19th July, Domenico had gone to his work in the fields and Filomena was preparing the first batch of peperoni from the new crops now beginning to ripen, when a slim steely eyed stranger with a purposeful air strode into the yard and asked if this house was La Cabana the home of Tornelli Domenico. With trepidation, she nodded her assent and asked what he wanted.

"Is your husband here?" he demanded.

She quavered "What would you with him" with a sinking sensation gnawing at the pit of her stomach.

"Just answer my question" he retorted brusquely, then sotto voce he added more kindly,"Don't worry, I am a friend." and handed her the St. Christopher. Relieved, she invited him into the house saying,

"It is quite safe, my husband is in the fields and the one you would meet is upstairs."

Then,pulling a chair forward as she invited him to make himself comfortable, she said.

"Isn't the day hot? Would you like some vino?"

The bronzed hawk-like face of the stranger creased in a smile which robbed the refusal of offence as he declined the offer and said, "Some water if I may." before helping himself from a copper urn by the door. Remarking on the excellent quality of her supply as he returned the dipper to its place at the side of the urn, he paused to glance through the door at the valley below, where a moving blob of colour had caught his attention, and he idly watched a tiny figure working with vacche move slowly across his vision. How peaceful it all seems, he thought. Yet, in the midst of this there are secret fears to poison minds one against the other.

"Brian, you old devil!"

Tanky's ejaculation of surprise cut into the Immigration Officer's thoughts and he swung round to stare in amazement before rushing forward to greet his friend. With hands firmly clasped in the age old token of friendship, the two men looked into each other's faces and laughed. Suddenly the world seemed good.

"What on earth brought you here so opportunely?" Tanky asked.

Brian grinned. "Better ask la Donna she arranged everything.

Meanwhile Filomena stood by watching with a pleased yet puzzled air. Tanky glanced at her.

"But I didn't know who the Don would send or that it would be a friend of yours" she protested. Then indicating the Immigration Officer, she continued,

"Is he also from Milan?"

"Yes", lied Tanky and quickly changed the subject.

"I knew, of course, that you had arranged for me to go into hiding with the Priest, but I don't get how my friend comes into it." Filomena smiled knowingly.

"It is the will of God."

In her simple faith no further explanation was needed.

"Now you must go while it is still safe."

Now the time to part had come Filomena could scarce restrain her agitation and clung desperately to Tanky as if determined never to let him go. With tears dimming her eyes she begged him to return when he could and, with a sudden impulsive gesture, pressed the St. Christopher into his hand.

"Guard this well," she said, "and he will guard thee. Take it and when you look remember Filomena."

With an expression of mixed relief and sadness on her face, she watched the stocky figure she had grown to love until it disappeared through the trees overhanging the path.

As the two friends passed the well at the bottom of the slope, Tanky gazed back at the house already half hidden in the foliage, the peperoni drying on its roof making a splash of red amongst the green of the surrounding leaves. Surprised to find a lump in his throat, he turned and sadly fell into step beside the Immigration Officer who, sensing his emotion, remained silent as he took the Cingoli track.

They found Don Pasquale crouched over an ancient radio listening intently to a news bulletin which could only just be heard above the crackling of the set. Nodding a greeting, he put his fingers to his lips and concentrated on listening. The usually animated face looked tired and Brian noticed that some of the life seemed to have gone from his eyes. He guessed the news was bad and tried to catch the faint words as they came over the air but without success. Presently the Priest switched off the radio and greeted his guests.

"You must forgive an old man for neglecting his manners," he said, "but the radio is so bad that it takes all my attention. Do sit down for you must be tired. In a short while a meal will be ready and we can discuss the news while we eat." Then, turning to Tanky, he remarked,

"So you are Bruno, from Milan I believe?"

Tanky nodded. At that moment a comely looking middle aged woman, who looked after the Priest's house and saw that he ate regularly, came bustling in. Scarcely glancing at the two guests she announced rather brusquely that unless they came to eat now the food would be cold. Don Pasquale courteously thanked her then, turning to the Immigration Officer, remarked,

"As I explained this morning, Quintale is rapidly regaining his strength under the care of the Suore at Gubbio but I fear his face is too well known at Cingoli for him to return."

Then led the way into an adjoining room furnished with a long deal table laid in readiness for the meal. The white linen and gleaming glassware in the subdued light of a cluster of candles lent an air of luxury to the scene and Tanky tried to recall when he had last ate in such comfort, but couldn't remember. Probably, he thought, because I always took civilisation for granted and never realised how transient it was. He found himself humming Elgar's graceful 'Salute D'Amour' and nostalgically recalled an old man playing a harp at the door of the Finnish Restaurant in Cairo. The actual meal escaped him but the memory of a four year old French girl who had made friends and borrowed his napkin brought a smile to his lips. Her coquettish flirting had made his evening and he wondered how expert she would be when she got older.

The sudden silence as Don Pasquale prepared to say grace brought his thoughts back to the present. Taking his place at the table he remarked,

"These are indeed tragic times for Italy when brother shoots at brother."

The Priest looked at him with a slightly sympathetic air and said,

"I am an old man and in my time I have seen many evil things but I could wish I had never lived to see the day when civil war was imminent. Mussolini and Hitler had another meeting today but I fear it will do no good."

"I fear not," agreed Tanky, "I expect old Mussolini will ask for help in the south - as usual Hitler will refuse then, with nothing accomplished, our Duce will return to strut around for a day or two as he usually does after being with the Germans."

"Meanwhile, the steady disintegration of Fascism leads infallibly to the fall of the Regime, the alienation of the German/Italy pact and national dislocation," remarked the Priest. "If the unrest in our fighting forces explodes into open revolt, there will be civil war and the tramp of jack boots will be heard as the Nazis take the advantage to usurp our land, our homes and our independence." He paused and wagged his head dejectedly from side to side. "Today Rome was bombed again and this time the Bassilica of San Lorenzo was hit and destroyed. With it goes a little of the old way of life and this is but a beginning. Soon the Allied Forces, now in Sicily, will be on the mainland of Italy itself. What then will Il Duce do? Will he sue for a separate peace, or will he fight on?"

As Don Pasquale came to the end of his comment, he regarded his guests keenly as if inviting opinions.

"As I see it," said Tanky, "whatever Il Duce does, the result must be the same. Make no mistake, the German Army will clash with that of the Allies on Italian soil whether Italy as a nation continues to exist or not."

"I suspect, that the Government will sue for a separate peace." said Brian, "If so, we are going to need people like Quintale and Volpe for, as Don Pasquale has pointed out, the Germans will undoubtedly march down through Italy and, in their animal way, will ravage everything in their path. Today it was the Bassilica which fell to the Allied bombs in Rome. Tomorrow, who knows what else will fall or be desecrated by those Jack Booted Nazi Bastards:"

"The whole situation is extremely worrying," responded the Priest, "every day I have people asking me for advice. What can I tell them except to pray? This eases their minds but does nothing for their predicaments. Far too many have grown up with Fascism so this is all they know; it is what they have been taught. Even so, many of them have come to regard it as evil. Now, in keeping with many others, I believe the Regime to be drawing to a close. The solidarity has been undermined by defection in the highest places. Everyone who stops to think must wonder why a meeting of the Joint Council has been called for next week. Many, particularly intellectuals, say that a move of censure is planned and Mussolini will be asked to resign."

Tanky exchanged a look across the table with the Immigration Officer, and grinned,

"I wouldn't care to be in the shoes of whoever moves a vote like that." he said, "I think I'd be dead scared of not getting any support."

"You'd probably get arrested on the way out," Brian chuckled. "I wonder who will beard the lion in his den? I reckon Kipling would have said - 'It's a rare old case of a Fascist wolf being hunted by Fascist hounds'."

"'Whatever the outcome, Fascism is likely to remain", remarked Tanky, "and if Mussolini goes they will probably put someone a lot worse in. Starace or Farinacci for instance. Then the fat will be in the fire and no mistake, particularly if a change renews peoples' faith in the Party."

"I don't think we shall ever see wholehearted support," interrupted the Priest, "for I believe those days are over. Fascism, after all, as far as Italy has been concerned, was never really Fascism in its true sense, it could be more aptly described as Mussolinism. Had it been otherwise, we should not be sitting here as we are now discussing the decline of Mussolini's popularity, and its effect on the Fascist Party. A new figurehead would have been put in power and the Party would never have been blamed for involving us in the war. However, as it is, if Mussolini falls then so too must Fascism. Knowing this, the anti-Fascists are practically certain to try and oust him when the Grand Council meets next week. I have reached the opinion that, if they succeed, a new Government will be formed and that its first job will be to negotiate for an armistice, since this is the only way that popularity with the people could be won."

Abruptly Don Pasquale rose from the table and said,

"Now if you will excuse me, I have things to attend to."

Then addressing Brian as Gino, the Pseudonym by which he was known to the Priest, he asked him to attend to his friend's needs, remarking that he should know his way about the house by now. Then bid the pair goodnight.

After about half an hour of amiable small talk, Tanky declared that he seemed to tire very quickly and, with the prospect of a long walk the next day, he thought he had better get his head down.

When Don Pasquale rose on the following morning it was not yet four o'clock, even so, his guests had already left but he was not surprised for such was the way these men came and went and he had come to accept it. Looking out of the window at the distant Sibillini range, he spared a thought for them and the dangers they must endure. "Mother here are your sons who have fought so hard, may they not be weighed as a soul is weighed, may they rather be judged as an outlaw is judged who comes creeping home along deserted paths." He uttered Peguy's memorable words aloud treating the poem as a prayer.

By mid-day the village of Stigliano had been reached and the Immigration Officer decided to call a halt. He was well pleased with the progress made for the route had not been easy and he had expected Tanky to lag. However, even the long jolting descent into the valleys, always more tiring than the steady climbs, had failed to bring a protest from his dogged companion who determinedly kept pace step for step. As he relaxed against a tree he rolled a cigarette and handing the makings to Tanky, said,

"Until now we have been in territory you know well but soon we will be breaking fresh ground on the other side of the Camerino Road where we take the track for a village called Palezzo then, leaving the track we follow a goat path to Pioracco at the entrance of a gorge where the river Potenza emerges from its rocky course. You'll find the way is rather rough and as we follow the river through the gorge the going gets progressively harder. In places the water is quite deep and extremely rapid in the narrower sections. How's your arm shaping by the way?"

Tanky moved his arm experimentally, "It's a little stiff but otherwise as good as new." he replied.

"Do you think it's up to a bit of rock climbing?"

Tanky thought a moment about this problem, then shrugged laconically.

"Depends on what you mean by rock climbing."

"Well, there's not much really, the only difficult part being a narrow ledge round a waterfall, but once past that point it's plain sailing."

Tanky laughed. "I expect it'll be alright, let's hope I don't have to put any weight onto it, but in any case we'll cross that bridge when we come to it."

Despite Tanky's assertions however, the Immigration Officer was worried. The old cave headquarters of the gang was comparatively close to their position so he decided that it would be best to retrace their way and spend the night at the cave in order that Tanky should be as fresh as possible for the second leg of their journey. Realising that Tanky would insist on continuing if he had any suspicion that the delay was for his benefit, Brian remarked, "Well so much for the route tomorrow but, of course, it's too far for us to try today. Normally we spend the night up at the cave then cross the road in the early hours of the morning. Then, as if it had been his original intention, he stood up and said, "Well we may as well get up there" and led the way through the forest.

. . . .

Throughout that Tuesday and the following Wednesday, Basil Holden anxiously scanned a small portion of track leading up to Laverino hoping for a sight of the Immigration Officer who had been due back on the Monday evening. John Hazelgrove had wanted to go in search of his friend but Basil insisted on his remaining at the camp pointing out with a cheery assurance, he didn't feel, that this was not the first time one of the party had been late returning from Cingoli. It was a long way and could only just be managed in a day's march. It was seven o'clock in the evening before his powerful glasses picked out two tiny figures walking along the track. The distance was too great for recognition even with glasses and Basil would have passed them over had the Immigration Officer not raised an arm in their recognition signal at a point half way along the small strip of track that was visible from the lookout point high on the slopes of Monte Fennino where Basil had made his H.Q. As he vainly tried to focus his glasses more sharply in an endeavour to recognise the heavily built figure that accompanied the immigration Officer, he wondered if it could be Quintale, then, as he watched, the Immigration Officer turned and faced the mountain and semaphored T.A.N.K.Y. As Basil read out the letters he frowned, mistaking the signal for advance information of tank movements. It was not until the message was repeated a moment later that he realised the word was Tanky. His great bellow of joy sent a flock of startled birds flying into the air and brought Jimmy rushing to his side. Shaken for once from his usual calm, Basil excitedly told Jimmy the welcome news and together they descended to the camp where they found Ernesto, who had just arrived back from a visit to

Nocera, showing Porky a leaflet which he claimed had been dropped on Rome a few nights earlier. Porky had already started to read through the leaflet but, seeing Basil and Jimmy, paused and grinned. "Hey fellows, listen to this ...

'Citizens of Rome, you have already been warned that military objects in the vicinity of Rome are liable to be bombed by the Allied Airforce. When this occurs the Fascist Government, which has consistently concealed from you the truth about the war, will pretend that we are trying to destroy those cultural monuments which are the glory not only of Rome but of the civilised world. It is moreover possible that the Italian Government and their German Ally may themselves arrange for bombs to be dropped on the centre of Rome, including the Vatican City, in order to give their lying statements some appearance of the truth. We leave it to your sound judgement to decide whether it is probable that we should waste our effort on the destruction of targets which are of no importance to the war effort. We have declared, and we repeat, that we are aiming at military objectives, including communications, war industries, military installations, and airports all of which are being used solely, in the interests of the Germans.' [12]

---

[12] This leaflet was dropped on July 19th, 1943.

CHAPTER 15

"It's fantastic!"

Basil protested as, on this hot day towards the end of July, he sat with his back against the flat rook enjoying the shade thrown by a group of silver birch near the entrance to a cluster of small caves, where they had made their H.Q. The icy current of a mountain stream which rushed precipitously towards a narrow defile in the rocks, before emerging into the gorge leading down to Pioracco, cooled his feet as he dangled them in the clear water; even here in the mountains the heat had been oppressive and he felt grateful for the respite.

"Are you sure you've got your facts right?"

He glanced at the stalwart figure who, with feet planted firmly apart, stood beside him, the erect stance, even when relaxed, being typical of his type. Jimmy, who had but a few minutes earlier returned from a scouting expedition in Gualdo Tadino on the other side of the mountains, nodded.

"Fantastic or not, it seems to be true. The village is in an uproar - at nearly every corner I saw groups either arguing or fighting - while in every street small groups were prowling in search of Fascists. A man, who only arrived from Rome yesterday, told me that the same sort of thing is happening there on a much larger scale."

"What's fantastic?"

Dumping a sheep filched from a flock grazing nearby and slipping his knife from its sheath, Porky commenced to skin the animal as he glanced interrogatively at the pair talking together.

"Old Musso's done a bunk or something very like it." Basil replied. Then, frowning, he spoke curtly,

"Watch that blood you clot!"

Basil believed in leaving nothing to chance and had made a strict rule that nothing was to be jettisoned into the stream for fear it should be noticed lower down and betray the presence of a camp some where upstream. Even though the risk of the stain remaining in the water was faint, it could not be overlooked for it was only by such meticulous attention to details that the location of their hideout could remain a secret. Flushing, Porky hefted the sheep away from the edge of the stream and carried it to the entrance of the small cavern which was used as a general store. As he hung the carcass on a specially constructed tripod and adjusted a bucket to catch the blood, he could hear the two New Zealanders talking together as they drifted into camp. He knew they had been out all day watching the road which runs from Foligno through Muccia and follows the Chienti Valley to Ancona, and wondered what news they would have to impart. John Hazelgrove's remark of,

"Hell of a lot of Tedeschi about, I think something big must be going on"

carried clearly to his ears, then the Immigration Officer cut in with,

"He said a mouthful! The focal point seems to be Foligno or beyond since that's the direction they're following."

Eager not to miss any titbit of news, Porky hurried back to the group, pausing on the way to wave cheerily to Tanky who, ensconced in a small cleft in the rocky walls of the miniature canyon, commanded a view of the narrow cutting through which anyone approaching the camp would have to pass. Since his return a week before he had spent the majority of his time at this post. Unless a stunt was on, the remainder took turns in patrolling the immediate area and brought back news of approaching search parties. On this day, the two Italians were doing their stint so would not be expected until nightfall. As he returned the salute, the binoculars hanging from their strap round his neck swung against his chest and a feeling of elation swept over him when no spasm of pain accompanied the movement.

Rejoining the others by the stream, Porky threw himself flat on the ground and dipped his hands in the sparkling water to drink, before rolling onto his back in an attitude of contented indolence.

"What's all this about Benito?"

He grinned happily up at Jimmy who, with knitted brow, was pondering over the New Zealanders' report. Ignoring Porky's question he remarked,

"German troop movements towards Rome seem to indicate that something has happened to worry them, on the other hand, the fighting in Sicily could account for the movements Brian speaks about and they could well be re-enforcements," he finished. Then, glancing towards Porky,

"Accounts vary, but there seems to be no doubt that Musso has vanished. Furthermore, according to a chap I was talking to in Foligno, many of the prominent Fascists have either fled from Rome or gone into hiding."

Porky sat upright with a look of incredulous amazement on his face as Jimmy paused to roll a cigarette before continuing his explanation.

"Apparently the old boy had an audience with the King last Sunday, which was the day after the meeting of the Grand Fascist Council that the old Don had heard rumours about. It seems that after the meeting with the King he was not seen returning to his car. Now it's being bruited about that he suffered a heart attack and died but this doesn't seem likely to me since no official announcement has been made. I'm inclined to believe the whisper which infers he was arrested by the Carabinieri and spirited away to their barracks in a blood wagon. However, whatever happened, the result is the same, Musso is out and Badoglio is in."

He allowed himself a chuckle of amusement and remarked,

"It seems that in Rome today nobody dare admit to Fascist leanings, yet it's obvious that some must have been quite fervent before the coup d'etat.[13] No doubt the hope of an armistice is a strong motive for the change of heart, particularly as the Allies have captured Palermo and threaten Catania. In fact, I should imagine that, if they keep up their present rate of advance, Sicily will be overrun in less than a week."

"Then what ho! my hearties across the straits and tierra ferma." chortled Porky who, when able, had been addicted to pirate stories and invariably referred to any mainland in the terms that his buccaneers would have used.

The conversation after this sally drifted into a discussion of the new situation and its collateral possibilities of peace terms. Only Basil didn't share the general optimism and, long after the group had settled down for the night, continued to worry over the difficulties which lay ahead. He could foresee problems and feared that some Italians would continue to fight with the Germans whilst others would lay down their arms only too willingly. In this case he guessed that the hills would become populated with refugees and, since not all of these could be trusted to keep silent if they chanced to stumble on their hideout, the pattern of their ways would have to be changed. Hitherto it had been possible to stabilise their H,Q., but, if there were odd groups wandering around the hills, they might have to keep on the move and avoid staying in any one position for more than two or three days.

During the ensuing weeks, as July turned to August and quickly gave way to September, Basil's fears proved to be groundless and though the story of Mussolini's disappearance and Badoglio's appointment as Head of the Government was confirmed, no light was shed on the whereabouts of the former Duce. Conditions remained much as they had been before except that German troops closed in around Rome as if waiting for the slightest excuse to open fire. Otherwise, the disposition of troops remained static.

---

[13] Historical note:

At the Fascist Grand Council, the first since 1939, Dino Grandi moved a resolution that the King should resume responsibility, he was backed up by Count Ciano. The meeting which, by all accounts, was stormy, lasted some hours and ended with the resignation of Mussolini. The Duke of Acquarone sent instructions to Ambrosio - trusted agents in the Police and Carabineiri acted - Key Telephone Exchanges, Police H.Q., and Ministry of Interior took over quietly.

A possible solution to the mystery of the whereabouts of Mussolini was presented during the first week of September while Basil was talking to a peasant who remarked that a shepherd was boasting of having spoken to Il Duce on the slopes of the Gran Sasso, where he was reputed to be held as a prisoner in the Hotel Imperatore overlooking the village of Assegio. Basil, however, took little notice of this story though he guessed it could possibly have some foundation of truth.

It became increasingly obvious that even if Italy did, surrender, the Germans were determined to continue the war in Italy and Basil noticed with dismay that the numbers of German troops in their area were steadily increasing. However, since the wholesale desertion of Italian forces he had expected did not materialise, the group carried on as usual, celebrating the news of the Allied landings in Calabria on 3rd September by staging a lightning attack on a German convoy which had halted for a rest on the Cammino road. By the time the unfortunate Germans - caught away from their vehicle - unprepared and in the open, were able to retaliate, more than half the vehicles were burning and the raiders were scampering back into the hills.

Six days after the attack on the convoy, while Porky was preparing the morning meal, the sudden spat of a rifle brought Basil hurrying out of the cave, as he ran, followed by Jimmy and the two New Zealanders, the Viler Perosa manned by Tanky split the peace of the morning with its rapid fire. Shouted instructions were not necessary for all knew their positions in an emergency. As he settled into a cleft in the rocks he noticed a small Storch spotter plane circling lazily overhead and cursed futilely beneath his breath. Then a movement on the track below caught his eye and he levelled a 6.5 Mannlicher rifle as he waited for the movement to be repeated ,

. . . .

John Hazelgrove wiped away the sweat streaking his face and neck with a bandanna which he habitually wore and grinned through the dust laden air at the Immigration Officer who shared the precarious perch with him.

"Those bastards are determined this time."

Taking a swig from the water bottle, he swilled the cooling liquid round his mouth before ejecting it in a steady stream onto the ground. Already the pitiless sun was beginning its downward curve as it passed the meridian, its rays reaching down into the rocky cleft now scattered with dead and wounded figures in the field grey of the German soldier, mute evidence of the determined attempts that had been made to rout out the eight intrepid men holding the natural fortress. The Immigration Officer grinned back and said,

"They're a different kettle of fish to the Ities. It seems a pity that such men should be wasted on the Fuhrer."

Even though Basil's foresight had ensured ample stocks of food and water as well as ammunition and spare weapons, at each of the firing posts, their position was desperate and more than once his anxious eyes scanned the skyline dreading the appearance of attacking forces who may have made the long trek over the hills to reach the rocks and crannies which overlooked them, and prayed that their retreat, which they could use only at night, would not be cut off. For the past half hour things had been quiet but he was not fooled into believing the enemy had left, so refrained from giving the 'stand down' while he waited anxiously for the next move.

From his position he could see the whole of his party who, despite the difficulties, looked cheerful. Even Ercolene had proved himself a useful member today and Tanky crouching behind the Villar Perosa seemed to be positively enjoying himself after his long period of inaction. From the look of his face he mused, Porky must be keeping up a regular supply of stories from a fund, he reflected which seemed to be inexhaustible. Suddenly, the quiet was disturbed by a dull thud, followed swiftly by the echoing explosion of a mortar shell and the frightened scream of Guiseppe, tethered behind the safety of a rock enclosure. His thoughts quickly came back to reality as he ducked instinctively behind a rock parapet.

. . . .

Lounging against the trunk of a tall Elm, Maggiore Mario Guiseppe Tenni, recently of the 77mo now stationed at Brescia, idly watched the float bobbing on the placid waters of the lake which stretched before him as far as the eye could see, until it merged into the V formed by the mountains whose terraced slopes shelved gently to its shores. The square red roofed house in which he was staying for a few days fishing before taking up his new duties at Matelica was just visible between the road and the shore of the lake.

Although the posting had brought promotion from Capitano to Maggiore, he regretted leaving the Luppi di Toscana, as his old Regiment was known, but reflected happily that, as he had brought a full platoon of well tried and trusted men with him, men he had selected personally and knew from past experience to be absolutely reliable, the example they would set would assist him to instil the confidence so necessary in attaining the high standard he would demand from the raw recruits which he hoped to turn into soldiers.

Behind the house and on the opposite shore, the cultivation of the terraces lent the hills a symmetric design tinted with various hues as they swept away from the waters edge until, dimmed by distance, they blended with the forested areas near the summit. He sighed contentedly as he reeled in the line then fixed fresh bait before casting into deeper water. Caldarola was a peaceful little town and made a pleasant change from the bustle of Brescia so, although the lake, justly famous for its fishing, stubbornly refused to yield its harvest, he remained sublimely unperturbed by his lack of success. Already after only three days he felt relaxed for ever since the collapse of the

Fascist Party he seemed to have been overburdened with work brought on by the new Administration and the re-organisation of the Fighting Forces, until the normal orderly routine had become a chaotic miasma and his office resembled a busy sales department with stacks of paper, mostly useless requisition forms, and messages piled on every available ledge. At length some sort of order had returned and he had snatched the chance of a few days rest en-route to his new station at Matelica.

Despite his resolve to forget everything, his thoughts persistently returned to the possibility of a separate armistice between Italy and the Allies and a worried scowl marred his handsome features as he thought of the dangerous possibilities. If the Germans retaliated by seizing control, Italy would become just another occupied country in which a war for liberation would have to be fought. On the other hand, if they resisted the Germans, who was to tell that the persistent bombing of all the major cities, which had continued with unabated ferocity throughout August and the whole of the past week, would not continue. In either event the destruction of their culture seemed inevitable.

Unlike many of his comrades, he was resolved to fight for the freedom of his country. He had been watching the almost surreptitious build up of German forces with some trepidation as discreet enquiries made him only too well aware that these were congregating around Rome and at key points along the coast. Despite his normal optimism, he could not delude himself into believing that the Germans would evacuate his beloved Italy if she suddenly dropped out of the war. On balance he felt they would be better off assisting the Allies to rid the country of the German hordes rather than trying to stop the avalanche already advancing up the coast of Calabria. As he deliberated, his fishing for the time being forgotten, the distant throb of a motorcycle impinged onto his thoughts and he absently watched the machine wend its way along the narrow ribbon of road which looped, and twisted out of sight, to reappear again further on. On reaching a point opposite the house, the motorcycle turned down a small track and stopped. With quickened interest he watched the Despatch Rider dismount and wondered why he should have come unless it was with a message for himself. Tempted for a moment to go for a long tramp in the hills, he shook of the reluctance that had overcome him and, having gathered in his line, set off across the rough grass towards the road where he waited for the machine, now plonking towards him. As the rider drew up he recognised him as a member of his platoon and the entrails of his stomach crawled as he speculated on what urgent matter could not wait until he joined his unit the following morning.

Almost snatching the small buff envelope from the courier's hand, he tore it open and scanned the simple message.

'Return immediately, important announcement expected'. Trembling slightly with a mixture of foreboding and excitement over-riding his disappointment at the termination of his holiday, he climbed up behind the rider and ordered him to return to the cottage where, in anticipation of a sudden call to duty, his valise lay ready packed. Within half an hour he was driving over the rutted road towards Serra Petrona and reached the Palazzo Valeria in Matelica at half past seven in the evening.

As he jumped out of his car and hurried towards the office, he was struck by an aura of excitement which contrasted strangely with the lethargy he had noticed on a previous visit. Small groups stood around furtively discussing the gossip and a couple of Italian soldiers were driving madly round the fountain in a captured military Volkswagen, their antics seriously impeding the legitimate bustle of traffic, which seemed to be passing hither and thither with exceptional urgency.

Infected by the atmosphere, he dashed through a colonnade shading the pavement outside the Admin. Buildings then, after taking the stairs two at a time, and without waiting for an answer to his knock, burst into the room which bore the legend 'Commandante'.

"Come in."

By the time the ageing Colonello who stood on a balcony outside the open window had called out the invitation, Maggiore Tenni was already half way across the room. As he joined the Commandante, he asked him what the excitement was about then, belatedly, saluted and introduced himself. The Colonello looked at him shrewdly, "Are you always so confoundedly precipitous?" He asked, then, glancing at his watch,

"You will know in a moment,"

As he spoke the loud speakers overlooking the square crackled and a voice called out,

"Attention ... attention. Today we are at peace with Gt. Britain and her Allies. The war is over. All soldiers will return to their units and await instructions. End of transmission."

As the loud speakers crackled into silence a profound hush fell on the square reminding Maggiore Tenni of the last time he had been to La Scala, when a similar hush had descended on the audience at the end of the finale. Then, with the suddenness of that applause, everyone in the packed square started to shout at once. Someone jumped onto the low wall of the fountain using one of the figures as a stepping stone and clambered up onto the centre piece. Waving his arms he began to harangue the crowd - "Citizens awake, the war is over, down with the Germans, down with the Fascists, long live the King and Italy. Viva Italia." With the same herd like chant that had once greeted their Duce, they shrieked back

"Viva Italia."

Interspersing their cries with snatches of song as they danced and hugged each other in that glorious moment when they became oblivious to everything except their joy. In contrast to the fervour of the crowd, a depressing feeling of foreboding assailed the Maggiore as he watched the revels in the square below. Noticing the stern features of his Colonello soften under the influence of a smile, he wondered irritably why no-one seemed to be aware of the immediate peril which threatened. If the Germans turn against us, he thought, those smiles and cheers will soon be tears. Instead of celebrating they should be preparing for the day of reckoning by readying themselves to drive the Germans out of the country before they have a chance to establish themselves as masters. Then, with no resistance, the inevitable occupation of Italy by the Allies may well be accomplished without the ravaging effect of a long campaign.

The morning of 9th September dawned bright and the heat of the coming day was already making itself felt with oppressive effect, when the Maggiore dipped his aching head under a cold tap as he tried to clear the fog created by insufficient sleep. The noise of the revellers had kept him awake long after he had gone to bed, but even without this distraction, the belief expressed by the Colonello that all forces would be disbanded within the next two or three days had so appalled him that sleep would have been impossible. Moving briskly, he completed his toilet and hurried down to the staff car which he noted with satisfaction was already drawn up outside the billet. As he was driven towards the barracks, the plan half formulated the night before took shape. He had already instructed his platoon to be paraded in marching order at 6 a.m, and breathed a sigh of relief when the car turned into the barrack gates and he saw that the lorries he had ordered were ready and waiting. Striding up to a young Luogotenente, he asked for the role and methodically ticked off the well remembered names which he refrained from calling since he knew each face individually. Then, praying that the Commandante would not put in an appearance, he strove to appear calm and unhurried, resisting the temptation to glance over often at his watch while he counted the minutes ticking interminably by. It was imperative to his plan that he should be well away from the town before his intention was realised. According to the map he had already studied, Pioraca was only about 15 kilometres by road and he hoped to have his men hidden in the ravines above the town long before the Colonello appeared on the scene. Before getting into the lorry, he handed a sealed envelope to the Luogotenente and, explaining that he was under secret orders, told him to hand it to the Colonello at noon. Actually all it contained was a brief letter to his family and a short note stating the reasons for his action.

By midday, the Maggiore was following the course of the stream and clambering over the boulders which strewed his path through the ravine above Pioraco. Each man in the straggling line which followed carried a portion of necessary supplies in addition to his normal equipment. As they panted and strained under the unaccustomed burden, they grumbled good humouredly amongst themselves referring in trite terms to the ancestry of the idiot who had thought up this lunatic enterprise. Though none would admit it, they were in fact enjoying the exercise, which made a welcome change to the monotony of barrack life. With amazed pride they remarked on the energy of their Maggiore who never seemed to need a rest and approvingly noticed that, as usual, he carried a fair share of the burden.

Later, when the supplies had been hauled by ropes up the sheer face of a small cliff skirting the ravine and everyone had traversed the narrow ledge above a waterfall, Maggiore Tenni deemed it safe to call a halt and in quiet level tones took the opportunity to appraise the men of his plan to form a guerilla band and fight the Germans from the hills if they took control of Italy. Talking to them, as was his wont, as equals rather than officer and men, he told them that the Italian Army would soon be disbanded and expressed the hope that they would stay with him in the venture.

CHAPTER 16

Maggiore Tenni checked at the point where the ravine opened into a dale some 200 yards wide and a mile in length and stared in delight at the scene before his eyes. The impression of peace too serene to sully held him spellbound. The ground lay level before him to a point where the rushing stream had widened to form a pool where the tumbling waters rested, before swirling past him to start again their headlong descent to the valley half a mile below. Beyond the pool, the ground rose gently at first, then steeply, to a line of rocky parapets beneath a jagged crest, clear cut and grey against the azure sky. He followed the thin ribbon of the stream with his eye noting how it swept away to his left as it hugged the gentle curve of the hills and saw how the dale narrowed at one end where, half hidden by a group of trees, the stream was lost to view. Using his glasses, he watched the water pour from a gap in the rocks and stumble down a steep broken stairway until, frothing in exuberance and sparkling in the sun, it emptied itself into the pool. Meanwhile, the struggling line of men closed into a compact group as they came level and gazed across the scene.

He sensed rather than saw a movement near the waterfall and stiffened as he swung the glasses back trying to locate the cause. For a moment his heart beat wildly as he picked out the unmistakable uniforms of Germans almost invisible against the grey background as they toiled up the rocky steps towards the gap. His suspicions now fully aroused, he focussed the glasses onto the cluster of trees then, warning his men to stay out of sight, watched carefully for signs of life. Before long his patience was rewarded and as he picked out nearly a score of men half concealed in the shadow of the trees, frowned in worried perplexity, wondering how many more were hidden from view. For a brief while the wild thought occurred to him that somehow the Germans had guessed his intentions and lay in ambush, then common sense prevailed as he reasoned that he had not shared his secret with anyone except the Commandante, who would not have had time to organise anything, even if he guessed his destination. The heavy crump of an explosion muffled by distance and the taint crackle of rifle fire galvanised him into sudden action as he realised that the Germans were engaging an opposing force.

His first impulse was to avoid becoming mixed up with the fight and he was on the verge of instructing his men to keep out of sight and work towards a track which could be seen at the other end of the dale, when it occurred to him that if the Germans had already started taking over the country the parapets could be put to good use. With the thought came the decision to lend his support and he scanned the cliff like crags above the slopes for a route by which he could gain access to the parapets where they overlooked the cluster of trees. He considered that the advantage of trapping the Germans in a crossfire directed from the vantage points offered would be amply rewarded providing he could get his men into position before they were spotted.

. . . .

The exploding shell did little, save raise a cloud of choking dust which sent Basil and Jimmy into a paroxysm of coughing as they tried to clear their lungs.

"Damn: That's torn it."

Jimmy swore and spat dust from his mouth. Pursing his lips to form a silent whistle Basil, who had instinctively ducked, straightened up from behind the parapet.

"Where in all hades did they lob that from?"

As he spoke, he cast his eyes quickly round the small rock enclosed area and noted with relief that no-one in his party had been harmed. Then glancing aloft to where the grey crags surmounted the walls of his fortress, he checked the skyline for signs of movement. Ignoring the sharp splat which preluded the high pitched whine of a bullet speeding on its new course, he anxiously watched for the tell tale puff of smoke that he hoped would betray the position of this new menace. Jimmy, who had also been scanning the nooks and crannies, peered intently for a moment then pointed excitedly towards the gap which formed the entrance to their camp. About three quarters of the way up the cliff like face which formed one of the walls of the cleft, a small smudge of smoke was easily discernible above a ledge some 60' below the rim. Snatching up his glasses, Basil trained them on the position in time to see a figure slide down a rope to the ledge, then duck out of the line of vision.

"I don't know how in hades they got up there, but one thing is certain," he muttered, "this caper will have to be stopped. If they've managed to place a mortar, what's to stop them adding a machine gun?"

Basil's brows merged together, and the deep cleft between his eyes seemed even more pronounced than usual as he assiduously searched the smooth rocks above the parapet for a route which would enable him to reach a vantage point. A fissure ascending the otherwise smooth wall caught his eye and he inwardly cursed the lack of proper climbing gear. Jumping back into the niche behind their parapet, he propped his Manlicher against the wall and packed a valise with a few hand grenades, then secured his Beretta across his shoulders tightening the strap to hold it firmly in position. With a cheery

"Keep your eyes peeled old chum!"

and a parting slap on the back, he gripped the edge of the rock above the parapet and hauled himself up to the base of the fissure.

At first the climb proved to be comparatively easy but as he gained height, the hand holds became fewer as the fissure gradually petered out. From their niche on the opposite side, the two New Zealanders watched him work his way to the top of the irregular scar running down the face of the rock. So slowly, that he scarcely seemed to be moving, he edged along a small ridge which extended towards the shelf. Meanwhile the double explosions of the mortar shells being fired at irregular intervals echoed hollowly from the rocky walls. The sweat streamed down Basil's face as, spread-eagled against the smooth surface, he groped for a hold on the edge of the shelf only 6" from his finger tips. Grunting in exasperation, he tried to edge nearer, but the narrow ridge supporting him canted and sloped so steeply towards the ground that only a fly could have found another foothold. Even though he tried bringing his feet together and leaned precariously towards the illusive goal, he still could not reach the shelf.

So deep was his concentration that he was unaware that the shelling had stopped, neither did he hear the shot that caused a tiny shower of rock chips to fall on his shoulders.150' below, the Immigration Officer voiced his disgust,

"Those bastards are trying to pick him off."

His keen eyes caught the glint of a rifle barrel between the jagged crests above the gap. Without a word, he left the niche and scrambled hurriedly down to the boulder strewn floor, then taking careful aim at the silhouetted figure on the skyline, he squeezed the trigger. As the figure dropped from view, the satisfied smile which quirked the corners of his sensitive lips, faded, and he slumped slowly to the ground. A thin trickle of blood issued from his mouth and spread rapidly, staining the ground around his inert body. At the same moment that John Hazelgrove lifted his friend to his shoulders, Basil sprang, his outstretched hands struck the edge of the shelf and clutched desperately as his body swung pendulum wise over the sickening drop, then taking a firm hold with the other hand he hung for a brief moment to regain his breath before hauling himself up. The shelf proved to be sufficiently wide to walk along with ease - he looked at his watch, then looked again. Surprised to find that the climb had taken nearly two hours, he hurried forward until a sudden burst of rifle fire brought him to a halt under an overhang which hid the crests from view. Unable to see where the firing was coming from, he proceeded cautiously, following the curved path into the gap and puzzling the while over the density of the firing which seemed to indicate that at least a score of men had got into a position where they were able to find targets.

As he approached the section which he judged to be opposite the mortar, he dropped flat on his stomach to worm his way forward until he could peer over the edge of the shelf. That he was very close to his objective was apparent from the sound of voices which seemed to come from immediately below. Across the gap, no more than 12' wide at this point, he could see a rope dangling from above and blessed the overhang which, while concealing the upper end from view, also served as excellent cover for himself. Carefully he peered over the edge, then froze as his gaze met the startled, stare of a pair of pale hazel eyes. For a brief interval both Basil and the blond giant, who could not have been above 15' away, remained transfixed.

"Du liebe zeit!"

As if the German's exclamation had released a spring, Basil came to life and nipped smartly out of view as an excited clamour of guttural voices reached his ears.

"Just my luck," he moaned, "that idiot would glance my way at the very moment I squinted over the top."

Crouching close into the rock face he reviewed the position as he freed the Beretta from his shoulder. He had, no fears that the mortar would be used against him at such close quarters, but recognising his vulnerability to stick bombs, worked quickly at the straps of his valise to remove the grenades. Then, taking aim from the dangling rope, he grinned wickedly and lobbed three in quick succession over the rim to the ledge below. When angry shouts, mixed with confused sounds indicated that at least one of the grenades had found a mark, he sprang to his feet and, taking advantage of the confusion, towered on the edge of the shelf, ready for instant action, a gaunt menacing figure behind the Beretta.

Two of the party of six were writhing on the ground, while yet another lay as if dead. Already the officer in charge of the party was attempting to tend to one of the wounded, while the blond giant, who had raised the alarm, stood dazed watching the remaining man placing the mortar upright. As if suspended in time, the tableau hovered on eternity, then a shot rang out and the giant slumped to the ground. The Officer gave one startled glance aloft and rapped out a command as he jumped to man the mortar. Rapidly elevating it to its highest trajectory. Before he had a chance to use it, the rapid fire from Basil's Beretta ended his life. In the momentary lull that followed, there came a shout from above.

"Mani in alto. Mani in alto. Hande hoch."

The remaining German raised his hands and an Italian soldier shinned down the rope, then jabbing a machine pistol into his ribs, herded him over to where the two wounded lay. A moment later another Italian soldier slid down the rope. On seeing Basil he flashed a smile of greeting which almost matched the brilliance of the small silver star set in the red tabs on the reviers of his tunic. Uncertain, whether these were friends or foe Basil withheld his fire and called across the chasm

"Who are you?"

The Italian's eyes sparkled with sheer devilment.

"Luppi di Toscana are the friends of all who fight the Germans."

Although at first inclined to mistrust the newcomer, Basil could not deny the evidence so recently portrayed - on the other hand, Italian soldiers fighting the Germans didn't seem to make sense unless, he thought, they've made a separate peace and their former allies have turned against them. Still half expecting a trap, he eyed the soldier keenly.

"You who wear the uniform of the Italian Infantry, why do you fight your allies?"

The eyes of the Italian hardened perceptibly,

"Since the armistice the Germans are not our allies. We fight them because they are now our enemies and because our Maggiore has told us that they will over-run us if we don't."

Bleakly Basil watched the other, his cool brain seething with possibilities.

"'Where is the Officer of whom you speak?"

he rapped. An alarming thought had occurred to him that, even if the newcomers were friendly, it would be fatal for them to attempt to enter the camp via the gap as the others would undoubtedly open fire with disastrous results.

"You must warn your Maggiore not to enter the camp until I have spoken with him. Better still, take me to him."

As he spoke he lowered the Beretta for the first time since the brief exchange had begun then, slipping the safety catch into position, he called to the other to catch the weapon as he threw it across the chasm where it was fielded neatly. Almost simultaneously, he retreated as far as he could, then running forward leapt before the surprised Italian had guessed what was contemplated. Almost snatching his gun back, he snapped,

"Alright friend, let's go!"

They found Maggiore Tenni directing mopping up operations in the spinney outside the entrance of the camp. Beneath the shade of the rocks a disconsolate group of Germans stood disarmed and under a guard.

CHAPTER 17

At 6 a.m. on 27th September, 1943 the sun, which had already begun to disperse the mist from the undulating hills of the distant Sibillini Range where it curled wraith like in the ravines, shone on a compact group of men on the slopes of Mt. Pennino. Basil took a last lingering look across the dale, past the pool to the entrance of the camp. A fleeting glimpse of sadness crossed his features as his gaze dwelt on the spinney and he thought of the simple wooden cross which marked the resting place of the Immigration Officer. He turned abruptly towards the Maggiore who stood at his elbow and thrust out a hand.

"Arrivederci Mario, perhaps we will meet again in better times." Taking the proffered hand, Maggiore Tenni smiled briefly.

"Who knows? Remember to keep to the countryside close in to the hills and you should avoid the Germans."

A hint of the old laughter returned momentarily to Basil's eyes as he gave the hand a final squeeze before hurrying away to join his friends already filing into the ravine. Falling into step beside Jimmy, he walked silently for a while wrapped in thought. Not a convoy had passed along the road since the arrival of the Italian soldiers and the idleness had been getting on his nerves, until he was glad to be on the move. With little or nothing to do and the Allied Forces only about 200 miles south near Foggia, there seemed no point in remaining in the area, so he had decided to follow the hundreds of liberated soldiers from the camps who had already trekked south to meet the advancing armies.

Inevitably, as his thoughts went back over the past weeks and the events which led to the death of the Immigration Officer, he became depressed, cursing the twist of fate that had taken a comrade such a short time before the Germans had left. Strange, he mused, how they vanished overnight. Mario seems to think they are being massed to stem the British advance - maybe he is right. Then there was that proclamation by Badoglio to the Italian people asking them to help and succour the P.O.W.'s who were being released from the camps before they fell into the hands of the Germans. Surely the time could not be better for their attempt to cross the line.

The prospect of once more being with his own people changed the sombre mood and a flicker of grim humour showed in the grey eyes as he recalled a party of P.O.W.'s encountered just outside Lavorino. The scared look on their faces and the way they had dived for cover until he called to them in English caused him to chuckle reminiscently. Then, later the same evening, well fed and at their ease, they had told of how the Italian sentries deserted the camp leaving the gates open and of the excitement which prevailed as the prisoners prepared to leave. They also told of their fear of recapture by the Germans who were said to be converging from the north. He had advised them to change the scarecrow uniforms they wore for civilian attire but they had been reluctant and gave the odd reason that their tattered uniforms would serve as camouflage.

"Camouflage be damned!"

Basil spoke his thoughts aloud and Jimmy, who had been waiting for his friend to break the moody silence, strove to keep a straight face as he looked at him quickly.

"What's all this about camouflage?"

Basil grinned, half shamefaced.

"I was just thinking of those walking adverts hanging on to their uniforms."

Jimmy chuckled,

"It was a bit daft." I wonder how they're making out."

Basil shrugged,

"Couldn't care less really, people like that deserve to be caught." His eyes twinkled with quick humour as he added, "What price Ercolene? He couldn't leave for home quickly enough. Not that I blame the lucky blighter, I think I'd be inclined to do the same given the opportunity."

Then continuing in a more, sober vein,

"I'm really more interested in whether Ernesto managed to contact Quintale on Mt. Ingino. You know, I was half tempted to join his Brigata Partigiani myself if only to see that ugly mug again."

Jimmy's eyes danced with merriment.

"He's certainly a glutton for punishment. Incidentally, I wonder if it's true that Mussolini has been rescued and is setting up a rival Government at Salo? If it is Quintale will certainly be busy."

Basil replied thoughtfully.

"It makes sense doesn't it. For all Hitler's great pal act with Mussolini, I don't imagine the rescue was organised for friendship sake particularly when one considers that a revival of the Fascist Party in Italy couldn't suit his book better, because a Government under the original leader could declare the Badoglio set up illegal."

"Which would make the armistice void!"

"Exactly. Besides there must be quite a few ardent Fascists only too happy to pick up where they left off, especially as the chances of promotion within the Party must be pretty fair."

"What will they do to the blokes who voted him out I wonder?"

"Shut them up in the Bloody Tower and hang them for treason."

Porky's voice cut across the conversation as, tired of playing gooseberry to an involved discussion between Tanky and John Hazelgrove, he had quickened his pace and joined the leading pair in time to catch Jimmy's remark. Basil shot him a shrewd glance.

"You're probably right at that."

Then, as if suddenly aware of the passage of time. "Hallo Porky, you look hungry, want a rest?" Suiting his action to the words, he selected a smooth rock and sat down contemplatively watching the ever changing shape of the stream as it glided past.

"Have a Player?"

As Basil took the proffered cigarette from Porky, he turned it over in his hand to read the familiar inscription 'British Red Cross'. "Hallo, where did you scrounge these? Watch it mates, someone's been holding out!"

Porky grinned delightedly.

"Those characters that came to the camp - I swapped a couple of jack knives for this tin of fifty."

Basil frowned.

"You had no call to do that, there are more than enough knives in the store for anyone that may want one."

Recognising the annoyed tone of Basil's voice, Porky flushed.

"So what, I didn't notice that tight fisted bunch offering anything around and anyway they had plenty of cigarettes." he retorted.

"Come to think of it neither did I,"cut in John."In fact, thinking they were out of smokes, I gave them about half a pound of leaf."

"So they got their knives free after all." Basil commented dryly. Then joined the general laughter over Porky's crestfallen face.

Had an interested spectator followed the five on the first stage of their journey south, he could not have been blamed for thinking they were on a hiking tour. Their relaxed and easy gait carried them through the remote village of Polverino and along a winding mountain track with splendid views of Lago di San Lorenzo to Bolognola in the heart of the Sibillini. They slept at night in peasant homes, accepting, with some humility, the generous offers of food to help them on their way, and chatted amongst themselves as if they were on a holiday. Even when they left the mountains near Communanza to cross the lower foothills, no signs of the Germans were apparent. It was not until they reached the tiny village of Vena Piccola, near Ascoli that they came across evidence of the rapidly increasing hold that the Germans were establishing over Italy. As they entered the village, a young lad playing five stones on the cobbled street took one startled glance and fled in terror yelling. "Tedeschi, tedeschi!"

Basil compressed his lips and, for the first time, began to wish that he had not left the machine pistols at the camp, as he stared at the suddenly empty street and waited for his companions to draw level. "Rum show this." he commented. "It looks as if these people have had an almighty scare."

At the far end of the deserted street a man, who Basil judged to be in his late twenties, hove into view, and came striding towards them. Halting a few feet away he showed strong white teeth beneath a friendly grin.

"Where have you come from and where are you going?"

Basil eyed the stranger coldly, taking in the hard eyes and firm lines around the mouth which the friendly smile failed to disguise. The clothes, though clean and neat, were patched and didn't look like those of a town dweller. Having already learned that the average villagers were not particularly inclined towards Fascism, he was not overly suspicious, nevertheless, he didn't respond to the other's smile as he rapped,

"To Ascoli, what business is it to you?"

Still smiling, the stranger said.

"If you're English, it is dangerous to pass near Ascoli."

He nodded his head towards the distant town.

"The place is filled with Germans and even here in Vena Piccola, there are Fascist spies."

"And whose to say you're not one?" snapped Basil.

As the smile whipped off his face, the hard eyes of the stranger glittered momentarily.

"Most people hereabouts will tell you differently for there are many friends who would obey Badoglio and help the English, while there are also many enemies who bow to Il Duce. Believe me when I tell you, you must be careful."

Then, indicating the charred ruin of a farm house which stood bleak against the sky.

"Last week, two English slept there. Those who helped them are now dead, their house burned and their live stock driven away. Now no-one dares help openly."

Something in the way the man spoke convinced Basil of his sincerity and he relaxed.

"Sorry my friend, but we too must be careful. We have no wish to bring trouble to your village and will pass on our way without delay."

The stranger pointed towards a distant pinnacle, which despite a nearby range of hills that masked its lower slopes, continued to dominate the scene. Then indicating the comparatively lower group in the foreground, said,

"If you keep that height in line, you will come to a few houses scattered on either side of the road which loops round these hills. Ask for the home of. Gianni Nello. I will join you later and take you to a safer place. Tell them Lepre sent you."Gazing at the height, Basil thought it still seemed no nearer than when he had first selected it as a bearing shortly after leaving Communanza.

The light was already fading, for it was nearly 7 p.m., when Basil caught sight of a figure coming down the road between the scattered houses. From his position in the almost dark day room, he watched the man approach the house and breathed a sigh of relief that his fears of a possible trap seemed unfounded. The latch lifted and their acquaintance of the afternoon walked in, nodded to their hosts, a middle aged couple who hovered in the background, and scooped up half a loaf and some cheese which he commenced to devour. Between mouthfuls, he asked Basil if they had fed, and when satisfied that they had had sufficient said,

"We must hurry while it is still safe - follow me and keep close." Still munching the food, he led the way outside and, scarcely glancing to see if the others were with him, made off at a brisk pace towards the hills now only a dim blur in the darkened sky. Within an hour of leaving the house, the open country gave way to trees and the track they followed began to rise steeply. Presently the trees began to thin and the party found themselves walking along a narrow rutted path which skirted the side of the hill.

The moon, which had suddenly appeared above the hill, shed a silvery light on the surrounding landscape which now lay far below; a study in black and grey, relieved by a single shimmering thread which lost itself in the deep shadow of the mountain range beyond. All six paused to gaze at the view and savour the calm of the night. For a space of minutes, they ,remained silent, content to just look. Then, in a hushed voice, as if afraid to break the spell, Lepre commented,

"It is beautiful is it not? The river is the Tronto which flows through a valley between the Sibbilini and the Laga mountains. The road; which follows the course of the river, is an important link with Rome and has been raided on several occasions by the Yugoslavs on Mt. Vettore, consequently, the German patrols are extremely alert. But come, we must move - I shall point out the landmarks tomorrow."

As they advanced, the gradient of the path steadily increased until it became almost impossible to remain upright then, all at once, they were walking on a flat surface towards a large house perched precariously on the edge of a cliff.

Lepre, who was now a few paces ahead, called back softly,

"Keep closely bunched and join me."

From somewhere to the left came a high pitched whistle.

"What was that?"

Basil's voice came in a sibilant whisper as, with eyes darting from left to right, he looked for the source of the sound. Lepre raised his hand, then replied,

"It is nothing. We have lookouts placed against discovery."

Approaching the house, he rapped twice on the door before lifting the latch to enter, then beckoned the others to follow. The door led directly into a large square room. Lit by small oil lamps, it was sparsely furnished with a few cane bottom chairs and a massive table. At one end of the table two men were locked in that curious game of strength sometimes called Indian wrestling, while a further group used the other end of the table for a game of cards. Stacked in one corner was a pile of equipment, ammunition boxes, rifles and various paraphernalia which a heavily built fellow seemed to be sorting into various piles.

"Sevan".

As Lepre called the name, the man in the corner straightened and Basil realised with a start of surprise that he was much taller than he had first supposed. Despite the huge appearance, the man moved with an almost feline grace. Taking in the thick neck and shoulders, the barrel like chest, which topped a tapering torso above slim hips and the complete absence of any fat, Basil eyed him with approval. A massive hand shot out to grasp Basil's in a vice like grip as they were introduced.

"You are welcome amongst us."

Although Sevan spoke in Italian, a certain inflection in his voice left an impression that he was from other parts. Completing the introduction, Lepre continued,

"Sevan is a good friend of ours. He is a member of the Partisan Group on Mt. Vettore and has persuaded them to help equip us for our own group of the Rebelli."

He then proceeded to introduce the other inhabitants of the room, leaving Basil with a head which swam with a confusion of Italian names.

Later that evening, Sevan, who had taken an instant liking to Basil, produced three bottles of a home distilled whisky which he dumped on the table and invited the five to share. Although the whisky was raw and extremely potent, tasting more like methylated spirits than a decent Scotch brew, John and Porky seemed to find nothing wrong. Happily they swigged the spirit down with rapid and disastrous results. Tanky, however, took one sip, wrinkled his nose in disgust, and promptly diluted it, a precaution which the other two were quick to emulate. Sevan himself, seemed to thrive on the concoction which brought an awed comment from Jimmy that the man must have a tin lining. Certainly the only effect it appeared to have was that he became more and more talkative. As he recalled the mountainous area of Serbia where he was born and spoke of the fierce guerilla warfare which his people had waged against the Turks for several hundred years, he became more subdued. Then, splashing more liquor into his cup and pressing the others to help themselves, he asked,

"What could be more natural than that we Serbs should resume guerilla activities when the Germans invaded our land in 1941 and our young King Peter was forced to flee to England? When General Mihailovic began to organise a resistance movement, the Germans retaliated by taking hostages who they brutally murdered, among these was my sister Miria."

The Serb's eyes flashed angrily as the memory hit him and his huge fist smashed down on the table upsetting Porky's drink. As, by this time, the little gunner was slumped out on the table, he took no notice, the glass remained on its side, while the liquor spread into tiny rivulets along the uneven surface of the table.

"This only made me more determined to kill the German beasts." Sevan scowled.

"So, when many of the Cetnik Commanders made, a no resistance agreement with the invaders, I took up with Tito's Partisans."

"Pardon our ignorance, but we're not very well up on Yugoslav politics though, of course, we knew that you had a good guerilla organisation. What is the difference between Cetnik and Partisan?" Queried Basil.

Sevan looked at him as if surprised that anyone should not know the difference.

"The Cetniks are the Serbian followers of Mihailovic; while Tito was a well known Communist along the Dalmatian coast where he was active at one time fermenting strikes. When the Germans came, he developed into a Partisan leader, and what a leader!" he rumbled, "Under his guidance, the various bands began to pull together and fought the German and Italian troops whenever they met them."

Eyes glinting with hate, he went on,

"We fight without mercy and ask for none. All we desire is freedom and if we can't win this, then death doesn't matter."

Dashing off his drink, he glared at the intently listening trio. Then, roared with raucous laughter at the sight of John sitting bolt upright with bleary eyes beside the recumbent Porky.

"Your friends, they cannot drink eh?"

Leaning across the table, he clouted Basil a friendly clump on the shoulder that should have felled an ox and brought a grunt of pain from Basil's lips. Splashing whisky into the empty glasses before filling his cup, he said,

"Come, we will drink to our ultimate victory." and raising his cup to his lips took the contents down with a single draught.

From fierce belligerence, the mood changed to one of melancholy.

"It is a sad thing we have also had to fight our fellow countrymen. Sometimes the Cetniks would make an agreement with the invaders which we Partisans would violate" he explained.

"Inevitably the Cetnik hostages held by the Germans, would be shot," he continued, "and, in revenge, the Cetniks would give the Germans information about us. All too often bitter quarrels ensued and there would be fierce fighting between Cetnik and Partisan."

Then, as if suddenly tired of talking, he rose abruptly to his feet and tilting the remaining bottle to his lips drained off the remnants before striding purposefully towards the door. On returning a few moments later, he made straight for a pile of straw in the corner and in a trice his stertorous snoring filled the room.

The clear serenity of the night gave way to an overcast morning and a few drops of rain, coupled with a distinct chill in the air, gave warning that the long summer with its hot dry days was nearing its close. Sevan, seemingly unaffected by his heavy drinking of the night before, was already up and about when Basil rolled himself into a. sitting position, stretched luxuriously and hurried outside for a wash where Jimmy joined him a few moments later. On re-entering the house, they found Tanky trying to stir Porky and John into reluctant life, while Sevan watched the process in obvious amusement. Sleepily Porky looked up at the grinning Serb.

"Talk about knock out drops. What the hell was it?" he grumbled. Then finding the effort of talking too much, slumped back on his straw. Jimmy exchanged a look with Basil and grinned. As though by pre-arranged consent, they pounced and hustled Porky outside where, ably assisted by Sevan and Tanky, and watched by an audience of half a dozen Ribelli, they unceremoniously ducked his head in a pail of water. The howls of laughter from the onlookers drowned his spluttering vows of vengeance and brought John to the door in time to save himself from the same treatment.

By the time Lepre, who had spent the night at his own home, returned to guide the party to a place where the Tronto could be crossed in comparative safety, the sun had broken through the clouds and the day promised to be fine. Soon they were descending the path, accompanied by Sevan who, disappointed that Basil refused to join forces with Lepre's outfit or his own, declared his intention of coming part way with them.

At first the route followed a stream through a narrow wooded valley with occasional clearances where sheep, tended in the main by children or young girls, grazed on the verdant grass. Leaving the banks of the stream, they parted company with Sevan and climbed steadily for an hour before descending to the Tronto valley.

From an obscured position on the heavily wooded slopes a few yards from the road, Lepre pointed out a heavy wooden plank set across the river which flowed swiftly at the bottom of a narrow ditch and drew their attention to a square brick building which showed through the trees on the opposite slopes.

"Take great care in crossing the plank, the river is very deep and swift at this point although only about 5 metres wide". he warned.

"When you are safely over, you will have to take a path which passes close to the brick building. It is sometimes used by the Germans as a check point so you will have to be careful how you go. Once beyond that, you must make for Valle Castellana, then across the mountains to Rocca and Cortino."

Hidden behind the trees, Lepre watched the five as they crossed the road and slipped down the gently sloping banks to the riverside, negotiating the narrow plank bridge one at a time. He saw Porky go first, then Jimmy whose weight set the plank swinging up and down, followed by John. Then, in dismay, he saw a German patrol suddenly appear as if from nowhere down the stretch of road on his left as they approached the bend which would bring them into view of the bridge. Knowing only too well that anyone found within the immediate area of the road would be shot on sight, he watched with trepidation as Basil patiently waited for his turn to join the others standing in a bunch on the opposite bank, wholly unaware of the danger. The distance was too far to shout a warning and there was absolutely nothing he could do to help; he could only stand by and hope.

The first car reached the corner just as Basil started across the plank. Transfixed to the spot, Lepre wept in impotent rage as the small group scattered and Basil fairly raced across the bridge. As in some horrible nightmare, he heard the shouts of the German crews above the squeal of their tyres when the cars came to a standstill, and the sound of their shots as they opened fire. His sigh of relief as Basil reached the opposite side in safety and paused a moment to tip the heavy plank into the stream before zigzagging his way at incredible speed towards the sanctuary of the wooded slopes, changed to a groan of despair as the runner sprawled to the ground.

CHAPTER 18

Immediately on reaching the obscurity of the trees Tanky darted to one side, placing a staunch oak between himself and the road while he waited for Basil to catch up. A short way ahead Jimmy and the other two crouched in a small hollow which afforded a view of the rear of the brick building through the trees. Since there were no windows facing them there was no way of telling whether it was occupied. Each carefully checked his automatic pistol then, while Porky and John remained in the hollow keeping an alert watch on the path, Jimmy melted silently away through the trees to reconnoitre the building.

Meanwhile Tanky, becoming apprehensive over Basil's continued absence, returned to the edge of the trees, peering through a screen of bushes as he anxiously scanned the area.

Three of the Germans were milling about at the point where the plank had been, while yet another seemed to be trying to retrieve something from the water. The main body of the patrol stood about in small groups by their cars. Puzzled, Tanky looked for Basil and checked over the groups near the cars to see if he had been captured. Suddenly a throaty chuckle drew his attention to a slight movement in the long grass close to where he stood, then he heard Basil's unmistakable voice.

"Stay where you are, I'll be with you in a moment."

The movement in the grass increased; Basil's head appeared, followed by his body, as he wormed his way quickly towards him before springing to his feet behind the screen of bushes.

"Near thing that!"

then, urgently

"Come on, let's get going."

Together they joined the others in the hollow, at the same moment that Jimmy returned to report the building empty. Then, leaving the path to avoid any chance meeting and hamper the Germans should they cross the river and follow, they stole away from the road. Barely 100 yards had been covered when sounds of the Germans threshing around in the undergrowth came to their ears. They pressed on quickly and gradually the noise receded and died. Only when a good two miles had been covered and it seemed obvious that the Germans had no intention of continuing the search into the hills, was the silence broken by Tanky when, unable to restrain his curiosity any longer, he asked Basil what had happened to delay him. Basil grinned cheerily.

After a pause, he said, "I tripped - which was a bit of luck really. Some of those boys could certainly shoot. As I lay winded by the fall, I noticed a small ditch running the way I wanted, so rolled into it and crawled along the bottom until I came up with you."

"Trust you to find an easy way out" grumbled Porky. "I had to run every damned inch of the way."

"Do you good, might help to get some of the booze out of you." Basil responded quickly.

Tanky snorted in disgust.

"Booze he calls it. 'Poison more like."

Porky laughed infectiously.

"Call it what you like, whatever it was it's a sight stronger than that muck they used to dish up at the Melody Club in Alex." John shot him an amused glance.

"You can say that again. I still feel half cut every time I take a short drink of water."

"Me to" commented Porky. "It's certainly economical if only it didn't feel like red hot needles every time I......"

The burst of laughter that cut across Porky's words drowned out the remainder of his sentence and started off a session of badinage with Porky on the receiving end, all of which he took in good part.

Despite the hilarity, their vigilance never relaxed; the wary alertness which always lurked beneath the surface had become second nature.

By using his watch as a compass in conjunction with the sun by day and the friendly constellation Orion at night, Basil was able to keep a fairly accurate course even when all signs of habitation ceased and there were no tracks, but only miles of rocky terrain.

When fortunate, they slept in the homes of friendly peasants and ate from their table; at other times they went hungry and were glad if a projecting rock would give them protection from the biting wind.

They climbed until it seemed their backs must break and jolted down the long descents until the muscles of their stomachs ached. Still they kept doggedly on, mile upon mile, always moving south. Now at last, they overlooked a wide valley, backed by the Gran Sasso d'Italia with its towering Corno Grande. Below and to the left lay Teramo with its network of railway lines, and a road which joined yet another road beside the river Vomano, before following the contours of the hill through the rising valley to the Capanelle pass. Keeping to the lonely tracks, they descended at night close to Montorio, then ascended the slanting path through the Passo di Croce beyond Arsita and so came by Farindola to the valley which shelves gently down to Celiera.

Now the Corno Grande lay behind, its lofty peak still visible above the rims of lesser hills. Near exhausted, they slept in a derelict barn close beside the winding path. Basil, who never seemed to need much rest, was the first awake. Moving quietly, lest he disturb the others, he wandered out to ease sleep stiffened limbs. The late afternoon sun cast its shadow from the jagged rocks which lined the rim scarce 50' above and glinted on the stream below the barn. Climbing easily, he reached the crest, then gazed toward a series of fir girt slopes with barren peaks and marvelled at the resources of the Germans who had somehow landed gliders and a tiny plane beneath the highest peak to snatch Il Duce from his guards.

Turning, he looked down the ever widening valley, patterned with the shadow of the hills on the cultivated terraces. Here and there small groups could be seen tilling the soil and he idly watched them at their work until three men sauntering along the path caught his interest. Although he followed their progress as they steadily grew nearer, he took little notice of them, for his mind was on other things. Gradually he became aware that the valley was deserted, yet several hours of daylight still remained. The three men were still continuing their stroll. Then, as they drew nearer so that he was able to see in more detail, he gave a start of surprise as he realised with horrible certainty that they were not only armed but wore a uniform he couldn't recognise. The path they followed must take them by the barn. Unless the others were warned their voices, if they were awake, might attract investigation. Worse, if the trio chanced to glance inside the barn and caught them all asleep ... The mere thought stirred him into action and brought a crawling sensation to his stomach as he scurried back, only to find that the others, as if warned by some sixth sense, were already alert and waiting for his return.

Peering through a crack in the wooden walls of the barn, Basil watched the men approaching. Above the rustle of his own breathing he could hear an unintelligible murmur as their voices carried through the still mountain air. Every now and then one of the leading pair would glance back impatiently to the third member who lagged some twenty yards behind limping awkwardly along.

"Come on Tex, we ain't got all day."

The unmistakable English words, spoken with a strong American inflection, produced a gasp of surprise from Porky and, with the unusually mild expletive,

"Hallelujah, Yankees!" he started to sing,

    "Yankee Doodle came to Town

      Riding on a pony ..."

as he made for the door of the barn.

"Shut up you fool!"

Basil rapped. A pained expression crossed Porky's features as he halted.

"What the hell? They're Yanks alright, I've seen that uniform at the flicks."

As the sound of Porky's far from melodious voice carried to the ears of the men on the path, the leading pair stopped short. One, with a shock of red heir, who appeared to be in charge, shouted,

"It's O.K. buddy. It's O.K. now. We'll get you boys out of here."

Striding forward, he pushed open the barn door grinning broadly and came face to face with Basil's mocking gaze. He took a pace forward, then stopped, the grin gradually fading as his glance dropped to the Beretta pistol levelled at him.

"Wha-..."

"If you're genuine, there's no need for alarm."

Basil's voice was quiet, yet flat and deadly. The American blanched but nevertheless, called to his friend outside.

"Bunch of Limeys in here don't believe I'm a Yank!"

Someone chuckled.

"Aw, quit joshing Red."

then the speaker stuck his head through the door and found himself staring down the levelled muzzle of a Luger beneath a pair of intensely blue eyes. Jimmy inclined his head almost politely and said,

"Walk right in friend".

Then the blue eyes took on a steely glint as he added,

"If you know what's good for you, you'll allow your mate to join us."

By the time the third member limped unsuspectingly through the door the first pair had been disarmed and sat dejectedly in a corner of the barn.

"Right, now the party's complete. Let's see your documents,"Basil eyed them bleakly "and no tricks."

Red started to bluster.

"You can't treat us like this, "Uncle Sam ..."

"I have" Basil cut in cryptically.

"Aw, show the sonofabitch your papers and get this crap over."

As he spoke, the last arrival fumbled in his pocket and produced American Army documents which Basil glanced over perfunctorily before returning them. Then, having examined the papers of the other two, lowered his pistol and, with his face screwed in a singularly disarming smile said,

"Sorry friends, but you're the first American soldiers we've ever seen. I hope we're forgiven. Name's Basil."

Then, nodding towards the others,

"Jimmy, Tanky, John, Porky."

Red, quick to recover his temper, chuckled, his laughter easy and without embarrassment as he grasped Basil's proffered hand.

"Guess you got us with our breeches down! Name's Larry, but they call me Red on account of my hair. The little Mexican is Miguel and the other lanky sonofabitch we call Tex, guess I don't know his real name."

"Alfonso." the other supplied " and no wisecracks!"

Pulling out a crumpled packet of Camel cigarettes, Red passed it round, then viewed the depleted contents wryly and passed the remainder to Basil.

"May as well keep 'em, I've got some more."

Basil began to light his cigarette, it tasted strange and toasted but better then the raw leaf to which he had become accustomed. He inhaled deeply, allowing the smoke to drift through his nostrils while taking stock of the apparently recently laundered denims and the excellent footwear of the Americans. A nagging doubt crept into his mind - they looked altogether too well dressed for P.O.W.'s and much too clean and fresh for an advance recce party. Then there was the way they had sauntered up the valley as if out for an afternoon stroll. If the Allies had advanced overnight, the valley by now would be overrun with Infantry engaged in mopping up. The whole position seemed wrong. He drew tentatively at his cigarette and wondered whether they might be Germans posing - he knew this had been done before. Masking his thoughts, he turned to Red.

"Where are our Forces now then?"

The American looked surprised that Basil shouldn't know. "River Sangro, of course."

"But surely that's all of 70 kilometres from here?" Don't try to kid me you walked."

Miguel giggled nervously.

"Red walk? That's a laugh!"

This caused a stir of merriment and even Basil grinned. Miguel felt pleased and slightly encouraged.

"Only time he walks is with a dame in the park."

"Shut your clap!"

Red spoke harshly, he felt annoyed and irritable once again, eager for a fight. Why did that Dago, always have to butt in with his wisecracks. This big fellow with the hard grey eyes looked dangerous.

"Can't you tell the guy's serious?"

He turned his attention back to Basil. He felt chicken, which was a new experience for him. 'For Chrissake what's up with me?' he muttered to himself and forced his eyes to meet Basil's, which seemed to probe into his guts.

"Special mission. We dropped last night by parachute." He felt better now he was talking.

"We're on joint operation with S.A.S. - Special Air Service – to assist P.O.W'.s across the line."

Basil relaxed, the story made sense and accounted for their clean appearance. Gaining confidence, Red went on.

"We're supposed to try and contact guys like you and pass you on to a contact."

The realisation that the Americans had been safe behind the Allied Lines only the previous day prompted a barrage of questions from the news starved men,

"Where was the line now?"

"Did they know the extent of the Winterstellung?" [14]

"Was it true that Deanna Durbin had been killed in a road accident?"

"That London was raised to the ground?"

"Ark Royal, Hood etc. had been sunk?"

These and many others were fired at the Americans who laughingly answered as many as they could.

---

[14] Winterstellung :

German line of defence which ran behind the River Sangro on the Adriatic side, across the mountainous spine of Italy to the mouth of the Garigliano on the west.

(See Churchill's 2nd World War' Vol. V.)

Later that evening, shortly before Red guided the party to their contact, he outlined the sequence of events since the Allied launching in Calabria. He told them of the American Fifth Army landings at Salerno which followed the British Eighth Army's foothold at Reggio and Toranto on the previous day and of the rapid advances by the Eighth Army which had ended in a deadlock when they had come across the strongly held Wintetstellung on the heights beyond the River Sangro. He also proudly told of the fierce fighting against stubborn German resistance that the Americans had employed in their endeavours to cross the River Volturno. Characteristically, Red made no mention of the X British Corps which, with the VI American Corps, constituted the Fifth Army. The omission gave the impression that only Americans had been employed in the section. He went on to tell them of the fighting in the hills south of the River Garigliano until at last, a week later, they had come to grips with the forward defences of the Winterstellung. Now a stalemate had been reached which the approach of winter was unlikely to resolve.

It was quite dark for it was nearly 9 o'clock and the usually bright stars were obscured by heavy cloud, when the Syndicate arrived at the farmhouse below Penne where they were to meet their guide. The small Italian, whose enthusiastic greeting belied his dour expression, produced Vino and glasses and bade them make themselves comfortable, then introduced himself as Dieci, which Basil guessed to be a code name, explaining as he did so that a guide was expected very soon on a routine call. While waiting, Basil reflected on the surprising ease with which Red had guided them to the rendezvous and couldn't help wondering whether this should be attributed to excellent briefing or a wonderful memory since, if he had only dropped the previous evening, he could not have had much time to learn the trails. His thoughts then turned to Tex, whose injured ankle had. looked so swollen that even Red had been forced to admit rest was essential.

Overcoming his intolerance of anyone not as strong as himself, he had suggested Tex should rest at the barn until his return, meanwhile Miguel could rustle up supplies of food in case the enforced rest became prolonged.

A soft tap on the door interrupted Basil's train of thought. Subconsciously he strained his ears in the effort to pick up the gist of a whispered argument between Dieci and the new arrival and absently watched his companions who seemed to be in a sort of suspended tension as they craned forward in their efforts to hear.

Only Red, who couldn't speak Italian, was making no effort to listen. With mounting impatience he fidgeted with a piece of paper, twirling it incessantly between thumb and forefinger until it formed a pellet. Abruptly, almost savagely, he flicked it away and started to his feet, then sat down again. Scowling at the table he fumbled for cigarettes, then remembered he had left them with Tex at the barn, and emitted a snort of exasperation. John pushed the makings towards him and watched in idle amusement as the American's spatulate fingers expertly fashioned a cigarette. He was in the act of offering a light when Dieci re-entered the room, he seemed to be angry and paced rapidly up and down before speaking.

"The guide who should have taken you to the H.Q, refuses because he says the road is busy and it is now too risky. I tell him tonight is the last opportunity, but still he refuses."

He resumed pacing, stopping every now and then as if seeking inspiration.

"What's he bitching about?"

Red rose impatiently to his feet.

"Guide won't take us."

When Basil explained, Red looked relieved and said,

"O.K. O.K. I'll take you to the H.Q. myself."

When Basil interpreted this, Dieci became even more agitated.

"No! No!" he protested. "In that uniform it would be best if he kept away from the roads tonight. Make him return to his friends."

Basil grinned, he could imagine the response from the impetuous American. Nevertheless, he passed the message on.

"For Chrissake! Don't he know there's a Goddam war on?"

Red glared at the Italian.

"Think I'm chicken, or what?"

"Come off it Red!"

Basil spoke sharply, "The man's right you know. You've got a job to do, and that doesn't include taking stupid risks."

Red's eyes blazed as his face suffused with blood.

"I'll say I've got a job to do and no Goddam wop's going to stop me."

Basil's voice took on a new note, one of controlled anger. "Nobody has said he's trying to stop you. Suppose we find out first what he has to suggest."

Red snorted.

"O.K. it's your neck."

Still angry he stomped to his chair and sat down glaring at all and, sundry until Basil, having exchanged a few words with Dieci, told him that the Italian had offered to act as guide. Red, now mollified, grinned sheepishly.

"So I blew my top for nothing. Guess I'd better be getting back to Tex. Tell the guy I'm sorry."

Shortly after Red had left, Dieci announced that he was now ready to leave. Outside the night was very black with a tense quality about it; they walked silently down a bullock track which followed a gradient to the bottom of a shallow trough where the trees grew thickly beside a rivulet. Under the trees it was even darker and it became difficult to make out the phantom faces suspended apparently in the air. No-one spoke. There was only the rustle of clothing and the scuffle of feet on the mud packed track, which rose gently on a winding course. Even the leaves were silent, hanging motionless in the still air.

"Wait!"

Dieci's voice came eerily through the darkness. A faint scuffle sounded in the night and a vague outline vanished.

Almost before they knew it, Dieci was back urging them to hurry while there was yet time. A road loomed beyond the trees where they thinned on either side, the gravelled surface crunching beneath their feet as they crossed. Turning to the right and keeping close to the tree lined edges, they walked in single file along the road, ready to dart under cover at the first alarm. A meandering path where bushes clutched at clothing as they passed, led to an open space where the blurred silhouette of a large house could be discerned. Dieci placed a hand on Basil's arm, halting him.

"Come quickly now and keep together." he murmured.

Together they approached the house and Dieci knocked softly. Then, answering a challenge from within.

"S.A.S."

The door opened and Basil got a fleeting glimpse of the interior which was crowded with soldiers in British Uniforms. He paused to allow Dieci to enter first. The Italian shook his head.

"I shall not go in."

Then turned and hurried into the darkness.

"Come on, look snappy!"

hissed the man who had opened the door. Basil slipped in, followed by the rest.

Upwards of a dozen soldiers were sprawled around the room, some sleeping, others sitting on their equipment strewn about the floor, with rifles pointing in every conceivable direction from the confusion. A Lieutenant sat at a table where he had turned a part of the room into an office. In contrast to the dishevelled appearance of his men, he appeared almost dapper, even the cravat at his neck, which was hardly Regulation, didn't seem incongruous. On seeing them, he came forward with hand outstretched in greeting. As

Basil shook the hand, he was not surprised that the clasp was firm, going all the way in. His voice, when he spoke, had just a trace of that enthusiasm found in a certain type of Officer, while he had merry eyes in which more than a hint, of devilment lurked.

"Good show chaps. Let's have your details for the record."

When the names and Regimental Nos. had been recorded in a book, which Basil noticed was almost full, the Lieutenant cast a critical eye over their clothing.

"You seem to have got yourselves fixed with gear which is just as well, my stocks are running low."

Basil chuckled - "Hardly Moss Bros. but they serve."

He glanced towards a map spread on the table and added,

"What's the stunt? Escape route?"

"Come, I will brief you," the Officer replied.

Then, addressing one of the soldiers.

"Get ready to set these chaps on the way."

As they crowded round the table, Basil said,

"If you think we would be more useful helping, I can speak for my friends when I say we'd be only too glad to assist."

The Officer eyed him keenly, and liked what he saw. Reluctantly he shook his head.

"Sorry Holden, orders are to get you home. The exercise is nearly over anyway."

Then, indicating a point near the mouth of a small river with a stubby forefinger.

"This river is the Foro. As you can see it is quite small and lies just south of the River Pescara which you will have to cross. There is a bridge here."

He moved his finger to a point just outside Chieti.

"It is patrolled by sentries and on no account are you to attempt to bluff your way through. Any suspicion of what we are doing could wreck the enterprise. The river is wide, but shallow on the seaward side of the bridge and is quite fordable, in fact I came through it myself only two days ago. An M.T.B, will call here just outside Francavilla, between 24.00 and 00.30 hours."

He indicated a further point beside the mouth of the Foro.

"Make sure you get it, the concentration of German Forces along the Sangro make a land route impossible without specialised knowledge of the dispositions. The entire forward area has been evacuated, so even your civvies would not help."

Basil nodded - "All clear."

A soldier with a Tommy Gun slung across his shoulder joined the group round the table. The Lt. glanced at him.

"Ready Nobby?"

Then, turning his attention back to Basil,

"Right, send me a postcard when you get back and don't forget to keep your eyes peeled."

Within half an hour of arriving at the house, they were again in the dark. The wind had begun to rise and a few drops of rain spattered them as they followed Nobby, who seemed to be nervous, jumping at the slightest sound. He talked rapidly and monotonously in an undertone as if afraid to stay silent too long. Under the trees the leaves rustled and a sudden gust of wind caught Basil's face as dead leaves scurried before the driving wind. By the time Nobby left them on the edge of the road to Chieti, rain was falling steadily.

CHAPTER 19

The wind rose and its force increased to a crescendo of sound as it whipped the rain into a maelstrom of fury which allowed no quarter from the needle-like jets lashing the five men as they trudged along the lonely road.

Three hours of battling against the elements had reduced them to bedraggled robots who had forgotten what it was like to be dry. Sometimes a flash of lightening unveiled a storm swept scene; a scene where trees submissively bowed their heads. Seemingly it had no end.

Step after weary step they plodded on until, at last, the wind abated with the coming day and they saw the bridge against the first grey streaks of dawn.

A muddy track led them to the river bank and they paused a moment to watch the dark water swirling by. Linking hands to form a chain they waded in.

Fifty yards to the right lay the bridge, the details of its structure and the helmeted sentries becoming rapidly more discernible as the light increased. With each successive step the current grew stronger until, near the centre, it flowed with such appalling force that Porky was swept off his feet. Instinctively each handclasp tightened and muscles tensed to take the added stress as the river, now more than, waist high, tried to win its prize. The human chain bent beneath the strain and formed an arc as first Tanky, then Jimmy, stumbled and ran awkwardly before the torrent. Miraculously they kept their stations and, finding anchorage for their feet, leaned against the swirling water until Porky regained his balance. Moving cautiously, they edged forward until the quiet shallows of the further bank were reached. Only then did they have time to realise that daylight had come, and the rain had stopped.

Utterly weary, they stood in a small group on the river bank and looked first at the water, then at each other. Suddenly Porky wanted to giggle; it started deep down inside him, he didn't know why, for there was nothing funny in the haggard faces of his friends. He tried to stop the laughter rising but it fought its way up. Desperately he endeavoured to control the irresistible urge, but it was no use. A quiet chuckle escaped his lips. Basil stared at him anxiously wondering whether the rigours of the night, coming on top of the months of tension, had finally proved too much. Men had been known to break down under prolonged strain and the possibility that this could happen to any one of them had often been in his thoughts. It never occurred to him, however, that the irrepressible Porky, who took everything so light heartedly, would be the first to crack. Although satisfied by his scrutiny that the laughter was prompted by genuine humour, he realised that the dividing thread between laughter and hysteria could easily be snapped. Laughter to hysteria, courage to fear, each equally infectious and equally dangerous and the one could lead to the other. He spoke sharply and with more than his usual authority.

"Cut the cackle and make yourself useful for a change."

The rebuke, coupled with the implied injustice, had the desired effect, it made Porky annoyed and with the annoyance the laughter died. Yet Porky's anger was short lived. Essentially mercurial in temperament, quick in humour and in anger, he was incapable of holding a grudge. By the time they had reached the railway he had forgotten the incident.

Even though the railway lines were deserted, the little party spread out crossing the series of tracks one at a time to avoid arousing the suspicions of any chance watcher. Nevertheless, they felt conspicuous in their sodden clothes and were thankful to reach the comparative safety of the countryside beyond the Chieti/Pescara road.

. . . .

"I don't like it:" Basil commented for perhaps the fourth or fifth time. "Too many seem to be aware of what's on."

Jimmy grunted non-committally. It was late afternoon and he felt pleasantly warm for all signs of the storm had passed and the sun, which had dried his clothes, felt hot on his back. The sleep beneath a haystack during the morning had removed the drawn lines from his face and the prospect of an organised route to safety filled him with a sense of well being. All the same Basil's remarks triggered off a nameless anxiety which intruded into his thoughts and he too began to wonder if everything would be as easy as it appeared. Every house they passed seemed to have its quota of workers, threshing corn or de-husking maize, who called to them as they passed offering food or water with a hospitality which reflected their thanks for a good harvest. All seemed to know more about the scheme than they did themselves and the repeated question,"Are you going to Francavilla for the Boat?" became monotonous with its regularity. At one house where wine was being made, they learned that many had passed before them and the route, far-from being secret, was common knowledge. With these points in mind, eventually - Jimmy replied dubiously.

"Alright, I suppose. If it's only the Ities along the route that know about the scheme."

Browsing silently as the possibility occurred that if the Italians knew, so also could the Germans. He began methodically to check the scraps of information supplied by the friendly workers against the briefing they had received on the previous night, and scowled as he realised the startling fact that even the most minute details of the plan seemed to be known. The time of the arrival, the exact point, even the route suggested to ensure that the rendezvous was reached. It all tallied. How much then, he wondered, was known by Fascists and how much of this had been passed on to the German Command. As the questions formed in his mind he started thinking. Basil, noticing the preoccupation, smiled grimly to himself and kept his silence for he wanted his friend to work things out for himself, since an unbiased opinion would be more valuable. At last Jimmy voiced his thoughts.

"If, as I suspect, the Germans are already onto the scheme, by continuing as planned we are almost sure to walk into a trap. On the other hand, it shouldn't be difficult to work out an alternative route. I've been trying to picture the map at the H.Q. There was the main coastal road and beyond. that the railway, a few dunes and the beach."

He enumerated the points on his fingers.

"If the weather stays fine there will be a moon and it shouldn't be difficult to pinpoint the rendezvous. I suggest we get into the dunes further south of the river, then make our way along."

I don't think that will be a good idea at all. "Basil replied.

Unwittingly Jimmy's thoughts had. followed precisely the same course that Basil's had half an hour previously, but Basil deliberately contradicted in order to draw out his friend's reasoning.

"It seems to me that if we follow the rail we could arrive at the landing point behind the dunes and, if everything is O.K., descend to the beach under cover." Basil suggested.

Jimmy stared at him for a moment.

"Alright, so far so good: but if the Germans are waiting, what's to stop them picketing the beach, the road, or the rail? As I see it, our only chance of approaching unobserved lies in the dunes. Even so it's damned dicey."

A small quirk appeared at the corners of Basil's mouth.

"And if you were the Germans would you leave the dunes uncovered?"

Jimmy frowned and pondered this a moment.

"Hardly, it seems to me the whole area will be cordoned off, with probably a passage through which we will be allowed to pass before the trap is sprung."

Basil nodded.

"Exactly! That being so, it's senseless to continue as we are. I suggest we hole up somewhere near here, for there can't be more than three miles to go. Then, before the moon rises, we'll have a nose around to see what's cooking."

. . . .

From his position in the long grass of the dunes, the beach could be plainly seen beneath a cloudless sky for, in contrast to the previous night, the sheen of the full moon reflected in the sea turned the night into day. Basil eased cramped limbs slightly and looked at his watch - the hands pointed to 11.30 yet still the beach was deserted.

Following the hunch of the afternoon, they had continued on the cart track till they reached a small grey roofed fishing village situated near the main road, then made a detour away avoiding the narrow streets to cross the coastal road and railway a mile south of the meeting place. There had been a small amount of traffic and once since they arrived, a train had gone through but nothing stopped. No Germans had been seen during their cautious scouting and it seemed his suspicions were unfounded. Yet deep within him a sense of foreboding prevailed; instinct warned him to take care and he glanced towards his friends lying alongside him. Since the days of the Concentration camp they had come a long way together. Now if everything went according to plan, the tight knit little band would be split up, the bond broken, as each picked up the threads of his old life.

On the beach something was moving. He watched closely as two figures made their way to the waters edge then walked along the firm sands until almost opposite their position, turned and walked back again. A flare from a match illuminated the face of one as he stopped to light a cigarette revealing tattered remnants of a heterogeneous uniform. Apparently tired of walking the pair, who looked like ex-P.O.W.'s, sat down near the waters edge, their voices carrying plainly over the still night air.

"Look at those idiots: Where do they think they are, Brighton Beach!"

Jimmy's scarcely audible voice sounded close to Basil's ear. He was about to reply when another figure appeared, the automatic weapon he carried showing plainly in the moonlight. The figure approached the two on the beach, who hurriedly rose to their feet then, after a moment, accompanied the newcomer to some further dunes to the left of the Syndicate's position.

Once more the beach was deserted and they lay quietly listening to the surf breaking on the sand below while they kept their vigil. Presently Jimmy touched Basil's arm and pointed towards the sea, where a tiny light flickered. To the left an answering flash beamed out across the sands.

"Better stay where we are until I give the word." Basil cautioned.

The throb of an engine, gradually growing louder, carried to the ears of the waiting men and Basil could feel the blood pounding through his temples as he allowed himself a faint tremor of excitement. Everything seemed to be progressing smoothly after all. Despite his determination to keep calm his excitement rose with anticipation as a small M.T.B. steadily drew nearer, until eventually the sound of the waves lapping against the sides of the craft could be plainly heard. Then came a harsh grating sound as the keel struck the beach scarcely fifty yards from them. Perhaps a dozen S.A.S. ran down the beach and spread out on either side of the tiny vessel to form a partial circle facing inland their Sten Guns held ready for instant use. With every nerve keyed to a fine pitch, Basil led the way down the dunes and across the sand towards the boat. They had covered about 25 yards and embarkation had already started when a sudden scuffling caused Basil to glance behind. There was no mistaking the helmeted outlines which stretched from the edge of the sea to the dunes. Pulling out his automatic pistol he experienced a dual feeling of satisfaction when the tiny gun kicked in his hand, which mingled with despair at the inadequacy of the weapon. Shouting a warning he fired at the advancing horde before running towards the comparative safety of the dunes to avoid the inevitable cross fire which would develop between the opposing forces. As always in moments of danger his mind functioned with ease and clarity. He could see Jimmy from the corner of his eye, sprinting alongside and a few yards beyond Tanky with John following closely behind. For one horrible instant Porky eluded him and he checked his stride, then heard a grunt as Porky swerved to avoid running into him. Already the sand was being churned up with bullets as the S.A.S. guard opened fire on the Germans now converging on them.

Above the noise, Basil heard the distinctive bark of Jimmy's Luger and caught a glimpse of the flash as a dark figure loomed in his path. He was vaguely aware of a bayoneted rifle coming towards him. His Beretta spat once, then the German was on him. Instinctively he grabbed the rifle with both hands and side stepped, yielding to the momentum of his attacker as he threw himself into a cartwheel. As the leverage took effect the unfortunate German, carried forward by his own speed and weight, somersaulted in the air and landed heavily with two distinct thuds as first the back of his head, then his body, hit the ground. In a flowing poetry of movement, Basil completed the cartwheel, glanced at the stunned German and stooped to retrieve the Beretta from where it had fallen when he grabbed the rifle. Still bent double, he dashed into a trough between the dunes where he almost collided with Jimmy who, having seen the German lumbering from the side of the dune had turned to lend his assistance. Although his response had been immediate, however, Basil's throw had been accomplished so quickly that it was all over before he had time to come to his aid. With an ease born of long practice, Basil shifted his grasp on the rifle from the barrel to the butt and dropped into the long grass between the sides of the dunes, searching as he did so for a target.

By now, the raiding party was so close to the boat that to fire into their midst would only risk injuring the wrong people. Disappointed he contented himself with picking off the stragglers, but there was nothing he could do to change the situation. The cause was already lost. As he watched helplessly, a group of ex-P.O.W.'s pushed the M.T.B. away from the shore, while the S.A.S, retreated until they were waist deep in the sea. Two of these remained to fight a rearguard action, while their companions clambered into the boat and started firing over their heads towards the Germans.

Outnumbered as they were their chances were slim, yet they might have succeeded had the vessel not caught fire, for it was already under way when a rosy tint appeared, which rapidly spread into flames, illuminating the squad of Germans wading towards it, and casting its glare over those who were leaping to safety.

Amidst the confusion, a solitary figure stood out starkly silhouetted against the flames as he continued to fire from the stern of the vessel, then he seemed to topple backwards into the inferno. It was all over now and the firing stopped as abruptly as it had begun.

Basil took one last lingering look at the blazing vessel on which their hopes had hung and the pitifully few wading ashore with hands held high, then made his way through the trough to rejoin his companions behind the dunes. Disgustedly he threw the rifle away, quite useless to him now and only a source of embarrassment. Without it there was a small chance of passing themselves as country folk, but first they must get away from the coast before search parties started combing the area.

On the railway track a solitary sentry remained on guard, they waited their opportunity then dashed across reaching the road in a compact group which they crossed at a run before losing themselves in the plantations of olives on the opposite side.

Swollen and angry from the previous night's rain, the river swept beneath the bridge near Chieti creating a phosphorescent wake under a brilliant moon as it eddied round the pillars. Lower down, where Basil stood, it was oily in appearance with an iridescent sheen which hid its treacherous strength. To Basil in this hour before the dawn, it seemed incredible that less than twenty-four hours had passed since, full of hope, they had crossed. Their hopes had been high then with the prospects that lay before them but now they must return to the hills and attempt to cross the Line near the upper reaches of the River Sangro as originally planned. 36 valuable hours had been lost. Hours during which time the Line could be consolidated and correspondingly more difficult to filter through. Already the countryside teemed with the refugees from the many towns and villages now in the German forward area. The feasibility of trying to steal a boat and row down the coast had occurred to him, but the idea had been instantly dismissed. The chances of finding a suitable vessel were remote and would entail too many risks for the probable negative result.

Remembering the force of the water on the previous night, he was tempted to use the bridge but a road block had been set up and no one was allowed to pass. Finally it had been agreed that a chain should be formed to cross as before.

They entered the water together, even near the edge the added strength could be felt tugging at their legs. Towards the centre, the current hit them with torrential force, tearing apart the human chain and whisking each individual member down stream as if they were mere pieces of straw. Basil was a strong swimmer but even so he felt himself dragged under by the terrific current and bowled along the river bed. All sense of direction gone, he fought desperately to reach the surface then, when he thought he could hold his breath no longer, the water suddenly calmed and he shot to the surface. Gulping in great lung fulls of air, he struck out for the bank no more than 15' away, only to realise rather foolishly that John was wading only waste deep beside him. He staggered to his feet and cast his eye round for signs of the others. A short way up river Tanky was also staggering ashore but there was no sign of the other two. Then something hit his leg nearly unbalancing him and he groped beneath the muddy surface. His hands came into contact with a heavy mass which could only be one of the missing pair. Calling to John to lend a hand, he clutched frantically, striving to find a grip on the clothing. With quick response John came to his assistance and together they lifted the unconscious burden, who proved to be Porky, from the water and with renewed strength born in the urgency of the moment, carried him quickly to the bank. While John cleared the debris from Porky's mouth, Basil felt for a pulse before rolling him over to commence artificial respiration.

Forward, press, back and release - forward, press, back and release .. the rhythm went on without stop for ten minutes with no sign of response. Suddenly Porky began to retch.

Meanwhile, Tanky had gone off down the bank in search of Jimmy who he found clinging weakly to a branch overhanging the river too spent to clamber out although the water was only about 6" deep.

"Hallo Jimmy, feel alright?" His voice was soft, almost inaudible, yet had a cheery sound which carried.

Jimmy nodded and managed a wry grin. "I'll be O.K, in a moment, legs seem to have turned to jelly and I can't manage the bank."

"That's alright old, son, give us your paw."

Somehow Tanky hauled Jimmy up the almost perpendicular bank then assisted him back to the clearing where Basil was still working on Porky who was now retching violently.

"Whose sitting on my chest? Get off!"

The voice sounded querulous and surprisingly strong and brought a gust of laughter that was a combination of humour and relief.

Only now did Basil realise how much the river had taken out of him, as he straightened from the task a wave of vertigo hit him and he staggered momentarily before he fought it off. Dimly, as in a dream, he became aware that the river had carried them nearly half a mile down stream before a sharp turn in the bank created an area of quiet water which seemed to be a collecting point for every kind of debris imaginable. - masses of foliage intermingled with drift wood and branches of trees, which floated placidly on the sluggish surface.

There was perhaps half an hour of darkness left, only half an hour in which to get away from the river and the proximity of the road and find a place to dry their clothes which clung dankly to them irritating the sores where the flesh had been rubbed raw by the incessant rubbing during the previous night's march. Yet still Basil sat content to rest, filled with a strange reluctance to move, his reasoning for once fogged by an apathy which left him content to watch the river flow by. Deep down within him a sense of foreboding stirred and as the years of habit asserted themselves, his numbed mind began to function. He pondered introspectively, seeking the cause of his alarm and idly watched the debris as it drifted to the right. At first the direction of the flow failed to register; when it did he was filled with dismay. "Surely it had flowed to the right before they had started to cross, "he muttered to himself." Instantly alert now that he was aware of what had been bothering him, he stood up and gazed across to the opposite bank. A complete tree swept by carried in the grip of the centre current its roots pointing grotesquely to the sky. An audible sigh of relief escaped. his lips for the tree was apparently moving in the opposite direction to the current and the knowledge came that he had. been watching the slow back wash of the eddy that had carried them to safety.

The realisation that they had indeed crossed the river filled him with renewed hope and some of his normal energy returned. With increasing certainty he knew that to remain beside the river a moment longer would be to court disaster. He goaded the other four into life and encouraged them as they waded through the heavy scrub which scratched at their faces and. hands. Yet, tired as they were, there was no need to remind them to pick up their feet and place them softly heel down to move with the minimum of noise.

When daylight broke, they found themselves beside a great tract of land planted with beans. The thick growth offered concealment so carefully parting the plants lest they leave a trail, they made their way several yards into the 4' high growth and at last, secure from prying eyes, stretched out beneath the cool green foliage.

CHAPTER 20

The stone and plaster houses of Villa Celiera cascaded down the hillside in a hotchpotch of narrow alleyways, cobbled stone steps and tiny courtyards.

In the morning, the men of the village left to till the soil on the fertile slopes of the undulating valley surrounding Civitella Casanova and the black gowned women carried their baskets of laundry down the well worn path to the foot of the hill where a mountain stream burbled briskly over large flat stones worn smooth by eons of kneading and slapping.

Here, with the mechanical motion of peasant women at work, they beat their wash against the stones and exchanged local gossip with their neighbours from Celiera, or friends from the nearby village of Vestia. Sometimes a relative from one of the farms would join them and they would talk of their families or chuckle over a, scandal.

In the tight community of country folk and villager where everyone knew everybody and each knew the intimate details of the other's life, they greeted one another with an air of familiarity, yet beneath it all lay an undercurrent of suspicion; tongues were guarded for the fear of free speech remained. Even though their simple faith imbued them with honesty and a trust in those they considered their friends, there was still the risk that a chance remark might reach the ears of the Fascists in the Paese.

The Strada Nuova linking Civitella Casanova with Penne had attracted the Germans to the small one street town and every week new arrivals crossed the bridge which spanned a deep gulley outside the town. Sometimes troops stayed overnight. More often they rumbled through the narrow main street past Brittoli and through the Foka di Penne, but their presence had alerted the Fascist elements who were anxious to ingratiate themselves with their German masters, so, as Annina stooped beside the stream, her plump young body bending rhythmically to her task, she took care not to mention the sick stranger beneath her Father's roof. How, when returning to the small two roomed cottage beside the rutted path which for centuries had been the shortest route from Celiera, to the small town in the valley below, Fistola his dog had nosed in among the long grass which grew from the banks of the stream, his excited barking drawing attention to a small party of refugees resting there.

She worked silently, lost in thought, What cold grey eyes the Condottiere had, and that other one they called Jimmy, whose eyes were blue, both so tall she had doubted from the first that they were Italian, although they said they came from the north. Then her suspicions had been confirmed when the sick one, who had been carried home on the donkey, had babbled in a foreign tongue which her Father, who had lived in America, declared to be Americano. This didn't matter, for were not the Americans the friends of the English who Maresciallo Badoglio had asked them to succour.

A whimsical smile layed around the sensitive lips and her eyes softened tenderly as she thought of the sick man who had been lying in her bed for two days now, his head resting on the fine linen pillow covers she had so carefully embroidered. with 'Bacio d'Amore'.

"What are you thinking?"

The shrill voice of Concetta cut into her thoughts, she started guiltily and bent energetically to her task without replying. The other woman laughed spitefully.

"You have another lover?"

Annina stopped working and met the eyes of the older woman angrily. The thin lips beneath an angular nose were curved in a sneer and Annina dropped her eyes again as she recognised the malevolent gleam.

"If I had it wouldn't be any business of yours" she muttered.

Concetta cackled harshly and swept her eyes over the young girl's plump form. The inference was obvious and Annina flushed wondering bitterly if the evil bisbetica would ever let her forget that her eighteen month old son had been born out of wedlock. Maybe if Giovanni had returned she pondered wistfully, and shook back the tears of frustration as she hurried to finish her work.

Most of the women had been very kind; to these a baby was something to be cuddled and fondled, they had vied with each other with their gifts of tiny clothes, offering help and advice, knowing she had no mother to turn to, but this Concetta was different, she never lost an opportunity to vent her spite. It wouldn't do to let her see so many shirts in her basket.

Still angry with herself for allowing the older woman to upset her, she finished off the last item, then placing the heavy basket on her head hurried down the winding path towards her home. As Annina walked quickly away, Concetta watched her lithe figure swinging with the rhythm of her movement. She felt sure the girl was hiding something. Why else should she look so flustered? she asked herself. If there was another scandal she was determined to be the first with the news. The thought brought a gleam of anticipatory pleasure to her eyes as she hastily packed her basket. Then, keeping carefully out of sight, she followed the unsuspecting girl, biding her time until Annina entered the cottage, before darting forward to peer through the crude wooden door which, as was customary, had been left ajar.

If she had expected to see a lover she was disappointed, apart from the furniture and the basket of washing on the earthen floor, the room was empty. Glancing furtively round to make sure that she was unobserved, she stepped into the house and tiptoed to the ladder set against an opening in the ceiling. Her straining ears caught the sound of voices and her heartbeat quickened with excitement as she recognised the deep inflection of a male voice. She was tempted to climb the ladder and peer into the room and was still debating this when the distant barking of a dog sent her scurrying outside lest it be Gianni returning.

In the tiny bedroom, the air was heavy with the flat sour odour of sickness which even the open window failed to dispel. Annina glanced towards Jimmy and smiled a greeting as he rose from his seat beside the window then, as she turned towards the bed where Porky lay, she shuddered at the change two days had wrought. The flesh seemed to have fallen away from the face and when Jimmy joined her beside the bed there was no light of recognition from the sunken eyes, only an unnatural brightness. Annina looked helplessly up at the tall man beside her.

"He looks like my Mother did before she died - they said it was il Tifo." Then added, " You know; the water illness." By way of explanation.

A sudden fear for his friend gnawed at the pit of Jimmy's stomach then, becoming concerned for the safety of the baby.

"If it is Typhoid you must keep away from him. I shall tend to his. needs."

Annina shook her head, and wiped the beads of sweat from Porky's forehead with a damp cloth,

"There will be no danger to the child. Since my Mother died we boil all water and anyway he is with his 'Nonna, I shall let him stay there."

Yet still Jimmy was not satisfied. He had a typical Englishman's horror of Typhoid, but knowing that argument would be useless, said nothing.

Shaken from his normal calm, he strode over to the window and stared out towards a low scarp rising steeply from the depths of a fosse which opened into a pleasant valley meandering gracefully between low green hills, until it merged with the distant shape of the mighty Maielli. Yet he saw nothing of this. He only saw the road where it shot from behind the scarp and the bridge it crossed before entering Civitella Casanova. The thought that the town would have a Doctor was with him and the urge to fetch help was strong. Were it merely his own freedom at stake he would not have hesitated, for to him the sacrifice would have been a small price to pay for the care of a friend, but there were other factors. The safety of Annina and her baby, of Gianni, her Father, who had cheerfully accepted the risks involved when he offered shelter, knowing that German reprisals against those caught aiding ex P.O.W.'s were harsh, without mercy for man, woman or child.

The fate of Dieci remained too fresh in his memory for him to ignore the dangers of involving the family in this way. He could still smell the charred ruins that had once been Dieci's home and lived again those moments of horror when they found the Agent hanging upside down from a tree with a notice - 'He helped the enemy'- pinned to the riddled corpse, as a token of what to expect. Basil had been furious, ignoring the risks, he had cut down the remains and handed them over to a small group of mourners who kept a sad vigil but were too frightened to approach the grim reminder.

Porky he knew would deem the bargain hard if the kindly family paid for his life in a similar manner.

Inevitably as he gazed from the small window onto the Maielli scarce 30 miles away, he felt depressed, for the advance units of the 8th Army were only just the other side of the mountain range, yet they seemed as far away as ever. The 30 miles might just as well be 300.

With the goal in sight, it seemed that luck had run out, first there had been the fiasco at Francavilla, now Porky was seriously ill. Until he was strong again, it would be unthinkable to continue, yet soon the winter would hold the land in its grip and the opportunity to advance would be lost until the spring, for it would be impracticable for any man to tackle the mountainous route they had planned once the passes were blocked and the ravines filled with snow. It seemed that the delay would of necessity, be longer than they had anticipated.

A deep frown etched itself between his brows as he tried to reason a way out of the difficulty, for the cottage was small and it would overburden their host if they all remained until Porky was well again. Yet, on the other hand, the mountains would be no place to stay during the winter months. As Porky was unlikely to make a rapid recovery their only real hope lay in an early advance by the 8th Army, but to imagine this happening in time to give him the care he needed would be to indulge in over optimism. It seemed the only way to reach a Doctor would be for him to carry Porky into Civitella and surrender to the Germans, trusting they would be treated honourably as soldiers, then Basil and the other two would be free to continue as planned.

Vaguely aware that Annina stood at his elbow, he looked at her, his blue eyes still sombre with thought. She smiled shyly up at him, then as if guessing his purpose, shook her head gently.

"You must not even think of it, there will be another day. Perhaps Basil (she pronounced it Bazeel) will think of something. "Her voice had a musical lilt with just a trace of huskiness and she spoke softly to avoid disturbing the sick man. Jimmy smiled briefly, her very nearness was soothing.

"Meanwhile, I shall collect the herbs we use for this illness."

She had no great faith in the efficacy of the wild herb remedies used by the peasants. They worked well enough for the usual ailments but they hadn't helped her Mother. Possessing the peasant's humble resignation to the Will of God, she felt no rancour, only an overwhelming sympathy for the man standing next to her. She spoke soothingly as a mother might to a child who wakes and is afraid of the dark as she sought to alienate his thoughts from the sad ones which beset him.

"He will soon get better when the Doctor comes."

"Doctor?"

Annina nodded. She seemed surprised.

"Did not Papa tell you he would fetch one?"

Jimmy stared blankly,

"But wont that be dangerous for you?"

"Of course not, Paolo would not betray us, he is an old friend."

"Can you be sure?"

She shrugged, spreading her hands deprecatingly.

"No-one can be absolutely sure of another in Italy today, but Paolo is a man who hates the Germans."

The casual announcement brought such a surge of renewed hope to Jimmy that he could scarcely suppress the elation in his voice as he asked Annina how soon the Doctor would come.

"Shortly after dark, he would not delay." she replied confidently, then laughed happily because of the obvious relief on Jimmy's face.

Nevertheless, it was nearly midnight before a low murmur of voices from the path outside the cottage announced the arrival of Gianni with the Doctor. Doctor Paolo was not a tall man, he was in fact short and rather tubby. Dressed in shabby ill-fitting clothes, he would have passed unnoticed in a crowd. But his eyes were shrewd and compelling and exuded a confidence in his own capabilities. They peered from beneath a pair of bushy eyebrows and seemed to take in every detail of the room and its occupants. Such was his personality that the small stature and untidy dress didn't notice.

As he glanced round the room, he knew instinctively what manner of men Basil and his friends were, and if he wondered whether gunshot wounds would be found upstairs he made no comment. Though already overworked, he was devoted to his calling, so made a point of visiting two or three times a week until he was satisfied that Porky had passed the danger mark. He even provided the medicines necessary from his own slender resources and brusquely refused to accept any payment for his time and trouble. Basil's offer was brushed aside with the comment.

"I don't need payment to help those who would liberate us from the Nazi yoke:"

It was in the third week of their stay at the cottage below Villa Celiera that a chance remark by Tanky brought an excited ejaculation from Annina.

"Ercolene, not Maldini Ercolene surely?"

Basil, who was occupying his hands by re-caning a chair, glanced up, from his work his brow lifting in interrogation.

"Do you know him?"

Annina nodded, her eyes round and accusing.

"Why yes, we grew up together, but you told me you only arrived here the morning we found you, how can you know him?"

Basil shrugged non-committally.

"It's a long story, but we knew him from other parts. He invited us to his home if we ever came to Civitella but forgot to give us his address."

He chuckled.

"We could hardly go around asking all and sundry where he lived could we?"

Annina's eyes twinkled merrily, she thought how like Ercolene that was.

"You could have asked me."

Then, beckoning him to follow her outside, she pointed towards that part of the scarp where the sides of the fosse rose less steeply and a Peperone festooned roof made a splash of colour between the upper leaves of the trees that covered its slopes.

"Casa Tufa, that is his house. You see he lives quite near."

So it came about that, later that same evening, Gianni led the way into the fosse, guiding them unerringly in the dark to a place where a plank spanned the small stream that trickled through its depths. Avoiding the bullock track which led to the house, he approached via a path which was little more than a goat trail through the Ginestra covered slopes.

They found Ercolene bedding the cattle for the night.

At first he stared in incredulous amazement then, let loose a whoop of delight and enthusiastically saluted each on the cheek. The smile of greeting faded and was replaced by a look of concern as he asked why Porky was not with them. Relieved by Basil's explanation, he invited them into the house, where, armed with a glass of Vino each, they became the centre of a babbling throng as Ercolene's family gathered round talking excitedly amongst themselves and gazed upon the men they had heard so much about.

In the confined space of the living room the family seemed enormous as, one by one, Ercolene introduced them. There was Maria his Mother, a small thin-faced self effacing woman with deep sunken eyes which lent a prominence to her cheek bones; his Father, Roberto, approaching 50, with a round almost cherubic face; and his three sisters, Giuseppina, Concettina and the eldest Teresina, not yet 20. Then there was Antonio, an Uncle, who lived under the same roof and seemed to be something of a rogue. His white moustache and silvery hair were set off by a pair of faded brown eyes which danced with devilment. He had apparently served in France during the 14-18 war and was inordinately proud of the few French words he knew, using them whenever he could, no matter how irrelevant. Emma, an Aunt, and her daughter Vincensina about three years old, completed the assembly.

Looking round the sea of faces and at the house, which was not very large, Basil couldn't help wondering where they all slept. The wonder increased still more when Ercolene hinted that the Syndicate should move in with the family, pointing out as he did so that even the mercenaries of long ago used to seek their winter quarters. With Christmas less than a month away, the winter snows would soon arrive and he vowed there was more room than there appeared as they would see for themselves if they decided to stay. As it was situated on a hill, it would be cut off from the outside world until spring melted the snow, so would provide a secure retreat for the winter months.

To Basil, Ercolene's reasoning seemed sound, already the bitter tang of winter could be felt in the night air and, until Porky was fit again, he had no intention of starting any activity that would advertise their presence in the area. Furthermore, Casa Tufa was more secluded than the cottage where, sooner or later, they were bound to be spotted. He had been increasingly worried lately because he had noticed a woman who seemed to be hovering around watching the house. He had, also noticed that although Annina seemed to know her and greeted her in the customary way, she never stopped to talk, her quick "Giorno", rather than the friendly "Salve", being as brief as it could be without being rude. They had all been careful to approach the cottage only at night, but the possibility that one of them had been seen could not be ruled out.

Basil's suspicions were well founded, the next day a squad of Germans surrounded the cottage ransacking inside the house and the surrounding area. They layed waste the meagre haystack as they searched in vain for the men that the woman who accompanied them insisted she had seen, but they found nothing. The Syndicate might never have been. Two hours earlier they might have seen Ercolene driving a bullock cart and if they had searched beneath the load of firing they would have found Porky, but they had arrived too late. Baffled, they questioned Annina who declared boldly that Concetta was known to be a trifle mad.

"Of course she washed several shirts at the stream, they were her Father's and he liked a clean one every day." she protested vehemently.

Even when one of the Germans twisted the defenceless girl's arm behind her back so that she blanched with the pain, she stuck to her story and would. say nothing. Meanwhile Concetta watched with malicious enjoyment, her eyes gleaming with anticipation as brushwood was brought and piled in the tiny living room in preparation for the incendiaries which would be placed behind the closed door.

. . . .

On the other side of the valley at Casa Tufa, Ercolene pulled the large wooden chest, in which the family stored their grain, away from the wall of the living room, revealing a small aperture just large enough to admit a man crawling on his hands and knees. Stooping to crawl through, he called to Basil and the others to follow. They found themselves in a small room some 15' long and perhaps 6' wide. In the dim light which filtered through a small iron grating set near the ceiling, Basil could make out two or three sacks of grain leaning against what appeared to be an old manger. A crude bed had been erected along one wall.

"Shades of Cromwell, a priest hole!"

Tanky's voice sounded hollow as he stuck his head through the opening prior to entering the small room. Ercolene grinned.

"This used to be the stable when my Grandfather was a boy, but when the entrance began to give way his Father was afraid that if he took away the lintel to replace it, it would weaken the house and, as a new stable was needed anyway, this one being too small to house an extra cow he had bought, he shored up the entrance with wooden supports and built a new stable along the side of the house where you see it now. The old entrance would have been about where the mangers are. When the Fascists started. imposing their heavy taxes, my Father needed. somewhere to store a supply of food for the winter months, where it would not be found by the tax men and taken away. Most of the peasants have hidey holes of some sort, if they hadn't they would have long since starved! He covered up the old entrance and knocked a hole in the wall; by this time trees had grown up around the gratings so that they could no longer be seen from outside, so he left them for ventilation. Until today no-one outside our own people knew about this place and those that would remember the old stable have long since gone."

While Frcolene had been speaking Basil, who was already weighing the possibilities, clambered onto the old manger which, despite its age, remained sound, to peer through the iron grating. Because of his position, he was the only one who heard the rifle shot which followed close on the dull thud of an explosion. He called to the others to be quiet a moment and strained his ears to listen but, hearing nothing, jumped down from his perch.

John looked at him an expression of surprise on his face and said,

"It's only blasting where the Germans are constructing the new defences."

Tanky felt dubious, he turned a questioning look towards Basil whose face was set in that grim expression which could portend trouble and said,

"I'm not so sure, come to think of it the explosion sounded too close."

Basil frowned momentarily as if not quite certain.

"I thought I heard a rifle shot, did anybody else?"

His glance passing from face to face inviting an answer as they individually returned his question with blank stares or negative shakes of the head.

All at once the semi-jocular air died. Each face wore a serious expression, for they knew Basil too well to suspect he might be mistaken, as far as they were concerned, if he thought he had heard a rifle shot then the probabilities were that he had.

Ercolene felt the blood drain from his face as a tremor of alarm shot through him. Until now he hadn't fully taken into consideration the risks which would be the inevitable outcome of helping his friends, but the months spent in the hills around Cingoli and Pioracco had left their mark ; his mind had become conditioned to danger and though he still felt the tug of fear, he had learned to ignore it. His voice when he found it, was barely audible - somehow he managed a wan smile - it seemed important that he didn't let Basil see he was afraid.

"It might be a rastrellamento[15], hadn't we better get Porky in here?"

Basil nodded, feeling for the Beretta he always carried in his jacket pocket, as a shadow fell across the entrance, then his hand fell away again as Roberto's face appeared. He seemed excited, gesticulating wildly before blurting,

"There had been trouble at Gianni's place, Pasquale just passed by, he says there was a squad of Germans there and they had Annina. prisoner. Now it looks as if the cottage is on fire." Basil swore, using his own peculiar oath.

"'What about Jhanni?"

Roberto shook his head.

"I don't know. Antonio has gone off to see what he can find out."

They scrambled through the entrance and without troubling to replace the chest, dashed outside where a small knot of women folk were standing wringing their hands and gazing at a pall of smoke which smudged the fair sky. Even from this distance, the explosive crackling of roof timbers could be heard as they sent showers of sparks into the air and, here and there, in small irregular groups, people could be seen watching the conflagration from their various vantage points.

As Jimmy watched he could feel a cold unreasoning anger rising in him, an anger which was directed as much against Pasquale as it was against the

---

[15] Literally, 'Combing out'.

Germans. He reflected bitterly that the man must have seen the captive girl yet done nothing to help. Seemingly he was more interested in scurrying from house to house with his tit bit of news. Yet, at the same time, he knew in his heart that it would be a foolhardy man who, lacking firearms, attempted to rescue the girl from her plight. How long he stood watching while his fury raged within him and he fought to control the urge to rush into Civitella in an attempt to wrest the girl back, he didn't know. For a while time stood still, as his mind dwelt on a hundred instances which had involved the girl - he remembered her gentle ministrations to Porky and the dreamy half smile, almost secretive, which curved her moist lips when she was thoughtful, an expression somehow demure yet sensuous as if her thoughts were too intimate to discuss - the way she would cast down her glance when embarrassed revealing luxuriant lashes which somehow accentuated the golden radiance of her cheeks, and his fists clenched into two hard balls as he thought of her helpless in the grip of her captors, while the haunting memory of the horror that had once been Dieci filled him with a nameless nausea as his imagination pictured what the Germans might do.

Basil's voice asking Antonio what had happened to the girl seemed to come from a great distance, as if in a dream he heard Antonio saying,

"Although the girl was taken prisoner, no-one seems to know what has happened to her. She wasn't with the Germans when they returned to town, and there's no sign of her at the cottage."

"And Gianni?"

Basil queried.

"Is safe, I found him cutting wood in the forest and told him what had happened he has gone to his parents at Catignano, he, seems to think that as the baby is staying there, it'll be the place to find her."

At first the possibility that Annina might have escaped brought a surge of relief to Jimmy's conflicting emotions, and his anger subsided. Then, remembering the rifle shot Basil had heard, he wondered dejectedly if the girl's dead body had been thrown into the flames. Suddenly life seemed empty, devoid of meaning, there wasn't even anguish, only a, sense of irretrievable loss he was unable to explain and a cold implacable determination to seek out and kill the man responsible if Annina had been killed. As if to match his mood, the sky gradually clouded over obscuring the sun and the leaves stirred restlessly in the trees with the first few drops of rain.

By nightfall, the rain, brisk at first, had degenerated to a fine drizzle which had an icy quality about it. It spread a drenching blanket over the countryside saturating the paths, turning them to mud, and hissed defiantly as it settled on the smouldering pyre that had been a cottage.

Two miles away up the mountainside where the forest belt began, moisture dripped from the trees in an irregular pattern of sound. Annina shivered, partly from the cold and partly from the fear that still held her in its grip. Her lips were bitten where she had clenched her teeth to stifle the screams which struggled to rise from her throat. Her mud smeared face and arms were covered in scratches where she had caught herself on the brambles that clutched at her as she fled, and she had torn her dress revealing one honey coloured shoulder and the curve of a breast while wrenching herself from the grip of the German that held her.

She rose to her feet and stood listening in the darkness hearing only the steady fall of water as it fell from the overladen leaves with staccato abruptness. She felt a strange unreality as if her own flesh was something alien, it was a singular sensation, a vivid awareness of her own fingers and toes, even of her teeth chattering in her head. She realised dumbly that the rushing noise she could hear now was her own blood coursing through her veins and that she was alive and must get help, but her In-laws place at Catignano was a good two hours walk away and there was nobody she could trust-except the Maldini family.

Slowly, hesitantly, she began to move, bit by bit her pace quickened to a run; she ran as a frightened doe runs when fleeing the hounds, without thought for the obstacles that strewed her path and oblivious to her own exhaustion. Stumbling frequently and sobbing pitifully, she came out of the forest and descended a steep path. She had to pass her home and, on reaching the well beaten track paused as the acrid tang of wet ashes and charred wood caught her breath. Some unknown force seemed to prevent her from moving forward, then, with a small strangled cry, she broke the spell and rushed by.

Spent and near fainting, it took her last reserves of strength to mount the steep path to Casa Tufa. Now the house stood before her dark and silent, no glimmer of light showed beneath the door as she advanced, hesitating whether to knock or enter the barn. Somewhere from behind a low growl sounded and hearing the pounding paws she knocked frantically, then turned to face the vague whitish shape looming out of the darkness. The dog stopped and growled menacingly, then, evidently recognising her as someone he knew, cocked his head on one side while he eyed her. Striving to keep the mounting hysteria from her voice Annina spoke quietly.

"Leone, come here."

The dog trotted up, sniffing suspiciously, then nuzzled his head into her outstretched hand so that she could feel the clipped ears wet with the rain. A light appeared under the door and she heard the grumbling tone of Roberto's voice as he came to open it.

She knew no more until the sun streaming through a crack in the shuttered windows touched her closed eyes and woke her. For a few moments, lying in that limbo between sleeping and waking, she was only partly aware of her surroundings, then as the memory of the previous day came flooding back she sat up. The steady drone of voices from downstairs seemed to indicate that it was yet early, otherwise the menfolk would have gone to work. Then she remembered that today would be Sunday.

CHAPTER 21

When the snow came on the eve of the New Year, blanking out the rifts and valleys and softening the contours of the foothills, the men of the district laid aside their zappe, the clumsy hoe-like instruments with which they tilled the soil, and gathered in their homes, for their work lay with the earth and the soil lay deep beneath the white surface.

Inside Casa Tufa, it was snug warmed by a blazing brushwood fire. If the girls worried about "La Vacca", those dappled purplish marks apt to appear on their legs if they sat overlong near the scorching flames, it didn't stop them drawing close to the fire as they spun their wool into yarn.

Although there was no radio and no news of the war filtered through during the seven weeks that the house remained isolated, there was no boredom and the time passed swiftly. Freed for a while from the long hours of toil which normally left them tired and taciturn in the evenings, the Maldini family, and in particular Roberto and his brother Antonio, treated the period as a holiday, taking the opportunity to indulge in the long and involved discussions which was t heir pleasure. At the end of the day when the small oil lamp was lit and the fire banked high, with chairs drawn round, the women, whose hands were never idle, took up their knitting or spinning spools while the men talked or yarned amongst themselves. Sometimes Leone sneaked in and, if unnoticed, hid beneath Annina's chair his great yellow eyes drooping as he dozed illegally in the heat of the fire. When conversation lagged a song would be suggested, then the treble voices would merge with the bass. Invariably one or the other would be persuaded to perform solo and the round of applause was always greater than the merit. Annina, who had a light clear voice and seemed to know every song that had ever been written was a great favourite and the way her eyes seemed to seek out Jimmy whenever she sang 'Non te Scodare di Me' was noted with glee, though no remark was ever made. When Porky treated them to a rendition of 'Old McDougal had a Farm' his voice, if nothing else, was remarkable and the applause was mingled with howls of delight. The honks and snorts of the various animals tickled the simple humour of the Italian family and they quickly picked up the melody joining in, each with his or her own version of how the animals should sound. They never tired of the song and thereafter no evening was reckoned complete without at least one performance. At ten o'clock Roberto would rise from his chair and announce that it was time to retire. As the head of the house he always led the prayers without which no day would be complete, gliding through the Latin Ava Maria with only a hazy understanding of the words but receiving that solace and comfort from his devotions which would have been denied to a man with a more complicated mind.

For the first time in many months the Syndicate was able to relax secure in the knowledge that few, least of all the Germans, would venture to make the difficult journey in snow shoes now necessary to reach the house. Yet there was not one of them who wouldn't have preferred the hazards of the trail to the enforced rest. Now that Porky, though thin and emaciated, was fully recovered they found the delay irksome and reckoned each day as a day lost.

It was towards the end of February that Roberto, who had. noticed Basil's habit of staring across the snow towards the Maiella, brooding and thoughtful, as he watched for the first sign of a thaw, mentioned his preoccupation to Jimmy.

"What's the matter with your friend, doesn't he like us that he is so impatient to leave?"

Before Jimmy could reply Antonio sidled up - he had a mischievous gleam in his eyes as he said,

"Maybe he is homesick 'cherchez la femme'."

Jimmy chuckled.

"Anyone less likely to be homesick I can't imagine."

"Not so you, eh!"

Antonio nudged him jocularly and shot a knowing glance towards Annina who was busy knitting a new heel into one of Jimmy's socks

"Che bella Mademoiselle!"

Jimmy could feel the blood rushing to the roots of his hair and hoped it didn't notice. He tried to change the subject but Antonio was in a teasing mood and felt encouraged by a certain sidelong look and titter of merriment exchanged between the three sisters. He had noticed the strong bond of friendship that had grown between the fair haired Englishman and the Italian girl, and was not to be put off.

"Voulez vous promenade avec moi?"

Cackling with his own humour, he minced over to the girl, casting leering glances towards Jimmy as he offered her his arm. Blushing furiously Jimmy took one horrified look at the ring of grinning faces that seemed to surround him and fled outside where he was joined a moment later by Roberto, still chuckling over his discomfort. Jimmy grinned sheepishly but said nothing as he slackened his pace to match the shorter steps of the peasant farmer.

As if by tactical agreement neither man spoke until they had reached the end of the barn where the bullock cart was housed and as this was the limit of the area that had been cleared of snow returned, passing the house to the higher ground. They paused beside the haystacks, a favourite spot of Basil's, and as Jimmy gazed at the view he thought he could appreciate how his friend must feel. Before them the ground sloped gently down hill, then fell away abruptly at the edge of the scarp which could be seen through the thinly populated trees. Seemingly only a few miles distant, the mass of the Maiela sprawled crescent shaped across the end of the valley; frowning as if in stolid anger at the foothills that tried to climb its massive slopes.

Roberto, who had been regarding him thoughtfully as if uncertain whether to speak, squeezed his arm in that ageless gesture of friendship, his eyes crinkling with a tiny twinkle as he said,

"You like her, eh?"

Slowly, almost reluctantly as if held by some hypnotic attraction, Jimmy drew his eyes from the distant scene to focus them on the face of his companion.

"Yes, she's a nice girl."

He spoke abruptly feeling slightly self conscious and, at the same time, angry with himself for behaving like a bashful schoolgirl. Before Antonio had acted the goat he had paid little heed to his impressions when Annina was around. Hitherto he had merely thought of her as a pleasant companion whose presence was agreeable, but the buffoonery had triggered off a complexity of tantalising emotions which left him bewildered - now he wanted time to think; to sort himself out.

Undismayed, Roberto went on.

"She is not betrothed, you should speak to her Father."

and then, as if suddenly remembering the baby,

"Her fiancé, the father of the child, is dead. She is a good girl - they would have been married ."

Suddenly, Jimmy felt oddly happy with a warmth towards Roberto which was almost affection. The Italian shrewdly said no more on the subject. Instead he glanced at the sky, serene with the expectation of Spring, then remarked as if it was a certainty,

"The thaw will start tomorrow." Then briskly, "Come, it is time we returned to the house."

Roberto's forecast was accurate, the snow, which had held the countryside fast in its grip for so many weeks, began to disperse but although it cleared sufficiently to allow free movement between the homesteads by the end of February, it was April before the mountain paths were negotiable. Even so, it still lingered on the higher slopes.

As the weather improved, the Germans became increasingly active visiting farm houses, usually in unofficial groups of two or three as soldiers will in an attempt to supplement their rations. They seldom caused any bother and usually went away satisfied with a few eggs or a chicken.

During this period Basil and the others roamed about the district, unobtrusively taking note and committing to memory any information they thought might be of use to Intelligence when they got through. Inevitably they came into close contact with the Germans but since even the Italians accepted them as refugees, if some suspected otherwise they kept a silent tongue, it was not surprising that those Germans they came up against remained unsuspicious of their true status.

It was towards the end of March, on a day that held more than a promise of the summer to come, that they met the Flt. Ltnt., a man of medium height, with that compact agile look of a trained athlete, his pleasantly alert eyes, neither blue nor grey, yet having something of each colour, seemed to invite confidence. Basil took a chance and spoke to him in English. For a moment the other man stood silent, quietly appraising the five who confronted him, then, as if suddenly satisfied, he smiled; it was a friendly smile, with a certain reservation which seemed to say - O.K, chum but let's have no tricks.

"Names Bernard Metcalf, what's yours?"

Basil told him then, having introduced the others, asked him which camp he came from. When he explained that he had never been in a prison camp but had crashed his plane, his actual words were

"The old kite pranged shortly before Xmas and I spent the Festive Season at a farmhouse which turned out to be a rendezvous for A. Force."

Basil's interest quickened. He wondered if a similar organisation to the L.R.D.G. was operating in the area, but instantly dismissed the idea as he felt sure he would have heard rumours of their activities if this was so.

"Interrupting, what is A. Force?" he asked,

Bernard paused - "Of course, you wouldn't know - it's a secret organisation for assisting people through the Lines. Some of our boys got back with their help, so I had heard of it before I pranged, but it was a stroke of fortune that I should contact them so soon." He stroked his jaw reflectively.

"You know, I've been helping them ferret out people like you, but its surprising how few are prepared to take advantage of using the organisation. I must have talked to nearly a dozen during the last few weeks, yet I've only found one man who is prepared to make the attempt - a chap named Ferris. I'll try and make arrangements for you to meet him. So many seem to be of the opinion that our Forces will soon he here anyway and as they are quite comfortable thank you, fed, clothed and entertained by their protectors, they might as well stay as they are. I suppose the truth of the matter is they've got used to the life and don't care much for the added risks involved in filtering through."

He broke into one of his rare smiles -"Of course, it takes all sorts to make a world. One chap I met has married into the family he's staying with, I reckon the Services have lost him for the duration. Still, instead of worrying about these, we should be thankful that several hundred have made the attempt and successfully reached the safety of our Lines, many of them with little or no assistance. Incidentally, I understand that the chap who is to guide us has made about 30 trips.

The lucky ones were those from the southern camps, there was one big camp of New Zealanders for instance, where they virtually started south one day and were home and dry the next; our Forces were advancing so rapidly."

Porky grinned.

"At least they did walk south, not like those coves from Sulmona, if ever anybody missed the boat ." he chuckled irresistibly.

"We heard that a bunch of them were actually living in the old camp, as if they hadn't seen enough of it. Apparently they would wander around during the day and return at night. Eventually Jerry came along and locked the door."

He went through the motions of turning a key then, beating his fists against imaginary bars, bawled,

"Let me out; Let me out;"

Bernard's eyes twinkled his appreciation and conversation became general for a while until Basil led the talk back to 'A' Force.

"It seems to me that the sort of assistance your friends offer provides a pretty fair chance of success. It's not as if everybody knows about it like that mess up at Francavilla."

Bernard shot him a quick look -"What was that?"

Basil explained and finished his account of the event by saying,

"You know, the average Italian is a born gossip, if he knows something he simply must natter," he drew his mouth down ruefully, "As we found to our cost. I feel morally certain that if the existence of 'A' Force were generally known, one of us would have heard about it."

"You're probably right."

"We had planned an attempt round the Maiella and thought of going by Caramanico, then through the Passo di Diavolo to dodge the Sangro, but from the appearance of the hills, there's going to be a lot of snow about."

Bernard nodded.

"Too right there's a lot of snow and a lot of Germans too. You've picked one of the most heavily concentrated sections."

"That being so, is there any chance of joining your crowd?"

"I will speak to ..." Bernard paused momentarily - "the man who's organising things and see if he will accept another five."

As he spoke he rose abruptly from the grass bank where he had been sitting and pulled the cloth of his breeches away from his buttocks where the dampness of the ground had caused them to stick. "See you tomorrow about 3 p.m."

Then, pointing to a dilapidated grain tower about a mile away

"By that point. If it's O.K. by you, I'll bring young Ferris along and you can get acquainted."

He finished by saying,

"I don't need to warn you to say nothing of this to anybody and that involves the people you are staying with."

So, during the last few weeks at Casa Tufa, no mention was made of 'A' Force within the hearing of the Maldini's. Even when Jimmy told Annina he would soon be leaving, he valiantly resisted the temptation to discuss the plan. If he had it is conceivable that he might have mentioned Doug Ferris or the name of his protector at the house beneath Ciliera then Annina might well have warned him to take care. With womanly intuition she knew that Jimmy was holding something back and that somehow, by doing so, his life was endangered. Because there was nothing tangible on which to found her mounting dismay she said nothing of her fears but, when goodbyes had been said quietly left Casa Tufa and followed. She saw the meeting with Bernard and the eventual entrance into a large farm house near Loreto and the uneasy state of her mind was not improved when a solitary Magpie settled on the roof of the building. She shuddered as she recalled the many superstitious tales recounted by the old folk. Convinced now that her friends were in real peril she waited with the nebulous idea that she could give warning if Germans came, but it was not until the following morning when, tired from her night long vigil, her suspicions were confirmed. Shortly after dawn, having watched the party leave the precincts of the farm house and move off towards Pianella, she saw Concetta. standing by the track. By then it was too late, they were already out of sight.

At the head of the column, Gino, his white sweater making an easy marker, set a brisk pace which Bernard, who walked beside him found stimulating as he settled down to enjoy the exercise. 100 yards behind, Porky talked happily with Tanky; he felt in great spirits and kept up an incessant chatter despite the difficulty it caused to his breathing, as they breasted the numerous long slopes. Every now and then Tanky would look anxiously at him, the long illness had sapped the stamina of the little gunner, but he puffed contentedly along, seemingly indifferent to his obvious discomfort. Some 50 yards to the rear, in contrast to Porky's joyful countenance, Jimmy strode silently beside

Basil his face downcast as he fingered the small gold cross which Annina had removed from her neck and hung round his when they parted.

"To remember me by."

He could almost hear her voice again - then he had said,

"Don't fret, when the war is over I'll be back" and she had promised to wait. When he kissed her, there had been the taste of salt on her cheeks and the lump in his own throat had been such that he could hardly speak. He wondered how long it would be before he saw her again, it was characteristic of him that it should never enter his thoughts that he might be prevented from keeping his promise. He looked so doleful that Basil nudged him jovially,

"Cheer up chum, there's nothing to superstition you know."

He was referring to Porky's jocular comments on the number of men who had spent the night in the commodious stable adjoining the farmhouse where their guide had joined them, introducing himself as Gino. He was a small man, no more than 5'2" in height, but what there was of him was all man. His face had that leathery look associated with climbers and though at first sight he looked fat, his stomach was flat and hard, the barrel chest and trunk like girth hidden beneath a white sweater gave a deceptive appearance.

Basil had been mildly surprised to find that there were four Italians included in the party and only one other Britisher, a morose individual who protested that as a Colonel in the British Army he should at least merit the dignity of a bed in the house and not be expected to share accommodation with twelve head of oxen and the accumulated dregs of the League of Nations. He gave it as his considered opinion that the arrangements were unsanitary and he would mention the treatment he had received in his report. When nobody took any notice of his ranting, he had finally stomped off to a corner of the stable, as far removed from the rest as he could and, taking a small note book from his pocket begun to write.

Flushed with anger, Gino had snatched the book from his hands and after thumbing quickly through the pages, had burned it on the spot.

"You call yourself an officer" he had said with virulent contempt, "yet you haven't the sense to realise what would happen if that fell into enemy hands. Now go to sleep, we have to rise early." To the amazement of all, the officer had complied, albeit sulkily.

By the time the sun had become a fiery ball in the east, they had by-passed Pianella; now it rode high in the sky and the heat of the day was making itself felt. The long slender bridge across the river lay far behind and Basil could feel the large veins of his hands swelling with the quickened flow of his blood as his system coped with the continued exertion. Jimmy looked at him, acknowledging his nudge with a smile.

"Porky's a priceless ass isn't he? I do believe he had one of those Italians worried with his talk of the Last Supper."

The long straggling crocodile moved slowly towards its destination. Half a mile behind the leader, John was paying only part attention to the involved story about a shaggy dog Doug Ferris was relating. There was an indefinable something about his companion that disturbed him. Doug had a head of sandy coloured hair which fell untidily over his ears; it looked as if it had become estranged from its marriage partner, the comb, and by mutual agreement the two had elected to stay apart; but this in itself was no reason for the antipathy John felt. Nor was the slightly superior almost arrogant bearing, and oblique references, oft repeated, to large estates in Scotland which Doug claimed his father owned. John had met many boastful men and enjoyed their company, he was thinking - the fact that his eyes are set rather close together doesn't make him a criminal, though the way they never seem to meet one's gaze but dart about apparently looking everywhere except at the person to whom he is talking is not endearing. There was that evening when Basil spotted him trying to follow us to Casa Tufa, despite our repeated refusals to disclose where we were staying. John's eyes twinkled momentarily as he thought of the long walk that had ensued, then hardened, becoming watchful once again, as he puzzled over an almost imperceptible movement of Doug's head, which he felt sure had been some sort of signal to a woman standing beside the track. Yet when asked who she was Doug had professed ignorance, pretending at first that he hadn't seen her.

As the day wore on and the miles passed underfoot, John's suspicions subsided, he came to believe he had been mistaken and had probably imagined the movement.

Gradually the terrain changed from lush green to barren grey on the slopes that climbed into the Maiella. Now, with the river Sangro only 15 miles away, the fertile valleys had that neglected look peculiar to land near the fighting zone of a nation at war. Ground that should have been populated with workers and bright with the early growth of spring was almost deserted but not quite, here and there a coloured shirt proclaimed that some had remained.

With each mile covered more and more houses stood empty, forlorn ghosts that but a short time before rang with the laughter of children. Now no flurry of scampering hens or warning bay of barking dog disturbed the silence as they passed. The only people they saw on that lonely track which follows the sweeping curves of Colle Spaccato, mounts La Maielletta by easy stages and leaves Pretoro far below with its huddled houses shrunk to matchbox size, were a peasant, his donkey loaded with a few household goods, who, driven from his home by the fear of fighting to come, trekked to join his family already evacuated to a safer area; a lone German soldier enjoying a few brief hours of respite - he passed the time of day with each pair as they drew level seeming not to notice the unusual number of men about that day and, at varying intervals, the A. Force scouts whose functions were to report to Gino any unusual activities along the next few miles.

'When they reached the ancient stone built dwelling overlooking Guardiagrele, the sun had ploughed its way well into the afternoon.

It was dim inside the house, with occasional streaks of sunlight piercing chinks between the wooden slats of the closed door and the air had that fusty smell of a building that has not been in use. Nevertheless, it didn't detract from the enjoyment of a meal that had been prepared in readiness for their coming. Even the Colonel had no acid remarks to make though, as the senior British Officer he insisted on taking the head of the table. It did much to restore Porky's usual liveliness, the long walk had taken more out of him than he would care to admit. Gregarious as ever, he couldn't resist cracking a joke about the Hotel Moderne as he signed his name in what he called the 'Visitors' Book' before adjourning to await the coming night when the last stage of their journey would be tackled.

'When John picked his way through the crowded room, Gino had already gone out intimating that certain points along the route had to be checked and Basil sat talking to Jimmy in that quiet way he had, his chair positioned so that he could see the door. Catching Basil's glance, John pitched his voice low to avoid being overheard, and said,

"Either of you two seen Doug lately?"

"Can't say I have, what about you Jimmy?" Basil replied.

Jimmy shook his head slowly -"Probably having a kip somewhere." Then, addressing John - "Have you asked any of the others?"

"Only our own crowd, neither Porky nor Tanky have seen him since we ate, they're having a sniff round now."

As he spoke, Bernard came hurrying into the room and approached the corner where they were talking. He wore a worried frown and his cheeks looked flushed with annoyance. His voice sounded sharp.

"What's this about young Ferris?"

His eyes sought out Basil's. Basil shrugged,

"You're as wise as I am, better ask John."

Bernard's gaze flicked over to the New Zealander.

"Well?"

John almost drawled and his Kiwi twang became more pronounced, a habit he had when affronted.

"Now hold hard chum, it's your party so don't get blaming me. The jokers disappeared, that's all I know."

At that moment, Tanky bustled in with Porky following hard on his heels. By now some of the Italian contingent were casting questioning glances towards the group in the corner as if wondering what all the activity could be about. Even Porky looked grave as he said.

"Nary a sign of him, we've looked just about everywhere. He just isn't in the place."

The red spot of anger faded from Bernard's cheek and the line of his chin hardened.

"Damned idiot had no right to go out. Sorry I got uppity John, I fear I flapped a bit."

John shrugged - "Forget it."

Then, building a cigarette, passed the makings to Basil who spread the cut leaf expertly along the paper. He was about to lick the edge when he paused, the half made cigarette mid-way to his lips. His keen ears had detected the sound of running. The door flew open and Gino burst into the room.

"Scappa...scappa.., vengono i Tedeschi."

Without slackening his pace, he made a stupendous leap for a small window set high in the wall and vaulted through. Instantly all was confusion as men collided with each other in their efforts to reach an exit or find a hiding place in one of the other rooms. Everything seemed to happen at once. Catching a glimpse of field grey uniforms through the open door Basil raced to slam it shut. Before he could drop the heavy bar into position, a terrific jolt shattered the flimsy latch and almost wrenched the door from its hinges, the shock sending a spasm of pain through his tensed muscles. Two of the Italians leaped simultaneously for the window, effectively blocking the opening as they struggled to get through.

Belatedly, as if actuated by some delayed action, the Col. galvanised into life, whatever his faults, he didn't lack courage. He charged to Basil's assistance and braced himself alongside shouting a warning to the others to keep away from the door. Together they succeeded in closing it again and as Basil dropped the bar into position Jimmy grabbed a threshing leg and hauled one of the Italians away from the window, the other scrambled through.

Pushing the Col. to one side, Basil dived for the safety of the wall. A split instant later, a hail of bullets tore through the flimsy wood. Miraculously no-one was hit as they scattered away from the line of fire.

At best the effort could only produce a delaying effect, had the window not been blocked, the delay might have allowed most of those in the room to get out before the raiders encircled the house, as it was, when the door crashed open only the two Italians had escaped. Basil fought down a fleeting temptation to use his Beretta on the owner of a forage cap that appeared at the window. Realising the futility of further resistance, he reluctantly raised his hands rather than risk the massacre of his friends.

CHAPTER 22

The darkness was complete until Basil struck a match to light his cigarette, then the tiny flame illuminated the mildewed walls of the shed glistening with moisture and reflected from the eyes of a rat which hesitated momentarily before scurrying off to darker regions of its own. When the flame died there was only the red glow from the cigarette as he thoughtfully drew smoke into his lungs. He lay on a filthy pile of straw, one hand behind his head and watched the glowing tip brighten and dull thinking that a cigarette never seemed to have the same flavour when you couldn't see the smoke.

At first there had been chattering voices, interspersed with laughter, which penetrated the thin wooden walls, then the rumble of a motor followed by a clatter of equipment as their escorts clambered aboard had brought comparative silence after the lorry had driven away. Now there was only an occasional voice and the scuff of feet as guards toured ceaselessly around the shed; and the little noises, the faint rustle as someone turned over, the heavy breathing of those who slept, merging with a myriad of undefinable tiny sounds which emanated from ancient timbers and various creatures of the night scouring for food.

"Got a light?"

The voice sounded eerily close and Jimmy's hand and face showed briefly in the glow as Basil sat up and tendered his cigarette.

"Thanks:"

For a few minutes neither man spoke ...

"What do you make of it Jimmy?"

"Damned if 'I know, do you think Doug Ferris tipped them off?"

"If he didn't someone else did! Why else would they only be interested in us and let the Ities go? What's more, they seemed to know just how many we were. Look at the time they spent looking for John."

Jimmy chuckled.

"The way he bolted up that chimney at the last minute is about the funniest thing I've ever seen. Beats me how they didn't see his boots scrabbling for a foothold."

"Priceless!"

They fell silent again and finished their cigarettes. Basil looked at the illuminated dial of his watch, it showed a quarter to ten. He closed his eyes allowing the deep mist of sleep to take over.

. . . .

When the hands of his watch had crept round till they pointed to three o'clock, he woke, every fibre alert as his ears strained to recapture the sound that had disturbed him. He heard Jimmy sit up, then the sound came again and he knew that someone was turning a key in the lock. The door opened and the outline of the guards showed briefly against the night sky before being masked by a blur of white as someone was pushed unceremoniously in and the door slammed shut.

The rasp of a match being struck seemed harsh and unreal and when the flickering light fell on Gino's face he squinted as he tried to pierce the gloom.

"That you Bernard?"

His voice sounded tired as if he had had enough.

"No it's Basil, what happened? I thought you were clear away."

"I was, but I tried to reach Melene and nearly made it too."

"Tough luck."

The match went out and in the darkness Gino shrugged.

"It's the penalty of failure. I'm sorry I didn't warn you in time."

"What went wrong?"

"I don't know. Someone must have talked."

"Exactly, any idea who?"

For a moment, the silence was pregnant. Then without answering Basil's question, Gino said,

"I shall probably be taken away in the morning, I must talk to Bernard, where is he?"

"Over here."

Bernard's voice came from the corner of the shed. Then a match flared again and Gino joined him.

For a while the steady drone of Gino's voice filled the tiny shed as he told Bernard of how he had become suspicious on the way back from the scouting expedition.

"I noticed that several sentry posts had been doubled since passing them earlier."

The voice paused as if he was thinking - he spoke slowly - punctuating each word ...

"I don't know what it was, but there was a subtle change in their manner. Somehow they seemed more alert than usual, it was as if they were waiting for something to happen, almost an air of expectancy."

Then, speaking more briskly,

"I was not unduly worried until I saw a small convoy of lorries making their way up the road towards the house. I should have returned to warn you straight away but when the lorries stopped I was intrigued and anyway we've had similar scares before and on this job it doesn't do to panic. So, to make quite sure, I hid myself and watched. It soon became evident that the soldiers were not just deploying over a wide area, they were in fact moving into positions which would prohibit anyone leaving the house without being seen, as if they knew about us and were cordoning off the house. When I realised what was happening, I made my way back intending to lead you into one of the gullies where you could hide in more security. It was slow work because I daren't let myself be seen. By the time I reached the door, the Germans were only about 50 yards behind and I knew for certain that we were rumbled.

After I had warned you, I hid in a thicket then, when it was dark enough to move, I tried to get through to one of the British outposts in the Palombaro area about six or seven kilometres south from here. Normally it is fairly easy to slip through since the hills west of Guardiagrele are only lightly held by a comparatively small group of the German 305 Inf. Div., their positions are fairly widely scattered and the activities of your patrols tend to keep them in their place.

Tonight it was different from normal, I don't know if they had got scared that the Indians might break through and had brought some of the 334 Inf. Div. down to stiffen it up or what, but the area between here and Pissadini simply crawled with troops. I managed to dodge them, however, and pressed on hoping all the time I might bump into one of the 5 Recce Regt, forays, I had met them before further out than this, but my luck failed, with only about 2 kilos to go in the Casatini/Capolegrotte area, I ran foul of a patrol.... Now I suppose they'll have me up for questioning........"

His voice shook a little, and he asked for a cigarette. Basil supplied one ready made and proffered a light. Gino drew deeply, expelling the smoke audibly through his nostrils. When he spoke again he had recovered his composure.

"Best not to think about it."

He laughed harshly.

"I've got the necessary if they get too rough!"

Then, changing the subject, he told them about himself, how he had been brought up in the little village of Castel del Monte, of his fiancée and the first time he had met a bear on the slopes of the Gran Sasso. The Hotel Imperatore was quite near his village and he had seen the gliders landing, then the take off towards L'Aquila when the tiny plane carrying Mussolini, though he hadn't known then who was inside, had nearly crashed. He talked on in like vein throughout the remainder of the night and was still talking when the guards came at dawn to take him away.

The morning had a clear quality about it that banished the haze and left an impression of unreality which drew the eyes of the seven men now standing outside the shed, irresistibly towards a scene that seemed as if an artist had spread his canvas overnight and painted in hills with tiny villages and numerous gullies against an azure background for a sky. Below lay Guardiagrele and to the south, seemingly no more than a stones throw away, the mountain town of Pennapiediemonte, its clusters of houses bright in the morning sun.

While they waited the signal to climb into a lorry parked on the road a short distance away, Basil watched two of the soldiers, who seemed to be little more than boys, skylarking around the tail board and couldn't help thinking how irrational it was that these young lads laughing and joking between themselves and playing the same sort of pranks as would their British counterparts, were the enemy.

A barked command from an officer sent them scurrying to the driver's cab and a prod in the back told Basil it was time to move. Soon they were hurtling down the road, little more than a track really, the wheels of the lorry churning up the white dust and forming a cloud which trailed behind them.

On reaching the lower road the going was better. As the lorry gathered speed Bernard surreptitiously ripped open the lining of his jacket and removed the chevrons of his rank which he had hidden there. Seizing a suitable opportunity he threw them out of the lorry saying,

"Without those as evidence we might be able to stick together."

Eventually the lorry entered the small village of Civitaquana and drew up outside a building which, if the petrol pumps were indicative, had been a service station during better times. Here they were separated from the Colonel and taken to a temporary cell on the upper floor of the building. A barred window overlooked the main street of the tiny township and commanded a view through the valley. There was an odd familiarity about the scene which puzzled them, then Basil, having gazed for some time, recognised a peak which he thought looked like Monte Corno and deduced that the distant villages, reminiscent of elfin castles, nestling in the foothills, would be Villa Celiera and Vestia.

Later they were taken before the Kommandant who apologised for the inadequate facilities at his disposal and generously supplied them with cigarettes. He told them he had been a chef at the Hotel Waldorf in the days before the war and had many friends in England. He hoped they wouldn't make a distasteful duty too difficult.

The following day he sent for them individually ostensibly for a chat, but in reality for interrogation relating to their route and those who had helped them. Some of the answers he received were so fantastically ridiculous that he would have been an idiot had he believed them. After Porky quite truthfully told him that they had been looked after by a chap called Roberto, then spoilt it by saying he thought the family name was Farinacci, the Kommandant admitted defeat by leaving them to their own devices.

It was on the third day of their renewed captivity that Tanky was staring moodily from the window trying to locate Casa Tufa when he startled the others with a yell.

"Hey chaps, what do you make of this?"

Together they crowded round the window. Down the middle of the street swaggered an Indian resplendent in German uniform with a flash depicting a tiger's head and the inscription 'Freie Inder'.

They stared in silence but as the Indian gradually drew nearer, Porky grew more and more excited, his neck suffusing with colour as he remembered the many Indians he had known. The idea that this might be a British one turned traitor irked him and his choler began to rise. He wanted to get at the figure which seemed to epitomise everything he hated. Squeezing his head through the bars he shouted.

"Hey nigger come here."

The Indian halted and looked about him as if wondering where the insult had come from.

"The bastard knows English anyway."

Porky sounded exultant.

"Let's try him with this."

Then, raising his voice again, called.

"Dhokebaag harami!"

Then the Indian spotted the face at the window and, even from their position in the room, his muttering could be heard as he approached. He let fly with a stream of filthy invective which must have been learned in British Army camps, mixed in with a Hindi that probably originated in that area of Bombay known as the Cages. In his diatribe he left no doubt as to his feelings towards the British Sahib who he said only used the likes of him to assist Imperialistic ambitions.

Porky, who had spent much of his boyhood in India, replied in kind. There followed a voluble tirade between the two which worried Basil for, though he couldn't understand what was being said, the rise and fall of the cadence was informative. He knew Porky of old and, remembering the countless times his tongue had led him into trouble, could guess the sort of things that were being said. For once, however, Porky took no notice of him when he told him to stop and he was forced to drag him away from the window.

When John, who had remained by the window, drawled "You've torn it now chum, the Joker's come into the building." Porky, looking not unlike a bristling terrier as he paced stiff legged back and forth in the small room, snapped back

"Good!"

This brought a sharp retort from Basil.

"Blamed pointless thing to do."

The incident had made him irritable, he firmly believed that nothing should be started which couldn't be finished.

It wasn't long before the door opened and two of the guards came in followed by the Indian who pointed out Porky as the man who had insulted him. As they hustled him along the narrow passage one of the guards, a youth of about twenty who looked after the keys and held the rank of Gefreiter, took the opportunity to let fly with a kick which landed painfully in the small of Porky's back and sent him stumbling towards the door of the Kommandant's office. They marched him inside where the same young German pushed him viciously then clubbed him on the shoulder with the butt of his rifle, saying in a curious clipped English "Stand straight in front of Herr Kommandant."

By this time Porky's fists were clenching and his eyes had a defiant gleam.

The Kommandant looked at the Indian with repugnance, he had a Teutonic dislike of coloured blood and his Prussian love of courage, stimulated by Porky's bearing, gave him a tendency to sympathise with his prisoner. He spoke curtly to the Gefreiter,

"Lass den mann, er ist kein feigling."

He would have liked to drop the matter and he chuckled to himself as he remembered Porky's recent avowal that the intensely pro-German Fascist leader Roberto Faranacci had helped look after him, but he hadn't reached his high rank by showing his feelings. Outwardly he appeared cold and ruthless. It wouldn't harm this young dumpkoff to cool down on his own for a while. He glared at Porky and, hoping the twinkle he felt sure was forming in his eyes didn't show, spoke harshly to disguise his feelings.

"If you can't behave yourself we shall have to teach you manners."

He was sure he detected a certain ironical glint in the eyes of the man opposite him - Du lieber Gott, he thought, I believe he's laughing at me, and gave a brusque wave of the hand,

"Take him below and lock him up."

When the door slammed behind him, Porky looked round the semi-dark quarters, the only light came from a small window barely 9" wide and 2' long. By standing on tiptoe he could just see through the grease smeared panes into a small courtyard, the pavement of which was only a few inches below his eye level. The smell of stale oil, grease and rotting rags seemed to be everywhere and the floor was littered with refuse. He wrinkled his nose in disgust and kicked morosely at a pile of oil soaked cleaning waste sending it scattering A few bars of 'Col. Bogey' flat and tuneless, escaped his pursed lips. The tune suited his mood and he whistled louder hoping his jailers would hear him and think he didn't care.

At one end of his prison a pair of ill fitting double doors took up the entire wall space, and when he peered through a chink between the doors he could see part of a road and the building opposite. The sound of movement in the courtyard attracted him back to the window and as he looked out a pair of dilapidated crepe soled boots, split at the seams and worn to the uppers, passed within inches of his nose. He grinned at the receding boots and whistled a few bars from 'Cuckoo', that delightful melody played on a tin whistle in the 'Laurel and Hardy' films, seized with enthusiasm by the male youths of Gt. Britain and whistled on every street corner to the embarrassment of passing girls. Now Porky used it to attract Basil's attention. The feet, as feet usually did when this tune was whistled, picked up the rhythm and Porky knew he had been heard. Presently Basil's face appeared at the window as he pretended to adjust a bootlace. He winked and his muffled voice came through the glass.

"How's it go Porky?"

Porky just grinned and shrugged then, noticing that Bernard was not amongst the group now clustered round the window,

"Where's Bernard?"

"Upstairs, he's been told to get ready to leave, I think they ..."

The end of Basil's sentence was lost in a guttural shout as the young Gefreiter barged in on the scene to send him flying with a kick. Porky saw Basil roll over and the bully advance and raise his foot to kick him where he lay then, so quickly it would have been difficult to prove it was deliberate, one of Basil's feet hooked behind an ankle and the other administered a hefty thrust on the knee cap. The German went down heavily, then sat up grasping the injured knee in his hand, his yell of anguish bringing the Kommandant and another guard on the scene.

Had Porky understood German and heard what was being said he would have heard the German, aware of his Kommandant's attitude to bullying, explain that he had stumbled and barged his knee on the ground. He watched the group disappear from view with the German limping behind and chuckled appreciatively, confident that Basil would steer himself out of trouble.

Left to his own devices, Porky stared moodily at the door, the knowledge that the road lay just beyond was tantalising, then the thought struck him that he was obviously in a lock up garage and, as it would have been designed primarily to keep people out, the locking mechanism might be accessible from the inside. He examined the door carefully, it seemed to be secured by a bar and padlock on the outside. Then his heart missed a beat and he wondered why he hadn't noticed before this that an interior hinge had been fitted. Excited now, he scrutinized the fittings carefully, they seemed to be held by heavy wood screws and a single coach bolt. He gazed at the nut securing the bolt and scratched his head contemplatively. Without tools of some sort it would be impossible to remove the hinges, but he seemed to remember when he kicked the cleaning waste he had heard a metallic clink. Rummaging among the pile of waste he got himself smothered in oil but eventually his patience was rewarded when he found a length of metal that had, at one time, been a case opening tool. Hiding his find back amongst the waste he sat down impatiently waiting for the dark.

He would have preferred to tell the others of the plan formulating in his mind and hoped that perhaps they would be brought down to the courtyard again for exercise, but in this he was disappointed, nor did anyone come near him until after sundown when a half loaf of bread and a cup of water was passed in to him.

Apparently he was supposed to do without bedding, but if his scheme went right he guessed he wouldn't need it.

When he thought the Garrison had settled for the night he started work. First loosening the screws, which proved to be no problem as the piece of metal made an excellent screwdriver. The nuts were more difficult, they would probably have been stiff even with a spanner, but a length of steel with only a fork cleft on the end was not an ideal instrument. By levering with the bent end of the tool and using the bolt, protected by a piece of cleaning waste, as a fulcrum, he managed to get one started. Working diligently, grinning to himself when the nut gave a little, and cursing silently under his breath every time he slipped or tore his hands on the jagged end of the metal, he was totally unaware of the passage of time.

It was 2.30 a.m. when, with the last retaining screw removed, he was able to ease the weight of the door to work the bolts free of the hinges.

Now that it was time to open the door, every sound seemed magnified and he imagined his own breathing was that of the guard outside. The slightest noise was sufficient to start the sweat from the pores of his hands and when the guard coughed or changed position, he would stand rigid for minutes at a time wondering if the door looked lopsided and if suspicions had been roused. Inch by inch he edged it open, swinging the two doors on the one pair of hinges and dreading the betraying clang of the padlock if it should sway with the movement.

At last there was room to slip through. Now that it was time to go, he felt calm, his recent fears forgotten. Scarcely glancing at the square shape of the guard standing back towards him, he doubled silently across the road and from the shadow between two houses gazed back at his recent prison. Everything looked normal, the guard unaware that he had lost his prisoner stood unconcerned ruminating no doubt on the off duty period to follow. Porky turned to go, then checked as he thought of his friends locked in a room upstairs. He looked longingly at the efficient automatic rifle held negligently in the crook of an elbow and remembered the rescue of Quintale. This time he would be on his own, but he thought if he could get his hands on that he would have a go.

Moving softly he slid from his hiding place back into the shadow of the H.Q. then silently advanced into the moonlight towards the back of the unsuspecting guard. Less than one minute later Porky died, there was no reason for the German to turn when he did, but the risk was always there.

The short burst of gunfire woke the four men in the little room on the upper floor of the building and brought a spate of activity to the Germans who garrisoned the H.Q. There was a tramping of feet on the stairs and voices were raised in the street. Together Basil and the others crowded to the window but they couldn't see much only a group of soldiers bending over something at the corner of the building too close into the wall to see. Eventually the clamour died down and they returned to their blankets on the floor.

The morning of April 4th, 1944 dawned as a thousand more like it have dawned throughout the ages, the sun rose catching the bars of the window and casting a zebra like shadow across one corner of the room which crept relentlessly round until the sun disappeared from view over the back of the building. When this happened it was nearly ten o'clock but on that morning, the usual pattern was broken. No-one came near them with a steaming jug of coffee and black bread at 7 o'clock. When a friendly guard they had nicknamed Fritz brought their breakfast shortly after ten, he said nothing, this again was unusual, he normally liked to practice his English, but for once he was silent and their questions about the happenings in the early hours went unanswered.

. . . .

Two weeks had passed since that day, but Basil remembered the date clearly because he had written it on the wall and remarked on all the fours being together. Tanky had suggested they meet eleven years hence on 5th May, 1955 and Jimmy had been amused, jocularly suggesting it should be 5 o'clock on the fifth step of St. Martins in the fields. Then the ensuing laughter had been rudely broken by the Kommandant coming in to tell them Porky had been killed trying to escape and he hoped they would take it as a warning not to try anything themselves.

Security had been even tighter after that and Basil reflected ruefully that five guards in a locked coach didn't give much lee-way for escape. Now he stared moodily through a wired window at passing scenery and wondered how long the four of them could stick together or whether they would be separated when they reached the camp.

CHAPTER 23

It was the first morning in the transit camp on the outskirts of L'Aquila, which would be their home for the next two weeks, and they queued with other new arrivals for the compulsory marking of their clothes. At the head of the queue the trustee, a dour little man with a taciturn manner and a convenient philosophy in life which permitted the end to be worthy of the means, if he gained an extra half a pound of bread a day then his conscience was stilled, dipped his brush liberally in a bucket of red paint and methodically daubed the distinguishing letters K.F.G. on trouser leg and jacket alike.

While waiting his turn Basil took stock of his surroundings. There were perhaps a dozen in the queue whose dull eyes reflected the shock of recent capture, they shuffled forward dissipatedly as if unsure what to expect. His eyes flicked over them with interest, then across the so called dining hall to the counter set in the wall, where the daily rations would be drawn, and the roomy kitchen that could be seen beyond. Hovering in the kitchen a huge American Negro was preparing a stew; the incongruity of a man of such dimensions trying to exist on prison fare brought an amused smile to Basil's lips, turning to Jimmy he remarked,

"Look at that chap, I reckon with a frame like that he needs a kitchen job!"

Jimmy nodded. "Yes he is a size isn't he. I wouldn't care to upset him. Incidentally, I gather he's a touchy customer, one of the chaps was telling me this morning that he nearly killed a lad for calling him Sambo, seems it's regarded as something of an insult where he comes from."

"I expect it would be" commented Tanky, "I believe the name is linked with slavery. You know, for all their talk of democracy, the Yanks keep their black population pretty well under the thumb, so it's not surprising that many view all white peoples as trash and resent any hint of a derogatory remark."

He gazed through the aperture admiring the splendid physique then, seeing the modern equipment, said

"Boy, look at those cookers, they're a far cry from the open air dixies at Macerata."

"By all accounts the feed is better too" John chimed in.

"These jokers give us the same rations as they get themselves."

"Next!"

The trustee's voice broke into the discourse as the Newzealander reached the head of the queue.

"Roll up a trouser leg."

"What the hell for?" John protested.

"Make sure you ain't wearing two pairs of pants. Now come on, we ain't got all day." rejoined the other.

When the clothing had been marked, they were free to wander about the camp and. Having arrived in the middle of the night, they were keen to get their bearings. Basil knew that L'Aquila stood in the centre of a valley between the Gran Sasso and the Velino-Sirente plateau, but he had not expected to see the vast area of flat ground which surrounded the camp. If a man ever got away from this camp, he thought, there would be a lot of ground to cover before he would be safe.

Across the wire, a score of miles away, the hazy shape of Monte Ocre stood out from its fellows and the rounded summits of the trio, Monte Velino, Magnola and Serente towering behind beckoned temptingly. The thought of freedom in those hills and the proximity of the Allied Forces beyond was galling. He turned his back on the wire in disgust, looking with interest at the diverse types in the camp and trying to judge their history by their dress. Unlike Macerata, where the majority had been taken in the disastrous collapse of the Gazelle Line, here there was a heterogeneous collection of nationalities to represent almost every sector of the front, yet the solitary Arab dressed in flowing Galabier, that curious nightshirt-like garment favoured by men of his race, seemed oddly out of place and Basil couldn't help wondering what he was doing there.

Among them were those whose raiment indicated that they had either escaped or been liberated at the armistice. Many had acquired civilian clothes or had their trousers died black. For some curious reason, practically all of these wore blue shirts. Jimmy remarked that it almost constituted a uniform. A few, having found friends of substance, sported natty city suits. Basil spoke to one who claimed to have lived in the heart of Rome where he wandered the streets as an habitue. His downfall came, so he told Basil, when he got drunk and started singing English ballads in the middle of St. Peter's Square. He had been in the camp for over a week and said that some, who still wore tattered remnants of old uniforms, had fought in the hills with the Partisans, and it was obvious to Basil that there were also those, whose pale faces and debilitated frames bore evidence of months spent in hiding, to whom recapture was a release from fear. He was to learn that not many had made an attempt to cross the line or join guerilla bands and, such is the way of human nature, those that had complained the least. Almost to a man they gazed upon the distant hills and cudgelled their brains for a way to escape.

During the time they spent at that camp, many and various were the plans Basil and his friends heard discussed. Nebulous, airy-fairy schemes in the main which held little hope of success and, if the truth be known, there was little intention of their authors to implement them. However, there were also those who said little and thought deeply. Bitter experience and a history of valiant attempts that had failed had taught them the wisdom of secrecy. Some had three or four breaks to their credit and the consensus of opinion would probably have revealed they considered opportunity more valuable than planning. They watched and waited for the day they would be moved for in transit such opportunities were more likely to occur.

The most publicised scheme of all and, because of the publicity doomed to failure, was the tunnel scheme. Boring had been started in a disused latrine and only had a matter of 25 yards to travel to clear the wire and the road beyond but, with the empty area surrounding the camp, it would take some weeks before a safe exit could be accomplished. Soil was disposed of in empty palliasses in the bedding store adjoining the latrine and the eventual discovery in the second week of their stay, was inevitable.

The discovery of the tunnel operation supplied a topic of conversation until it was superseded by the strong rumour that a large majority of those in the camp were to be transported north. The rumour had it that they would be travelling by road. Hearing this Basil's spirits rose, for if this were true it seemed reasonable to suppose that the drivers would have to rest and there was a possibility that an opportunity to get away would present itself. If it doesn't, he thought grimly, we shall have to chance it and he wondered if he could wangle the last truck in the convoy.

One evening, towards the end of April, the rumours became fact. The camp was mustered in the various compounds in readiness for the usual roll call but tonight, after a trustee had called out the names, a Weichmaster called out those who were to remain in the camp and ordered the others to collect what few possessions they may have and return to the compound. Then came the long slow business of drawing rations for the journey, after which they were told to stay in the hall and remove their boots. After the boots had been marked for easy recognition, they were collected by a fatigue party and placed in one of the trucks now waiting outside.

Somehow in the melee, Basil and his three friends managed to stay together and, after an interminable wait, found themselves in the same lorry where they waited until nearly midnight for the journey to commence.

Shortly after dawn, having travelled without rest since midnight, they pulled up at a small village but the halt was of short duration, soon they rolled on again, northward now and ever deeper into the hilly country that was Umbria. It was about ten o'clock when it happened. The convoy halted abruptly and the prisoners were told to lie down in the bottom of the trucks. Far away to the east a formation of tiny blots marked the sky. Basil, talking to Jimmy, said,

"See that? If they spot the convoy we might get our chance."

However, the planes flew on silently and the vehicles prepared to move then, as the first truck got under way, there was a sudden shout.

"Halt oder ich schiesse!"

Someone Basil recognised as one of the men who had worked on the tunnel, had leapt from the truck immediately behind and, running at incredible speed despite his lack of footwear, had almost reached the safety of a group of rocks half shrouded by the thick cane like growth. Even as the guards raised their rifles to fire he disappeared from view. For a few moments pandemonium raged as some of the prisoners sprang to their feet distracting the attention of the guards. Meanwhile the one who had shouted raced across the intervening strip of ground and entered the shrubbery. There came the sharp crack of a pistol, then he reappeared walking slowly now. As he passed the truck where Basil sat, he glanced up at the guard and grinned.

"Caput!"

Then sauntered unconcernedly to his own station.

The convoy started to move again, rolling on through the hills, but Basil had started to think. Apparently the guards with the rifles didn't leave the trucks when there was trouble and the man who had given chase was only armed with a revolver. If this was the pattern he would play on the weakness.

Shortly after passing Lake Trasimeno, the convoy halted again just outside Cortona in a place where the trees growing on the verges of the road afforded cover for the vehicles and shed a welcome shade for the weary travellers. Here they were shepherded out of their trucks and made to sit on the ground while a meal was prepared.

At this point the railway ran parallel to the road some 200 yds away and beside the track was a house with a clock set in the wall. Basil noticed that the hands pointed to 4.30 when one of the guards shouted for four men to carry water. He was on his feet in an instant, his shrewd mind already working out a plan. Jimmy and the others were quick to follow his example and as they walked together towards the guard, Basil said,

"Be ready for instant action." He spoke tersely, using short clipped sentences. "I've got an idea we'll be out of sight. The guard just came from that cottage."

He indicated a cottage on the opposite side of the road which was half hidden by trees.

"When I dawdle try to get ahead. When I start the ball rolling, run for it!"

Jimmy scowled and said,

"What about you?"

Basil glared.

"Shut up, he'll hear us talking." Then relenting, "Don't worry I'll make out."

On reaching the guard, they were presented with buckets and escorted across the road towards the cottage. As Basil had surmised, thick growth surrounding the building effectively hid the small party from the convoy. They passed behind the cottage and Basil began to walk more slowly. He glanced back at the guard with an ingratiating smile.

"Can I have a cigarette?"

The guard grunted and motioned him forward, so he made the action of a man smoking which brought a grin from the guard.

"Eine zigarrette?" a short laugh escaped his lips "Was du Nicht sagst:" Then impatiently, "March, march."

Now the other three were almost at a well 20 yards ahead and the guard, realising the risks was getting more impatient. Basil could feel the blood pounding in his temples, as his mind worked with a clear precision; every nerve of his being was dynamically alive, his muscles keyed to that perfect blend of physical readiness for the moment he had planned.

At this stage he knew it would be fatal to turn his head, one false move could close the grey eyes for ever. Already the others were at the well and were standing about, alert and watchful, then Tanky started to lower his bucket and Jimmy sauntered casually to the far side of the well where a dried water course extended a few yards before bearing sharply to the left. Desperately now, for the opportunity he had worked for was rapidly dwindling, Basil slowed almost to a standstill, it was imperative he didn't catch up to the others. At last the guard lost patience and prodded the revolver into his back.

It was the moment for which Basil had waited, like an uncoiled spring he whirled, sidestepping as his left arm swept the pistol to one side; Basil heard the crack of the explosion, but the shot went wide, then stepping in again, his right came across to deliver a punch on the jaw and backed by all the weight his experience had taught him to use. The guard staggered back and tried to bring his pistol into play but Basil's left shot out and his grip fastened with merciless strength, his thumb pinning the back of the hand and providing the leverage so necessary in the hold. The gun clattered harmlessly to the ground where Basil kicked it out of sight into the bushes as he grasped the elbow with his right hand before sliding down to the wrist in preparation for the whip which sent his opponent catapulting head over heels to land on his head with stunning force. There was no time to look for the fallen pistol, already shouts could be heard beyond the screen of shrubbery as reinforcements raced along the track, alarmed by the single shot which had loosed from the pistol. Feeling thankful that the well was now deserted he sped to the water course and, following the route already taken by the other three, rounded the bend. A short way ahead he could see

Jimmy waiting beside a break in the undergrowth, where a ditch debouched into the watercourse. He raced towards him.

When planning the manoeuvre, Basil realised that the pistol would probably be fired, but he had hoped for a somewhat longer margin of time before the alarm was raised. Ten minutes would have been sufficient time to put half a mile behind and the chances of being found in such a radius would have been remote. As it was, only a thin screen of bushes separated the pair watching the Germans pound by as they followed the bed of the water course. For a few tense seconds, neither dare move, for a stone could easily have rattled down to betray them then, before the searchers could return to commence a systematic hunt, they clambered up the steep narrow ditch where, at the edge of a small open patch of ground sparsely covered with bush, they joined the other two.

Before them, barely 50 yards away, lay the forest offering the concealment of its growth, but a barbed wire fence stretched mid-way across the open ground and Basil groaned aloud.

"In all these thousands of miles of unfenced country in Italy why does that have to be there?"

On closer inspection, the fencing proved less formidable than it looked, the wire was rusted with age and several gaps had been allowed to form in the coils at its base, so they managed to slip through without much bother, reaching the edge of the forest before the first German appeared at the head of the water course. There were no paths here where they had entered and sharp thorns tore their unprotected feet. They penetrated some 25 yards and finding no sign of a trail Basil called a halt saying,

"If we carry on like this we will all end up lame. I doubt if they'll search for very long because the convoy will soon have to get under way. If we wriggle beneath the undergrowth and lie still I think it extremely unlikely we'll ever be found."

A half hour passed and now that the shouts had died down no sound reached their ears. The forest might have been dead but for a cuckoo on a nearby tree who persisted in calling its mate. It reminded Basil of springtime at home and letters in the Press when people claimed to have heard the first call of the year. A whistle sounded shrilly in the distance and he guessed the convoy was preparing to move off. Even when sure that everybody had left, they took no chances; they remained till the chill of the evening descended and the air grew dark around them.

When they emerged from their hiding place, Basil had no idea where they were, but the constellation Plough was as near to being overhead as it was likely to get, and Orion's Betelgeuse was far down near the horizon. It was sufficient to tell him that Arcturus, just visible above the trees, would lie a little south of east, he reckoned about 115°. He gazed at the familiar star, thinking that it would be useful as a bearing to march on for about three hours, by which time it would be just about south and he would have to switch to Vega or, better still, Altair, if the skyline permitted. It would not be very precise, but, providing; they kept an approximate south easterly bearing, the actual destination at this stage was not important.

Following the course Basil had planned, the four men walked steadily through the night, climbing the easy gradients until, in the half light of dawn, they saw the wooded glory of Umbria lying before them and, far away, a lucent gem of pellucid serenity in a bed of dark green velvet, the great Lake Trasimeno.

Tired after ten miles of painful travel, they paused, glad of the brief respite, for jagged stones and clutching brambles had pierced the soft undersoles of their feet, while pine needles had worked their way between their toes to rub them raw until, in desperation, they ripped their jackets to swaddle their feet in rags. Now, with the ever brightening light, they felt conspicuous knowing that all who saw the betraying marks on their clothes would know what they were.

Somewhere below, the hollow cracked clonk of a sheep bell intruded into the morning sonata of a thousand birds to warn them that the world was coming back to life and it would be dangerous to linger on the edge of that path overlooking the lake. Too weary to speak, they stumbled on their way, four pathetic figures ludicrous in their tatterdemalion jackets and bundled feet as, faces grey with fatigue but determined in aspect, they sought out the denser parts of the forest that they might sleep without fear of discovery.

The next night they managed better, refreshed by a sleep in which dreams played no part, their hunger assuaged by the raw flesh of a lamb Basil had separated from its flock. Because they were deprived of knives, they were forced to tear the flesh away with their fingers and the pelt, which Basil had hoped to fashion into moccasins, defied all attempts to remove satisfactorily.

It was on their third night they found the remote stone built dwelling, almost obscured by trees lining the edges of a clearing. They would probably have passed along the path that cut across the open space and not noticed the tiny house had a dog not barked within and drawn their attention that way. Basil, who was a few yards ahead at the time, paused and scratched at the four day stubble on his chin, waiting for the others to catch up for, though the hour was late, a glimmer of light still showed beneath the door. He felt reluctant to rob peasant people who could ill afford even the small amount they so often willingly gave, on the other hand, the position was desperate. Even in the faint light of the night he could still see the letters blazoned on his trouser leg, despite strenuous efforts to obliterate with dirt. Before long it would be necessary to approach the populated areas in daylight and fix their position, but to do this in their present condition would be to court disaster.

As Jimmy came abreast he said,

"What's up?"

"Nothing," Basil replied, keeping his voice low. "we must sort ourselves out so I'm going over to that cottage to see if we can get something done with our togs and the loan of a razor. I'm hoping it wont come to violence, but if they're not prepared to assist us we shall have to help ourselves."

In spite of his words, it was with some misgiving that he approached the door then, standing well in the shadow lest his rough appearance should scare the tenant, he rapped on the worn woodwork and glanced back to where the others waited to lend assistance should a forced entry be required. A woman's voice called - "Who's there?" and the barking of the dog rose to a frenzied clamour.

"A friend." Basil replied.

Whereupon the door opened a fraction and he caught a glimpse of the baleful eyes of a huge yellow dog. The bark descended to a low menacing growl.

"Be quiet Forli."

The woman spoke roughly in the manner of peasant women and the dog cringed to the ground but suspicious still emitted sporadic subterranean woofs as he eyed the stranger with the flappy clothes.

"Who are you that you are afraid to show your face?"

The voice sounded sharp for all the tremor that lay beneath it as she added,

"Come into the light that I may see you."

Basil advanced a pace, feeling he deserved the rebuke and something at a loss, for he had expected a man to open the door. The woman gazed at him, her lips compressed; used as she was to seeing rough clothes and neglected beards, she had never seen an honest man looking like this, yet she thought the eyes are steady, not brown like ours, but grey and held the tiny light the better to see.

"Who are you?" she reiterated "and what do you want?"

Basil explained in a few rapid words.

"We have escaped the Germans and mean you no harm. We merely need to clean ourselves and the loan of a needle and thread maybe to patch over these markings." He indicated the letters on his trousers and added, "We shall be gone long before morning and no-one need know."

"You say we, how many men are you?"

Basil told her, saying "We shall cause no trouble."

"I don't know, we are small here, there is no room for you to sleep."

Basil felt irritated as he often did at the slow wits of some of the peasant women, but managed to keep his irritation from his voice.

"We don't want to stay here, I told you all we want is a clean up."

Suddenly the woman relented.

"Come inside, I'll ask Cesare, my husband."

Basil stepped inside the doorway and the action set the dog off again, as growling and snarling it stood, legs straddled, glaring at this intrusion.

"Shut up!"

All Basil's pent up feelings went into those two simple English words; surprisingly the dog obeyed. He grinned and said,

"You speak English eh?" then fished around his pockets to produce a piece of raw lamb which he offered to the dog who wolfed it greedily and looked around for more. By the time the Donna returned with her husband, they were firm friends.

Now it was settled that help should be given, she couldn't do enough. Despite the lateness of the hour, a meal of boiled maize and horse beans, this a measure of their poverty, was prepared and placed over the fire to cook. Then, having produced blankets, the husband bade them take off their trousers so that his wife could work on them. To do this entailed removing the bundles swathing their feet - the sight of which brought a gasp of shocked pity from the Donna who produced a bucket of warm water to clean them and insisted on dressing them herself with olive oil. For the most part they were only minor scratches, but one of Basil's heels had sustained a jagged cut when he pivoted on it to attack the guard. Resorting to native lore, she anointed it with a concoction compounded from wild herbs and covered it with a leaf before binding the foot with swift dexterity, taking care to leave the leaf free to breathe.

Having served the meal and made sure they were all eating, she went to work with needle and thread, placing patches cut from the remnants of Basil's jacket over the marks. When she had finished patching the trousers, she held them up to view, shaking her head and making peculiar little clucking noises.

"They should be dyed really then the patches will hardly show." She glanced towards her husband who said,

"Very well Emma, they may stay in the barn, no-one ever comes this way and their company for a while will be a diversion."

Jimmy couldn't resist a chuckle, he looked at the blanket wrapped figures round the table and said,

"God, no boots, no trousers. What next? If anything goes wrong whilst we're here Basil I'll blasted well slay you!"

"That goes for me too," John chimed in, but Tanky was feeling more serious.

"It's all very well to laugh, but right now we're in a fine old pickle."

His very seriousness brought another spurt of laughter from John and Jimmy and questioning glances from their hosts. Basil explaining the predicament strained to keep a straight face when a fleeting vision passed across his brain. The thought of the four of them bounding across the countryside dressed virtually only in a flapping blanket was too absurd. The husband nodded sagely, saying ponderously,

"I understand, but have no fear, this is a lonely place and we don't see more than one or two people in a month. If you will feel safer there is space beneath the haystacks."

Basil knew that he referred to the practice of building haystacks on a platform of cut saplings, which left a snug cavity frequently used as an extra room but, he thought, useless as a hiding place as it had only one means of entrance and would be the first place a searcher would look, so he shook his head and said,

"The barn will do, we can easily stay out of sight there."

Cesare shrugged. "You can please yourselves, it's not so snug as under the hay."

Then, emitting a prodigious yawn, said,

"Come, it is late, I shall put down some straw, then we must sleep."

CHAPTER 24

Jimmy eased cautiously from the shadow of a stunted tree, its gnarled branches grotesquely silhouetted against a sky thick with stars. Nearby he could just make out the bulk of Tanky and ahead the vague outline of Basil ascending the ravine. With wraith like silence, his bare feet testing every foothold on the steeply sloping shale strewn surface, he descended. the few yards separating him from Basil who turned, retracing the way he had come. No words were exchanged between them for they were in that place known as the Valle di Femminna Morta, where the German 305 Inf. Div. had a section of their forward defence.

Somewhere a hundred yards ahead he knew that John would be waiting at the limit of the path that had been reconnoitred. He would be ready to investigate any activity, or race back with a warning if he thought a detour advisable.

Following Basil's rapidly receding figure, Jimmy marvelled at the photographic memory of his friend, an attribute which made him wonderfully suited to this type of work. He went forward with such confidence that it was as if, having passed that way before, he now knew the precise location of every minor obstacle, an impression confirmed when he stopped so suddenly that Jimmy nearly cannoned into him. The thin thread of wire stretched across the path only a few inches above the ground was almost invisible to Jimmy even when he stooped, but Basil had known it was at this spot. Carefully stepping over, he signalled a warning to Tanky, for there was no means of telling whether it was a trip wire or the innocent communication of a field telephone and these things were best left untouched. Then, keeping close into the cliff like rock face on their right, Basil led the way forward once more as, with uncanny precision, he took them to a fault in the rock where John waited.

Now, while Basil and John went about the perilous task of spying out the way, Jimmy settled down with Tanky once more to wait for their return. He couldn't help thinking what a wonderful team the pair made, for both had that cat-like power which laughed at darkness and a phantom-like ability to come and go without a sound. With moderate luck tonight's work would see the culmination of their efforts. The thought was tinged with a certain nostalgic regret for the girl he had left at Civitella and a shadow passed across his face as he wondered when he would see her again.

During the journey from Maestrello, where their clothes had been dyed, they had dallied a while to bathe in Lake Campotosto before trudging through the snow line of the Gran Sasso, no more than 10-15 miles from Casa Tufa. It had been a great temptation then to deviate their route and go visiting, but Basil seemed obsessed by a sense of urgency, pointing out that there had been too much delay already and they should cross before the disposition of Forces changed materially from what Gino had told them and while the knowledge they had gained of defences under construction might still be useful to British Intelligence.

They had descended on the opposite side of the mountain, close to the cable railway which goes up to the Campo Imperatore, and entering the forests which clothe the lower slopes had come to the track leading out of Assergi, where they found a concrete built watering point to assuage their thirst. Then, without pause for rest, they had passed on into the foothills of the Maiella near Pietranico. Such is the distorting effect of distance on time, that, in retrospect, the two weeks since their escape seemed more like two months. He grinned reminiscently as he recalled the hideous clatter on the cobbled stones of a village near Perugia that their zoccolli had made and couldn't help thinking, what vile contraptions those wooden sandals were. Emma had insisted they wear them and they had served their purpose tolerably well giving the cuts on their feet a chance to heal but they had been tiring to wear, slowing down their pace until they had been glad to kick them off when the going was not so rough. Walking a few miles each day without the protection they afforded, their feet soon hardened and they finally discarded the footwear near Assisi. It was then they found they had much to learn in the art of walking as nature intended and Jimmy marvelled at the adaptability of the human kind as he wondered if the newly acquired skill would ever be needed after tonight. He was hard put to suppress a chuckle as he remembered how difficult balance had been at first, particularly on grassy slopes when still wet with dew; how, accustomed to digging their heels in when wearing boots, they had slithered and tumbled frequently until they learned to use their toes for grip and point their feet inwards when traversing the length of a grassy slope - as Basil had said 'like a dancing master' and Tanky insisted was pigeon-toed, discovering for themselves the value of the greater toe. Now nature, in compensation, had endowed the soles of their feet with a thick layer of skin, which had already begun to spread at the edges to form a pad. The only difficulty not solved was how to cross cut stubble or long grass without the stuff getting between the toes.

As John's approach broke his train of thought he came out of the fissure to meet him and saw the stars in the east had lost their brilliance. Meanwhile, Basil waiting near the bottom of the ravine had also noticed the lightening sky and was thinking that the trek through the hills was taking longer than it should for they still had to find a way down the escarpment which lay an unknown distance ahead. He reflected that it was fortunate Gino had been right when he said these positions were only lightly held but, not knowing the location of the sentries and machine gun nests it had been virtually necessary to recce every inch of the way and it had taken time, too much time. He scowled into the darkness and, looking towards the opposite wall which had been out of sight for some time, tried to judge the width of the ever widening ravine. Knowing they couldn't have descended the escarpment so soon he had been wondering whether they were on a suitable track. Observing the grey streaks in the east, he had doubts whether they would reach the level ground between the escarpment and the River Sangro before daylight.

A light cough somewhere ahead sent him edging forward to investigate. The possibility of such an exigency had already been allowed for. John would not bring the other two further than the scanned route but would wait as arranged till he returned. Only if he failed to show up within a reasonable time would the others continue without him.

He had only covered about ten yards when his sensitive nostrils caught the faint smell of tobacco smoke. The realisation that someone was evidently enjoying an illicit smoke was encouraging for if, as he suspected, it was a sentry, it could indicate that a relief was not expected for some time; it would probably also infer that he was alone so would be more easily handled. Then he saw it, the faint glow of a cigarette and, later, the vague blur of a steel helmeted outline. For a moment Basil was puzzled, the glow seemed to be much lower than it should be then, as it moved slightly and vanished, he realised that the smoker was cupping the cigarette - he grinned to himself thinking the German was like a guilty schoolboy hiding something from his master by holding it behind his back. The thought was irrelevant and Basil glided forward softly concentrating, on the task in hand. Drawing nearer so that he could make out the details more clearly, he saw that the picket stood with his back towards him at the head of a much smaller ravine which he guessed would lead to the bottom of the escarpment. Stealthily creeping closer, he slipped a length of telephone wire from his pocket. It was a crude weapon but in his hands efficient and it had the merit of complete silence.

When the German moved away a fraction before Basil was ready to strike, he little realised how close to death he had been. Unaware of the silent watcher, he entered the ravine and Basil could hear him clumping noisily down the rock strewn path as he followed, watching him join his companions in a machine gun nest commanding the whole of that narrow way.

After hearing the low murmur of greeting, Basil paused before creeping close enough to see the ugly snout of the gun and its crew of three. Staying only long enough to ascertain that it would be just possible to slip by unobserved if they kept close to the rock wall beneath it, he returned the way he had come to find the others waiting as he had expected. In a barely audible undertone he explained briefly what he had found and urged the imperative necessity of passing before the darkness faded and they were trapped.

By this time the grey streaks in the east had become tinged with silver; each knew that in ten minutes at the most they would be able to see each other, for already the blackness had a translucent quality about it. It took them scarcely five minutes to reach the nest and as they crept beneath the rocky platform where it had been mounted, they could see the shape of the sandbags with alarming clarity and hear the German voices whiling away the duty hours. They could also see where the path dipped steeply to form a hard ridge against the skyline before canting to descend to the plain below and, in the imagination, flattened hard against the rock face, they felt naked and exposed as if a search light had been turned on, realising the machine gun crew could hardly fail to see them when they wormed their way over that all revealing ridge for, with alarming rapidity, the light was getting stronger and their eyes, adjusted to the velvet blackness of the night, could now make out every detail of the path.

It seemed incredible that at any moment the venture could end in a crashing crescendo of sound, for in those narrow confines there would be no escape. Basil viewed the possibility with detachment and made use of every available bit of cover as he listened for the faint rustle of breathing which told him the others were still close behind. Inch by inch, deep in the shadow of a boulder, the four men worked their way by degrees towards the crest of the slope, hugging the ground as they crossed it lest their outline should show against the sky.

Now, in the first nebulous light of day, they could see the long descending track and fifty yards ahead a bend which would conceal them from the crew above. Crouching and moving swiftly, they dashed for the safety it offered rounding it as bright orange streaks of flame, accompanied by a hideous stutter of awesome noise announced that they had been seen. They had no time for finesse, for there was an urgent necessity to run before the clamour brought others on the scene to investigate; before the machine gun crew realised the futility of firing at a target that could no longer be seen and sent one of their number in pursuit. They ran as they had never run before with a speed and agility matched only by their determination to survive, and as they ran, the light strengthened inexorably coming on them long before they reached the end of that perilous descent, to reveal the gently undulating plain with its interlacing network of tracks and beyond the metallic gleam of a river, the riven slopes which merged into the hills on the distant horizon.

Soon after passing through the broken arches of a road bridge, where a sign canted crazily on its bent stem atop a pile of fallen masonry, indicating that this was the unlikely route to Taranta Peligna 2 kilometres away, they debouched into a wide river bed which paralleled the base of the escarpment. Half expecting to hear again the angry scream of the machine gun, or the crisp bark of a rifle, they splashed through the shallow water and sped up the long shelving bank on the other side, finding temporary refuge between the walls of a derelict building.

Now that they had time for a momentary rest, they noticed the brooding silence, it seemed as if even the wild life had fled this desolate place where the sky stared through broken windows of roofless homes which pointed their blackened beams forlornly into the air, or sagged dejectedly on their piles of rubble amid the lush extravagance of weeds growing in rank profusion on soil that had once been cultivated.

Taking advantage of the luxuriant growth to mask their movements, they worked their way towards some wooded country which lay ahead and, in half an hour, the escarpment lay about a mile behind them, looking from this distance forbidding and austere with its numerous ravines and stunted trees.

They entered the woods as the first rays of the sun making their début reflected redly on a moving column of dust beyond the river as if to assure them that the 8th Army was still there. Following the narrow woodland path, with the dank sweet odour of rotting leaves in their nostrils, they felt secure in the knowledge that, whatever dangers lay ahead, no sniper using telescopic sights could pick them off from the escarpment. As the peace of the forest seeped into them, relieving some of the tension they had known, it felt good to be alive. Contentedly they padded on, soft footed with that cat-like wariness which seemed to remain even when they slept, until a muffled exclamation which could have been a cough or a curse, brought them abruptly to a halt. Then, as Basil moved forward to investigate, the sound of movement, followed by the clash of a tin can fell harshly on their ears.

Dropping to his hands and knees, Basil peered cautiously over the edge of a hummock into a hollow which lay beyond. A light truck had pulled in beside an unmetalled road and someone was setting up a wireless aerial, while yet another carried a steaming dixie towards two others seated on a fallen tree. There was no mistaking the berets they wore or the markings on their Jeep. Basil turned, looking almost boyish again as a delighted smile erased the stern lines from his face, then, as he beckoned to his friends, a strong Mancunian accent came sweetly through the air,

"I don't know why I came 2,000 miles to join the 5th Recce Regt. I can brew up much more efficiently in Manchester."